STAGING AUTHORITY
IN CAROLINE ENGLAND

T0347529

Studies in Performance and Early Modern Drama

General Editor's Preface

Helen Ostovich, McMaster University

Performance assumes a string of creative, analytical, and collaborative acts that, in defiance of theatrical ephemerality, live on through records, manuscripts, and printed books. The monographs and essay collections in this series offer original research which addresses theatre histories and performance histories in the context of the sixteenth and seventeenth century life. Of especial interest are studies in which women's activities are a central feature of discussion as financial or technical supporters (patrons, musicians, dancers, seamstresses, wigmakers, or 'gatherers'), if not authors or performers per se. Welcome too are critiques of early modern drama that not only take into account the production values of the plays, but also speculate on how intellectual advances or popular culture affect the theatre.

The series logo, selected by my colleague Mary V. Silcox, derives from Thomas Combe's duodecimo volume, *The Theater of Fine Devices* (London, 1592), Emblem VI, sig. B. The emblem of four masks has a verse which makes claims for the increasing complexity of early modern experience, a complexity that makes interpretation difficult. Hence the corresponding perhaps uneasy rise in sophistication:

> Masks will be more hereafter in request,
> And grow more deare than they did heretofore.

No longer simply signs of performance 'in play and jest', the mask has become the 'double face' worn 'in earnest' even by 'the best' of people, in order to manipulate or profit from the world around them. The books stamped with this design attempt to understand the complications of performance produced on stage and interpreted by the audience, whose experiences outside the theatre may reflect the emblem's argument:

> Most men do use some colour'd shift
> For to conceal their craftie drift.

Centuries after their first presentations, the possible performance choices and meanings they engender still stir the imaginations of actors, audiences, and readers of early plays. The products of scholarly creativity in this series, I hope, will also stir imaginations to new ways of thinking about performance.

Staging Authority
in Caroline England
Prerogative, Law and Order in Drama, 1625–1642

JESSICA DYSON
University of Portsmouth, UK

LONDON AND NEW YORK

First published 2013 by Ashgate Publisher

Published 2016 by Routledge
2 Park Square, Milton Park, Abingdon, Oxfordshire OX14 4RN
711 Third Avenue, New York, NY 10017, USA

First issued in paperback 2016

Routledge is an imprint of the Taylor & Francis Group, an informa business

British Library Cataloguing in Publication Data
A catalogue record for this book is available from the British Library

The Library of Congress has cataloged the printed edition as follows:
Dyson, Jessica.
Staging authority in Caroline England: prerogative, law and order in drama, 1625–1642 / by Jessica Dyson.
    pages cm. — (Studies in performance and early modern drama)
  Includes bibliographical references and index.
  ISBN 978-1-4094-3332-3 (hardcover: alk. paper)
  1. English drama—Early modern and Elizabethan, 1500–1600—History and criticism. 2. English drama—17th century—History and criticism. 3. Law and literature—History—16th century. 4. Law and literature—History—17th century. 5. Theater—Great Britain—History—16th century. 6. Theater—Great Britain—History—17th century. 7. Law in literature. 8. Authority in literature. I. Title.
  PR658.L38D97 2013
  822'.4093554—dc23

                                                                    2013007743

  ISBN 13: 978-1-138-26882-1 (pbk)
  ISBN 13: 978-1-4094-3332-3 (hbk)

To Mr Wright, with thanks.

Contents

Acknowledgements

This book has accompanied me, in different forms, through several different institutions. The initial research was undertaken at the University of Stirling. From this stage, I owe a great deal of thanks to Professor James Knowles for encouraging, engaging with and challenging my ideas and arguments; to Professor John Drakakis, Professor Neil Keeble and Dr Robin Sowerby for their generosity of time and intellect, and finally to Professor Susan Wiseman, whose comments helped to shape further the arguments you read in this book. I also wish to thank the Arts and Humanities Research Council for their generous decision to fund my research at this early stage. Next, at Lancaster University, particular thanks to Professor Alison Findlay, Dr Liz Oakley-Brown and Dr Hilary Hinds for their friendship, encouragement and guidance, and to Dr Stephen Curtis for moral support and lively discussions on law, blood, monarchy and beheadings. Most recently, at the University of Portsmouth, I'd like to thank my colleagues, particularly the early modern cluster of the Centre for Studies in Literature. The editors and readers at Ashgate, in particular Erika Gaffney, have offered me more help than I could have expected.

Closer to home, thanks in particular are due to Dominic for his patience. Last, but not least, my family and friends have supported me through all of these stages, and I owe them more thanks than I can express here.

Abbreviations and Orthography

Abbreviations

JCS	Bentley, G. E. (1956). *The Jacobean and Caroline Stage.* 7 Vols. Oxford: Clarendon Press.
ODL	Martin, E. A. and Law, J. (Eds.) (2006). *Oxford Dictionary of Law*.
Oxford	Oxford University Press. <http://www.oxfordreference.com/views/SUBJECT_SEARCH.html?subject=s12>.
ODNB	*Oxford Dictionary of National Biography*. Oxford: Oxford University Press, 2007. <http://www.oxforddnb.com/>.
OED	*Oxford English Dictionary Online*. Oxford: Oxford University Press, 2007. <http://dictionary.oed.com/entrance.dtl>.
Plays and Poems	Massinger, P. (1976). *The Plays and Poems of Philip Massinger* (P. Edwards and C. Gibson, Eds.). 5 Vols. Oxford: Clarendon Press.

A note on quotations

I have maintained original spellings in quotations except where I have silently standardised 'v', 'u', 'i', 'j', 'vv' and 'ſ' (long 's'), expanded contractions (prescriptiõ becomes prescription) and corrected inversions.

Introduction

A Prerogative Royall, I take two wayes: 1. Either to be an act of meere will and pleasure, above, or beside Reason or Law: Or, an act of dispensation, beside, or against the letter of the Law.

  Assert. 1. That which the Royalists call the Prerogative Royall of Princes, is the salt of Absolute Power; and it is a supreme and highest power of a *King*, as a *King*, to doe above, without, or contrary to a Law, or Reason: which is unreasonable.

  1. When Gods word speaketh of the power of *Kings* and Judges, *Deut.* 17.15, 16, 17. *Deut.* I. 15, 16, 17. and elsewhere, there is not any footstep, or ground for such a power: and therefore (if we speake according to conscience) there is no such thing in the world: And because *Royalists* cannot give us any warrant, it is to be rejected. (Rutherford, 1644, pp.192–3)

The reign of Charles I saw significant changes in the ways that legal authority was perceived. An increased acceptance of established law as a legitimate authority independent from the king was demonstrated in Charles's trial in 1648, under a law to which some argued he could not be subject. The relative position of the monarch and the law had been under debate for some time. In the sixteenth century, Edmund Plowden's tracts and reports suggested that the 'political powers enjoyed by English monarchs were properly rights granted by the common law' (Cromartie, 2006, p.109): thus, royal prerogative was a part of the common law, allowing to the king to act against or around the established law in exceptional circumstances, if this were necessary for the common good. In this formulation, despite acting outside the law, a monarch exercising the prerogative would be acting entirely legitimately and in accordance with the law. By the time Samuel Rutherford was writing in the 1640s, 'the law and absolute prerogative had become [...] direct competitors' as the requirements of the common weal became increasingly seen as something that judges could – and should – determine: 'if the law [judiciary] were competent to judge the common good, then it was competent to judge the extra-legal measures that had traditionally been justified by reference to such considerations' (Cromartie, 2006, p.107). Moreover, the necessity of the royal prerogative to ameliorate the effects of an inflexible law, or to raise non-parliamentary funds in case of emergency (an external attack on the country, for example) was brought increasingly into question as Charles ruled without Parliament during the 1630s, raising non-parliamentary funds such as Ship Money in peace-time, and acting often in conflict with the spirit, if not the letter, of the law.

  Whilst legal and political historians have long noted the importance of the politics of law in the period, it has been conspicuously neglected in studies of Caroline drama. This book will explore the ways in which the claims made for the legitimacy of the absolute prerogative and the sovereignty of the common law were played out on the professional stage in the reign of Charles I. During this time, Rutherford's terms – 'will', 'reason', 'law' and 'absolute power' – become central to theatrical and political discourses of legitimate authority. The chapters which follow will place drama from 1625–1642 within the politico-legal context of its production, and in doing so not only emphasise the contemporary legal engagement of playwrights of the commercial theatre – particularly Massinger, Brome, Jonson, Shirley and Ford – but also suggest for the theatre a position of political importance in providing a forum for the public discussion of such issues.

Life and Law

Law defines relationships – person to person, person to property, individual to State – and as such overarches the social and political world. Indeed, historians have argued that 'law was perhaps the most important framework for understanding seventeenth century politics and society' (Hughes, 1991, p.78). Levels of litigation increased from the Elizabethan period onwards, and many people of all social strata came into contact with the law through local justices and assize courts, court mediation or litigation. This, Michael Lane argues, 'must have produced at the very least a veneer of legal knowledge' (1981, p.275).[1] There is evidence, he continues, that a more 'substantive and substantial' legal knowledge was part of the common culture: private libraries of people from a variety of backgrounds and professions contained a significant number of legal texts, from the rich and powerful to the middle and lower status merchants, shopkeepers and small yeoman farmers (1981, p.275).

The number of gentlemen entering the Inns of Court also increased during this period. Wilfred Prest notes that although numbers at the Inns had been rising from around 1530 and reached a peak during the reign of James VI and I, 'there is a rally in the 1630s and very little weakening before the outbreak of the Civil War' (1972, pp.5–7). Particularly important to the debates over common law and prerogative power in the period, and to the argument of this book, is the fact that the Inns, unlike the Universities that mostly taught only civil and canon law, educated their students in common law. Lectures were given on subjects of law to the newer members (inner barristers) by the more senior members (readers or benchers), and the students participated in moots and debates on points of law.[2] That a desire to

---

[1]   For information on the increase in litigation see Baker (1985, p.41 and *passim*). Lane also notes that we should not assume ordinary people went to court only in connection with prosecutions: 'Minor courts mediated in a variety of disputes, disagreements and simple uncertainties that we now regard as either inappropriate or too trivial to warrant seeking legal intervention' (1981, p.276).

[2]   For a fuller discussion of the educational activities of the Inns of Court see Prest (1972, chapter VI). J. H. Baker's *The Common Law Tradition: Lawyers, Books and the Law* discusses in detail the development of learning at the Inns (2000, particularly chapters 1 and 3).

attend an institution which provided an education in law should increase during a period of intense disagreement over legitimate legal authority exacerbated by Charles's personal rule cannot be a coincidence, whether the education or the discontent with royal legal activities came first. It was not the personal rule alone that caused discontent; James VI and I, Butler notes, ruled without Parliament for ten years (1984, p.13). Increased attendance at the Inns brought a broader spectrum of legally educated men, and many of these men took up positions at court or in the House of Commons. Lane notes that in 1593, two out of five members of the House had received some legal education; by 1621 this increased to half, and by the 1640 Long Parliament, more than six in ten Commons members had received some legal education, although Lane does include a caveat that far fewer than this had actually been called as barristers (1981, p.277).

Not all of those who studied at the Inns of Courts pursued law as a profession. The Inns were not structured legal colleges as such; they more closely resembled clubs or societies where young gentlemen went to associate with others in London. Whilst there were lectures on subjects of law, expected attendance was not enforced and many young men went to the Inns to round off their education. Indeed, the Inns provided not only the facilities to study law, but attendance was a route to high office at court, as the Inns also provided the opportunity to take part in other events which gave training for the well-rounded gentleman and would-be courtier (Finkelpearl, 1969, pp.51–2). One of these was the performance of Christmas revels, which often included masques, and were sometimes performed at court.[3] The interests of the members of the Inns in theatrical activity were not only in performance; they were also an important source of patronage for players and playwrights, 'mak[ing] regular use of professional companies in their entertainments' (Neill, 2007, para. 5). Several of the Caroline playwrights whose work is discussed in this book also had clear connections with the Inns: as a member of the Middle Temple from 1602, John Ford should not, perhaps, be described as a layman in law; James Shirley was admitted to Grey's Inn in 1634, possibly because of his work on the masque *The Triumph of Peace* which the Inns of Court presented to the King and Queen that year (Leech, 1967, p.278); Philip Massinger, although not a member of the Inns himself, had friends there (Garrett, 2007, para. 27) as he dedicated *The Picture* (1630) to 'My Honored, and selected friends of the Noble society of the Inner Temple' (*The Picture*, sig. A3r); Jonson was a friend of such political thinkers as John Selden and Robert Cotton (Butler, 1992b, p.171), and as Brome was closely connected with Jonson it is likely that he mixed in similar circles, or at least had access to these political and legal ideas.

Indeed, that the members of the Inns were avid supporters of the theatre and readers of drama is clear from Francis Lenton's suggestion in *The Young Gallant's Whirligig* (1629) that the Inns' students preferred Jonson's 'book of playes' to their law books (Gurr, 1996, p.139), and from records which show that at the

---

[3]   See Wigfall Green (1931, *passim*) and Finkelpearl (1969, chapters 3 and 4), for detailed descriptions of some of the Inns' revels, and their performance for the court.

Inner Temple, Edward Heath purchased ten play-books between 1629 and 1631, and John Greene paid numerous visits to the Blackfriars and the Cockpit whilst attending Lincoln's Inn (Prest, 1972, p.169). Gurr notes that under Charles I, 'playgoing became socially more respectable than it had ever been', and that 'when the literate and the politically eminent began to pay serious attention to plays, it was inevitable that matters of both state and cultural policy should enter them more strongly' (1996, pp.138–9). With increased attendance at the Inns, legal knowledge widespread in society, and the politics of law raging around the Caroline court, it is unsurprising that debates over law and legitimate legal authority should appear in drama of the period. What is surprising, given this social and legal context, the 'immediate proximity between the professional worlds of theatre and law in the cultural geography of London' (Mukherji, 2006c, p.3), and the dramatic explorations of the politics of law including wide-ranging comment on particular laws and proclamations in Caroline plays, is the relative paucity of comment on these issues in literary criticism.[4]

Early Modern Literature, Law and Culture

Such an absence is particularly surprising, given the expansion at the end of the twentieth century of the Law and Literature movement. The two main areas explored by this movement can be summarised as 'law *as* literature' and 'law *in* literature'; the former 'seeks to apply the techniques of literary criticism to legal texts'; the latter examines 'the possible relevance of literary texts, particularly those which present themselves as telling a legal story, as texts appropriate for study by legal scholars' (Ward, 1995, p.3). Antony Julius suggests the movement has four, rather than two, main elements: law relating to literature (laws of literature); the literary properties of legal texts (law as literature); methods of interpretation of legal and literary texts (legal and literary hermeneutics); and the representation of law and legal processes in literature (law in literature) (1999, p.xiii). This book is most closely related to the latter, although it also takes account of hierarchies of governance. Despite this more detailed categorisation, however, the 'law as' and 'law in' literature division is more common.[5] Although Richard Posner asserts that

---

    [4]   For example, Brome's *The Court Begger* presents issues concerning Projectors, and Shirley's *The Lady of Pleasure* deals with Charles I's proclamation of 1632, 'Commaunding the gentry to keep their Residence at the Mansions in the Country, and forbidding them to make their Habitations in *London* and places adjoining'.

    [5]   Although censorship, which would fall into Julius's 'laws of literature' category was, to a greater or lesser extent, an influence on playwrights throughout the Caroline period, it is not a primary concern of this book. See Richard Dutton's *Mastering the Revels: The Regulation and Censorship of English Renaissance Drama* for a discussion of licensing and censorship to 1626. Dutton's *Licensing, Censorship and Authorship in Early Modern England* further examines censorship until the closure of the theatres in 1642 and how censorship impacted the concept of authorship. For an overview of critical positions

'the study of law and literature seeks to use legal insights to enhance understanding of literature, not just literary insights to enhance understanding of law' (1988, p.1), the described approaches favour the use of literature and literary critical practice for a better understanding of the law, rather than examining law as a means to a fuller understanding of a literary text. However, literary scholars seem to be expanding the boundaries of 'law and literature' in a variety of interesting ways.

Lorna Hutson's highly influential study of drama and legal processes, *The Invention of Suspicion: Law and Mimesis in Shakespeare and Renaissance Drama* (2007) parallels law and literature through the idea of constructing a narrative from evidence, testing motives and the use of rhetoric. This connection between rhetoric, evidence and law is also discussed by Subha Mukherji in her *Law and Representation in Early Modern Drama* (2006). Luke Wilson's monograph *Theaters of Intention: Drama and the Law in Early Modern England* (2000) is concerned with the representation of the developing understanding of intention and agency in law in the early modern period on the contemporary stage, and such engagement with human agency and subjectivity is also a focus of Victoria Khan and Lorna Hutson's edited collection, *Rhetoric and Law in Early Modern Europe* (2001), which looks further at points of intersection between law and rhetoric.

These useful critical approaches to the intersections of law, legal practice, rhetoric and drama, however, do not address broader political arguments of legitimate authority, nor focus in any detail on Caroline dramatic texts.[6] Bradin Cormack's *A Power to Do Justice: Jurisdiction, English Literature and the Rise of the Common Law 1509–1625* (2008) is concerned with issues of jurisdiction in the common law, showing the resemblance between law and the literary arts, but again offers analysis of pre-Caroline literary texts (dramatic and non-dramatic). More closely aligned with my arguments are the essays in *Literature, Politics and Law in Renaissance England 1580–1660* (2005), edited by Erica Sheen and Lorna Hutson, which present concrete engagements with law and politics by examining the position of individuals, including the early modern authors discussed, in relation to the law, and indeed particular legal cases. Whereas in several of the writers discussed in Sheen and Hutson's collection there is what the editors call an assumption of 'the rhetorical position of martyrs in representing themselves as oppressed by common law' (2005, p.3), my argument in this book contends that in drama of the commercial theatre under Charles I, common law was associated with rights, liberty and freedom from an oppressive and absolute central law.

---

on the nature and extent of censorship, see Andrew Hadfield's 'Introduction' to *Literature and Censorship in Renaissance England*. The essays in this volume examine the theatre and censorship, religious censorship and political censorship. Martin Butler (1992a) also discusses Jonson's *The Magnetic Lady* in relation to ecclesiastical censorship.

6   Mukherji's essay 'False Trial in Shakespeare, Massinger and Ford' does, however, deal more closely with two Caroline texts: Massinger's *The Picture* and Ford's *The Ladies Triall.*

Legal scholarship, too, is offering literary analysis in relation to law and governance. Paul Raffield's monograph *Images and Cultures of Law in Early Modern England: Justice and Political Power, 1558–1660* (2004) examines the relationship between the law, the Inns of Court and theatrical entertainments. Raffield argues that the Inns of Court 'acted out' an ideal constitutional state in the structures and symbols of their own government, showing by example the benefits of such a state, and this was further illustrated in their presentations of appropriate use of law in their masques and revels through which they sought to influence the monarchy. This attempted influence, he argues, shifts to lawyers in Parliament under Charles I and to pamphleteering during the interregnum. This argument suggests that Inns' revels were less frequently used under Charles to influence royal policy; I would argue that Caroline theatre takes up the representation of such legal argument, not necessarily to influence the King, but to highlight and develop the debates of contemporary legal and political discourses of reason and rationality which Raffield notes as the concern of some Jacobean entertainments (2004, pp.138–9).

Reading Caroline Drama

Since Martin Butler's seminal monograph, *Theatre and Crisis 1632–1642* (1984), to which I am, of course, indebted for its insights and for 'breaking the ground' on political readings of Caroline drama, other literary scholars have taken on serious readings of these texts, and have each been influential in formulating my approach. Ira Clark's *Professional Playwrights: Massinger, Ford, Shirley and Brome* proposes to enlarge 'Butler's focus on political issues such as absolutism and social mobility, so as to include more social concerns, mainly family and gender relations' (1992, p.6), and examines the inter-relationship between individuals' roles in society and the structure of that society within his chosen plays. Julie Sanders's brief but informative *Caroline Drama: The Plays of Massinger, Ford, Shirley and Brome* (1999) is the most recent survey of Caroline drama, and succinctly combines Butler's political and Clark's social/socio-political approach in offering ways to read these plays in different courtly, theatrical and social contexts. Whilst all of these critical works necessarily paint with broad strokes, Adam Zucker and Alan B Farmer's edited collection *Localizing Caroline Drama: Politics and Economics of the Early Modern English Stage, 1625–1642* (2006) attempts to avoid grand narratives, instead offering closely focussed essays on individual texts, theatres and markets for plays in an attempt to reassess Caroline drama from the inside out.

Monographs on individual playwrights, too, have begun to appear. Matthew Steggle's *Richard Brome: Place and Politics on the Caroline Stage* continues the critical pattern of reading Caroline drama politically, paying particular attention to the importance of specific locations in Brome's plays. Lisa Hopkins's *John Ford's Political Theatre* examines the contexts of production of Ford's plays, and is concerned primarily, but not exclusively, with the politics of religion – an approach that Rebecca Bailey also takes in *Staging the Old Faith: Queen Henrietta Maria and the Theatre of Caroline England, 1625–42* which re-evaluates the drama of and around Henrietta Maria's Court to consider a politics of Catholicism directed towards the Queen presented in James Shirley and William Davenant's writings. Less obviously politically, although concerned with the politics of interpretation, Joanne Rochester's *Staging Spectatorship in the Plays of Philip Massinger* centres around three of Massinger's plays and explores differing levels of interpretive gaze in the relationship and interaction between audiences (on and off stage) with the action presented. In this book, I hope to uphold the growing academic investment in, and investigation of, the texts and contexts of Caroline drama.

Staging Caroline Legal Authority

To return to Caroline drama's political beginnings: in *Theatre and Crisis 1632–1642* Butler argues that, 'Drama of the 1630s, perhaps more than any earlier drama, did persistently engage in debating the political issues of its day, and repeatedly articulated attitudes which can only be labelled "opposition" or "puritan"' (1984, pp.1–2). He does, however, maintain that, throughout the period 1632–42, drama did not question Charles's power or authority, rather, that what he faced were problems of government (1984, pp.13, 16). In this book, I want to expand the 'oppositional' positions that Butler establishes to include a specific politics of law that did indeed challenge the power and authority of the King. By this I do not wish to suggest that Caroline England, particularly its theatres, was overflowing with republicans; indeed, there is a notable but deliberate absence of republicans in my readings of the plays. The modern meaning of republic, as a state in which supreme power rests in the people and their elected representatives or officers, as opposed to one governed by a king or similar ruler, *was* current in the period, but, as Sanders argues, it was also used to refer to the community of the commonweal, and had an inflected meaning in the sixteenth and seventeenth centuries which was more constitutional: 'a republic implied a mixed form of government ... even a monarchy – a limited accountable monarchy – might be republican in its politics' (1998, pp.2–3), so the slipperiness of the term makes its use problematic.[7] I have, then, avoided republics and republicans in the chapters which follow, in part because of the ambiguousness of these terms, and in part to avoid temptation or accusation of reading with hindsight in the knowledge that the Civil War and Interregnum were to come. No one in 1629 knew how long Charles would rule without Parliament; no one in the mid-1630s knew there would be Civil War within a decade, and no one in the 1630s anticipated an English republic.[8] Revisionist and post-revisionist historians of the period, although they

---

[7]   For a discussion of republicanism in a variety of meanings and interpretations in relation to Ben Jonson's plays, see Julie Sanders's *Ben Jonson's Theatrical Republics*.

[8]   There is evidence of thinking that a republic without a monarch was at least possible in the documents that were prepared by members of Elizabeth I's Privy Council whilst there was concern for her safety from the supporters of Mary, Queen of Scots. Usually

differ on ideas of overarching ideological differences, do agree that the Civil War, and the subsequent execution of the monarch, were in no way inevitable.

This is not to say that there was no republican thinking in the period. Markku Peltonen's *Classical Humanism and Republicanism in English Political Thought 1570–1640* traces republican discourse as an alternative set of ideas to those concerning absolutism and the ancient constitution, arguing that:

> Although classical republicanism as a constitutional goal was not fully developed
> in early modern England, a theory of citizenship, public virtue and true nobility
> based essentially on the classical humanist and republican traditions, was taken
> up, studied and fully endorsed throughout the period. (1995, p.12)

The only true nobility, humanist republican thought argued, is found in pursuing the *vita activa*, undertaking virtuous acts for the good of the commonwealth.[9] Such a pursuit was not incompatible with support for a strong monarchy (Peltonen, 1995, p.165), and thus does not necessarily imply the advocation of rule without a monarch. Nevertheless, a strain of republican thought was evident in literature of the period, particularly in poetry.[10] Caroline drama, however, whatever it might suggest about tyrannous monarchs, legitimate legal actions, parliamentary activity or constitutional monarchy, does not advocate government without a king. There is a possible exception to this in James Shirley's *The Traytor*, in which Lorenzo, the Duke's kinsman and favourite, uses republican ideas of nobility and active virtue set against the corruption and vice of the court to persuade Sciarrha to help him kill the Duke. Sciarrha believes his promises for a virtuous government but it is clear to the audience that Lorenzo's republican rallying is merely a ruse to gain support; his government would have been as corrupt as the Duke. At the end of the play, with the Duke, Lorenzo and Sciarrha all dead, Cosimo, as 'the next /Of blood' (Sig. L1v) becomes the ruler of Florence. Although the idea of a republic is posited, the play is not able, finally, to institute this kind of government.

Whilst arguments for the *vita activa* of classical humanism and republicanism were developed under James VI and I, Peltonen notes that the 'humanist tradition did not have as strong an ideological significance in the latter part of the 1620s',

---

when the monarch died, the Privy Council and Parliament disbanded and were recalled or reconstituted by the new monarch. Under the proposals put forward in a document which was never approved by the Queen or passed in Parliament, Burghley proposed that in the event of the Queen's sudden death without named heir, the Privy Council or Parliament or both would not disband and, with judicial officials, would rule in a 'quasi-republican state of emergency'. For a detailed discussion, see Collinson (1987, *passim*, p.418).

   [9] For a full discussion, see Peltonen (1995, especially chapter 3). The idea of the virtuous citizen leading the *vita activa* is set against the scholastic idea of the *vita contemplativa* which involved seclusion from public and political life (Peltonen, 1995, p.144 and *passim*).

   [10] For a detailed discussion, see David Norbrook's *Writing the English Republic: Poetry, Rhetoric and Politics 1627–1660.*

suggesting that one of the reasons for this was that 'the real issues at stake ... were such that a juristic vocabulary and more particularly one of the ancient constitution proved perhaps more efficacious in countering the king's policy' (1995, pp.286, 288). The challenges presented to Charles's authority in law were not challenges to his position as monarch, but rather to his ability to act above, beyond or outside the established laws of the country; it was a debate about the nature of kingship, not about whether there should be a king. One of the aims of this book is to highlight the ways in which debates over the extent of legitimate monarchical legal authority were played out on the Caroline stage.

Under Charles I, there was no debate over whether the country should be governed by rule of law; the conflict arose over whose law should take precedence: the law of the king or the common law. Many common lawyers believed that the king had no extra-legal powers, and the king's prerogative was nothing more than those rights which he possessed under the law. Absolutists, on the other hand, accepted no limitation to the royal prerogative. This was not a new debate. The extent of the royal prerogative and the relative position of prerogative and law had been under discussion for some time:

> The idea that the royal prerogative was derived from and limited by law was orthodox among Tudor lawyers. Moreover, the Tudor monarchs themselves accepted legal limitations upon their powers in practice, whatever high views of their authority they may have held in theory. James and Charles, by contrast, proved far more willing to test their theoretical claims at law. (Sommerville, 1999, p.99)

James's public professions of his commitment to customary ways and established legal methods, Roger Lockyer suggests, had the effect of preserving the image of the King as a constitutional ruler despite his recourse to unpopular prerogative measures such as Impositions (1999, pp.240–1), and whatever his claims to absolute rule may have been elsewhere. Charles, on the other hand, made no attempt to cushion his claims to the prerogative in terms of the common law, and it was this, Glenn Burgess argues, which disrupted the Jacobean political consensus. Burgess argues that under James, discourses of common law and absolutism were not contradictory because they were used within particular parameters; thus James could claim a right to absolute monarchy in the theological discourse separating him from the Pope, and still claim supremacy for the common law without contradiction. Charles, however, either did not know or chose to ignore these conventions of political 'languages' that maintained a steady consensus under James, claiming an absolute prerogative not only in the theological discourses, but also in discourses of common law (Burgess, 1992, pp.179–81).[11] I do not intend,

---

[11] For a detailed examination of these political languages, see Burgess (1992, chapter 5). J. P. Sommerville disputes the existence of these languages, but does not suggest an alternative reason for a breakdown in legal and political relations in the Caroline period (1996, pp.44–5).

however, to describe in detail here the theories expounded and arguments made regarding common law and prerogative; a fuller discussion of ideas of divine right and the ancient constitution will be given in the appropriate chapters where their importance in drama in bringing legal discourse on to the Caroline stage will be explored.

The argument of this book is structured around the decentralisation and fragmentation of legitimate legal authority as it was presented in drama of the commercial theatre. Beginning with the concrete expression of the crisis in legal relations between Parliament, the law(yers) and the King in the Petition of Right, the chapters then move in stages away from the dramatic presentation of divinely appointed absolute monarchy, through the establishment of an alternative legitimate legal authority in the common law, to the divorce of a benevolent local authority from an absolutist central authority and finally the destabilisation, to the point of absence, of a legitimate legal authority.

Chapter 1, 'Rights, prerogatives and law: The Petition of Right' takes as its focus the debates surrounding the Petition of Right in 1628. The Petition makes reference to several important legal issues of the period which tested the relative positions of the king's will and the common law, such as granting monopolies, military billeting, prerogative taxation and arbitrary imprisonment. In doing so, it provides a useful introduction to the ideas of right, privilege and law which form the background to the concepts debated in the subsequent chapters: the position of the king in relation to the law, and the foundations for arguments against an extensive royal prerogative in the ancient constitution and in Magna Charta. The dramatic engagement with the Petition of Right in Jonson's *The New Inn* and, less directly, Brome's *The Love-sick Court* demonstrates a theatrical involvement in specific legal and political debates, and, in the same way that the Petition itself points towards the main arguments in law, these texts are indicative of the ways in which contemporary debate over legitimate legal authority was presented on stage throughout the period. *The New Inn* nods towards a perceived wilfulness in the monarch which is explored in Chapter 2, and presents a mock-sovereign presiding over an imagined court leading towards the ideas of trial and judicial authority explored in Chapter 5. Chapter 3 develops the connection made between reason and law in *The Love-sick Court,* and this play's presentation of a separate but centrally-connected authority in the countryside opens the possibilities of an alternative local legal authority which is the focus of Chapter 4.

Arguments for and against unlimited royal prerogative in theories of divine right rule, patriarchalism and non-resistance are the subject of Chapter 2, 'Shaking the foundations of royal authority: from divine right to the king's will'. This chapter argues, through a chronological discussion of three of Massinger's Caroline plays, that during the period there was a change in the way that the monarch's authority was presented on stage. Whilst Massinger's *The Roman Actor* presents ideas of the irrefutable divine right and absolute power of kings, this claim to absolute authority through an intrinsic divinity is questioned in *The Emperour of the East* which presents the monarch as a fallible and wilful man. The decline from divinity in the stage-monarch to the point at which the insistence on the unlimited prerogative comes to be seen as the enforcement of the arbitrary acts of a wilful, and entirely mortal, man rather than the wishes of a divinely protected and authorised king is examined through a reading of *The Guardian*.

This decline from divinity to wilfulness allows the possibility of an alternative legal authority which functions to moderate the king's will. Chapter 3, 'Debating legal authorities: common law and prerogative', puts forward the common law as such an alternative. It begins by establishing the legitimacy of the common law as a legal authority through its connection with custom and the ancient constitution, explored in the theatre in Brome's *The Queenes Exchange*. Royal absolutism in this chapter is set against a rationality which contemporary legal discourse associates with custom and common law, and in this play and the others to be discussed here, *The Antipodes* and *The Queen and Concubine*, arbitrary absolutism comes to be represented as the opposite of reason: madness. This madness, I argue, is not only self-destructive but also creates a kind of madness in the country as the plays suggest that an effect of royal disregard for established law is the destabilising of legal authority. When royal will competes with established common law, what exactly the law is, and where authority lies, is brought into doubt.

Attempts to enforce prerogative laws were compounded by an attempt to centralise systems of local government. Chapter 4, 'Decentralising legal authority: from the centre to the provinces', is concerned with the idea and implementation of legal authority in the localities, and focuses on figures of local justice such as constables and Justices of the Peace. It argues, through a reading of Brome's *The Weeding of Covent Garden* and Jonson's *A Tale of a Tub*, that Justices of the Peace represent royal absolutism, and that constables are more liminal figures, selective in their implementation of established law and keeping a balance between the strict enforcement of law and local public relations. Like the destabilising of legal authority caused by wilful action discussed in Chapter 3, *A Tale of a Tub* suggests that the manipulation of law for their own ends by representatives of crown authority destabilises local order, and makes the local officers' positions untenable. In presenting the debates on arbitrary prerogative and reasonable law in a provincial context, I argue, plays such as Brome's *A Jovial Crew* suggest that Charles I's attempts to enforce central law more strictly in the provinces, and thus centralise legal authority, polarised legal positions, not only destabilising but potentially fragmenting legal authority.

Chapter 5, 'The theatre of the courtroom', discusses dramatic trial scenes in the context of contemporary court procedures, apparent perception of these procedures and the political and legal debates outlined in the chapters above. The focus of this chapter is the connection between the law court and the theatre, examining the interplay between court, theatre, law and legitimate legal authority. The trial in Massinger's *The Roman Actor* is essentially a trial of theatre, and reminds the audience of the precarious position censorship created for actors and dramatists. However, this chapter will argue that the theatre also provides a courtroom in which to judge legal authorities and processes. *The Roman Actor* acknowledges the Emperor as absolute judge despite his absence from the trial, but this position of authority is questioned and undermined in later plays. Ford's *The Ladies Triall* places the 'monarch as judge' into a domestic sphere to question unnecessary royal trials of loyalty, and to reinforce the need for a monarch to obey his own laws as established by the plays discussed in Chapter 3. The acted trials (as forms of 'plays within the plays') in Brome's *The Antipodes* and Shirley's *The Traytor* examine the ways in which trials were conducted, and find both the legal system and the judicial authorities wanting. More than this, though, the lack of a true figure of legal authority in these trials, this chapter will argue, is representative of the destabilisation and fragmentation of legal authority caused by attempts to enforce the King's will as central authority, circumventing established legal and local authorities. Such trials of authority exemplify Caroline theatre's legal engagement as a forum for political and legal debate.

Inclusions and exclusions

Finally, some words on the scope of this study: in terms of its literary coverage, my focus is chiefly on the works of Massinger, Brome, Jonson, Shirley and Ford as representative of the Caroline professional theatre. Their Caroline plays were primarily staged at the private indoor theatres of the Blackfriars, Cockpit/Phoenix and Salisbury Court by the royally patronised King's Men, Queen's Men and the King and Queen's Young Company (Beeston's Boys).[12] The more expensive indoor venues suggest a wealthy, well-educated audience; Blackfriars and the Cockpit were 'the favourite resort[s] of the gentry' (*JCS*, VI, p.47), and the gentlemen of the Inns of Court 'provided an influential segment of the play-going public' at these theatres (Neill, 2007, para. 5). Thus the plays concerning the law and legitimate legal authority to be discussed here were performed to an audience for whom they would be particularly resonant, in a place where this audience could interact less formally than at court:

> The theatres were neutral zones, independent of the court, where the gentry gathered casually, but also on a regular basis and with interests that were widely shared, and where ideas and attitudes were actively exchanged. They were both public settings and areas of unrivalled personal interchange. (Butler, 1984, p.110)

The theatres thus created a venue for development of a public sphere, in which legal argument and political discussion could thrive. Whilst it may seem that this only included the gentry, some of the plays were also performed at the Globe, as the King's Men alternated by season between the Globe and Blackfriars (Gurr,

---

[12]   The King's Men and the Queen's Men were adult companies; the King and Queen's Young Company was not a traditional boy's acting group, but a combination of adult and child actors (*JCS*, I, p.324, n.1).

1996, p.150), suggesting a broader, more socially diverse audience for the same legal arguments.[13]

In legal terms, my concern is with the competing claims of custom, common law and royal prerogative made central to Caroline politico-legal debate by Charles's insistence on the unlimited scope of his prerogative powers; the constraints of time and space prevent a discussion of civil, ecclesiastical and admiralty law. Whilst I have read widely in the legal texts of the period, choices of what to include here were guided to some extent by the discussion of these issues in the work of legal and political historians, particularly J. G. A. Pocock's *The Ancient Constitution and the Feudal Law. A Study of English Historical Thought in the Seventeenth Century*, Glenn Burgess's *The Politics of the Ancient Constitution: An Introduction to English Political Thought, 1603–1642*, J. P. Sommerville's *Royalists and Patriots: Politics and Ideology in England 1603–1640* and Alan Cromartie's *The Constitutionalist Revolution: An Essay on the History of England 1450–1642*. Except where English translations were necessary, wherever possible I have used for both legal tracts and dramatic texts editions that would have been available to contemporary readers and audiences, as the circulation of such texts in print provided further opportunities for the discussion of the legal ideas contained in them.[14]

The plays and playwrights to be discussed here were deeply concerned with issues of divine right, absolute monarchy, the ancient constitution, laws and liberties. In the chapters which follow, this book will argue that Charles I's attempts to gain greater and tighter control over the laws of the kingdom, asserting himself as the highest legal authority, led to an equal assertion of alternative legitimate legal authorities. The plays of the foremost playwrights of the Caroline commercial stage, by employing the terms of contemporary legal discourse, present and juxtapose these authorities, allowing their audience to see and debate the potential consequences of adherence to royal will or rule according to common law or local practice. In over-asserting kingly and central authority, the plays suggest, Charles's policies raise the possibilities of destabilisation, fragmentation and disintegration of legitimate legal authority.

---

[13] Brome's *The Northern Lasse* and Massinger's *The Emperour of the East* are known to have been performed in both theatres. Shirley's *The Doubtful Heir* was written to be performed in Ireland. On return to England a performance was planned for Blackfriars but it was actually played at the Globe. Massinger's *The Guardian*, Brome's *The Northern Lasse*, Jonson's *A Tale of a Tub* and Shirley's *The Dukes Mistris* were also acted at court.

[14] Where Caroline editions of the plays were not available, whilst accepting Steggle's caveat that later printing may include revisions reflecting the context of print production (2006, p.166), I have used the first printed edition. See David Zaret (1992, *passim*) for a discussion of the development of a public sphere through print.

Chapter 1
Rights, Prerogatives and Law:
The Petition of Right

'Soit droit fait come est desire' was the long awaited and sought after second response from King Charles I to the Petition of Right in 1628. 'Let right be done as is desired' recognised that wrongs had been done to Charles's subjects, and stated the King's will that the same wrongs would not affect his subjects again. In recognising the validity of the Petition in this particular way, Charles was seen to be acknowledging his subjects' rights under the law and the limits to his own prerogative, and as such, this response was met with joy by those who had fought for the Petition's acceptance. Francis Nethersole, member of the House of Commons, wrote to Princess Elizabeth that the bells of London were ringing and men were making bonfires at every door in celebration (Foster, 1974, p.22). That the King realised these implications was made clear in his decision to have the Petition reprinted after Parliament's authorised version, changing his printed response back to that of his first answer:

> The King willeth that right be done according to the laws and customs of the realm, and that the statutes be put in due execution, that the subject may have no just cause to complain of any wrong or oppressions contrary to their rights and just liberties, to the preservation whereof he holds himself in conscience as well obliged as of his prerogative. (quoted in Russell, 1979, p.377)

This first reply had been a royal attempt to respond to the Petition without limiting Charles's prerogative, admitting wrong action on the King's part or providing a written explication of the law. As such, it was not an appropriate answer to the Petition and was unacceptable to Parliament which began, as in the dissolved session of 1626, to debate taking action against the Duke of Buckingham whose influence they blamed in part for the divide between the people and the King. Finally, in the House of Lords, Buckingham and Saye arranged to petition the King to change his response, and asked the Commons if they would join them. This resulted in Charles's second, and much more acceptable, response, with the added qualification that he meant no more by it than his first, and that the Parliament neither meant to, nor could, hurt his prerogative. Charles understood his prerogative to be divinely given and invulnerable, and this was the understanding of some in the House of Lords: 'the king had "a royal prerogative, intrinsical to his sovereignty and betrusted him withal from God for the common safety of the whole people and not for their destruction"' (Russell, 1979, p.353). Factions in Parliament argued that they could not damage the King's prerogative in their list of grievances in the Petition of Right because in those things he had no prerogative

(Russell, 1979, p.362). This chapter investigates how Caroline drama staged the relationship between rights, prerogatives and law highlighted in these different responses and encapsulated in debates held over the Petition of Right.

Performed in the aftermath of the Parliament which passed the Petition of Right, and immediately before the meeting of the 1629 Parliament, Ben Jonson's *The New Inn* (1629) examines the use and abuse of prerogative through a background of common law rights based in Magna Charta, and addresses many of the Petition's grievances in the immediate court and parliamentary context of 1628–9. Theatrical engagement with the Petition of Right is continued in Richard Brome's *The Love-sick Court* (1636–8), which will be discussed in the final section of the chapter.[1] This play deals less specifically with the particular grievances and instead uses the Petition of Right and the idea of petitioning as a means to examine the structure of relationships between king, court and parliament, thus engaging not only in a discussion of earlier political structures and arguments, but also commenting on contemporary activity at court.[2]

Issues of Right; Problems of Law

Petitioning was a common way to approach the monarch or Privy Council for assistance. There were two main forms of petition: the petition of right, and the petition of grace. Private petitions of right asked the king to provide justice to an injured party, seeking redress for specific, identified and investigated grievances; those of grace sought mercy or exemption for a subject from an aspect of law. What was unusual about the Petition of Right in 1628 was that it was presented collectively by both Houses of Parliament on behalf of the country to gain redress for grievances caused by the King's manipulation of law regarding taxation and imprisonment. Members of Parliament sought a royal explanation of those laws by which he claimed to act, or the institution of further laws to confirm the liberties of his subjects. Although Charles was prepared to confirm existing laws, including Magna Charta (which was usually appealed to in cases of dispute between the sovereign and subject over rights and liberties), he was not prepared to create new laws, or to provide a legally binding, explicit elaboration of the meaning of

---

[1]   The dates given in parentheses for plays here and in subsequent chapters indicate dates of writing, licensing or first performance. The dating of *The Love-sick Court* is particularly unclear with suggested dates ranging from 1626–40. I would suggest that the play's reference to Tempe points towards a date of, or after, 1632 when the masque *Tempe Restored* was performed at court. Most critics now agree that the play was composed in the mid-1630s.

[2]   This more general engagement with the Petition may reflect the later date of the play, as whilst specific details of the Petition of Right might not have been so immediately clear in the 1630s, the issues of prerogative it involved were still current, and the political resonance of the Petition itself continued throughout the period. For example, the Petition was often cited in John Hampden's case in the Exchequer Chamber in 1637 and 1638 regarding his obligation to pay ship money (Reeve, 1986, p.261).

such existing laws, which could potentially limit his scope for interpretation or prerogative action. A further ratification of Magna Charta did not go far enough for many of those sitting in Parliament; it had been confirmed several times in the past by a number of monarchs, and had not provided sufficient guarantee of the subjects' liberties, depending as it did on the king's interpretations and enactment of its provisions. After some debate, the House of Commons decided to present the Petition of Right. In using this form of petition, they were not merely presenting a complaint over unsubstantiated grievances; rather, a petition of right was a statement that wrong had been done, and that the monarch had to take action to rectify the issues stated. Although the King had refused to clarify the law, the Petition also provided a bridge between complaint and legislation: gaining royal assent to a petition of right was an archaic method of passing law. Nevertheless, the extent to which the Petition could be seen as a statute was and is heavily debated.[3]

The Petition of Right does, however, provide a statement of the developing contemporary concern that the structure of legal authority was not sufficiently clear or defined. It was, L. J. Reeve claims:

> an early and clear sign of the problems of Charles's reign. They included his own inclination to govern of arbitrary will, his losing the support of powerful individuals in the house of lords… Perhaps the most critical problem of all was the widespread refusal to trust Charles, and the insistence by his subjects on legal guarantees, when fundamental interests or principles were at stake. (1986, p.275)

According to Conrad Russell, however, the problem that Parliament sought to resolve through the Petition was not merely a lack of trust in the King, but a lack of confidence in the law, particularly as a safe guarantee of liberty (1979, pp.350, 348). It was because the law no longer seemed to provide the legal guarantees Reeve describes that the Commons sought a clarification of the law from the King. The Petition described the particular grievances for which it sought redress, and asked:

> [t]hat no man hereafter be compelled to make or yield any gift, loan, benevolence, tax or such like charge without common consent by act of parliament, and that none be called to make answer or take such oath or to give attendance or be confined or otherwise molested or disquieted concerning the same or for refusal thereof. And that no freeman in any such manner as is before mentioned be imprisoned or detained. And that your Majesty would be pleased to remove the said soldiers and mariners, and that your people may not be so burdened in time

---

[3]   L. J. Reeve argues that using a Petition was a deliberately antiquarian attempt to revert to an older method of legislation (1986, p.369). In the 1628 Parliament, Coryton objected that legislation had not been made by petition and answer since the fifteenth century (Guy, 1982, p.311). William Prynne discussed the Petition as a law at a reading at the Inns of Court in 1661 because, he argued, 'it is a law originally framed, prosecuted and passed according to the ancientest and most usual parliamentary way; to wit not by bill, as of late times, but by petition' (Foster, 1974, p.24).

to come. And that the aforesaid commissions for proceeding by martial law may be revoked and annulled. And that hereafter no commissions of like nature may issue forth to any person or persons whatsoever to be executed as aforesaid, lest by colour of them any of your Majesty's subjects be destroyed or put to death contrary to the laws and franchises of the land. (Kenyon, 1986, p.70)

'Franchise', Coke clarified during the 1628 Commons debates, 'is a French word, and in Latin it is liberty. In Magna Carta, *nullus imprisonetur* nor put out of his liberty or franchise' (Russell, 1979, p.351).

In presenting a statement of his subjects' rights, the Petition of Right also implicitly brought into question the rights to the prerogative powers that the King claimed. One of the main crisis points between the asserted legal rights of his subjects and those of the King was the Five Knights' Case of 1627. Sir Thomas Darnel, Sir John Heveningham, Sir Walter Erle, Sir John Corbet and Sir Edmund Hampden, gaoled without cause shown for refusing to pay the Forced Loan of 1626, sought release through a writ of *habeas corpus*, which meant that the true reason for their imprisonment had to be made known to a court in order to determine the legality of their detention. Had the King's Attorney returned that they were held for refusal to pay the Loan, their writ should have allowed the judges the opportunity to make a ruling on the legality of the Loan, as well as on the legality of the knights' detention. However, the answer returned was that they had been imprisoned, and continued to be so, *'per speciale mandatum domini regis'* (by his majesty's special command). J. A. Guy argues that this form of words was a direct response to the prisoners' presumed strategy, and prevented a judicial review of the Loan's legality; rather, it shifted the debate to the extent of the royal prerogative (1982, p.291). As no further defence could be made, the prisoners were refused bail and returned to gaol.

Was imprisonment at the king's command without further cause stated acceptable under the law? Magna Charta, the Petition of Right reminded the King, stated that no man could be 'imprisoned... outlawed or exiled or in any manner destroyed, but by the lawful judgment of his peers or by the law of the land' (Kenyon, 1986, p.69); however, this left the problem of what exactly the law of the land (*lex terrae*) was. Coke argued that 'If I have any law, *lex terrae* is the common law' (quoted in Reeve, 1986, p.265), which meant that prerogative imprisonment was against the stipulations of Magna Charta. The King and Privy Councillors, however, argued that the King had the right to detain potential felons for reasons of state without giving more specific cause. There were precedents for incarceration without cause shown: Guy Fawkes, for example, had been held for reasons of state without complaints of infringement of liberties or applications of *habeas corpus* (Russell, 1979, p.347), and in 1592 the Elizabethan judges had explained the propriety of prerogative imprisonment:

> If any person be committed by her Majesty's commandment from her person, or by order from the Council Board, or if any one or two of her Council commit one for high treason, such persons so in the case before committed may not be delivered by any of her courts without due trial by the law, and judgement of acquittal had. (quoted in Guy, 1982, pp.293–4)

Guy notes, however, that although this allowed the monarch or the Privy Council to imprison without bail, it also points towards an intended trial (for which the cause of imprisonment would have to be given); it is not licence for indefinite arbitrary imprisonment. That Charles had returned an answer of '*per speciale mandatum domini regis*' to the knights' writ of *habeas corpus* meant that they would be detained indefinitely, as no defence could be mounted without substantive charges to answer. Reeve argues that 'the practice by which Charles had had the knights remanded constituted not the manipulation but rather the *prevention* of due process' (1986, p.267). It was in this prevention of due process of law that Charles contravened the stipulations of Magna Charta's *lex terrae* clause (Christianson, 1985, p.68). The further difference was that in this case the prisoners were not held on suspicion of plotting treason, but for refusal to pay the Forced Loan; Charles had clearly abused his right to prerogative imprisonment for reasons of state as a political tool to punish those who displeased him and to prevent judicial review of the Forced Loan (Reeve, 1986, p.263).

It was not only arbitrary imprisonment and the Forced Loan which led to the Petition of Right, however. Russell argues that the presence of so many soldiers billeted in civilians' homes, however 'unpaid and mutinous' and 'unfit to stand against a continental enemy' they might have been, carried the implicit threat of military force to impose the King's will (1979, pp.335–6). Billeting was, in fact, one of the specified grievances of the Petition:

> [O]f late great companies of soldiers and mariners have been dispersed into divers counties of the realm, and the inhabitants against their wills have been compelled to receive them into their houses, and there to suffer them to sojourn against the laws and customs of this realm, and to the great grievance and vexation of the people. (Kenyon, 1986, p.69)

Not only was billeting a great expense to those upon whom it was forced without adequate financial redress, it also brought military practices into a domestic sphere. Thus, closely related to billeting, the Petition also addressed the exercise of martial law. Although it was accepted that martial law was a suitable way of maintaining order amongst troops in war time, the concern was that such systems of law and justice were being, or would be, imposed upon the King's non-military subjects. Again, as with prerogative imprisonment, an arbitrary, summary law threatened to override the rule and due process of established statute and customary law which supposedly guaranteed the liberties of the subject. It is with the theatrical negotiation between prerogative, liberties, parliament and law in *The New Inn* and *The Love-sick Court* that the rest of this chapter is concerned.

Assuming Authority: *The New Inn*

The main plot of Ben Jonson's *The New Inn* explores the appropriate extent of the royal prerogative and parliamentary advice through the establishment of a mock court (potentially royal, legal and parliamentary), presided over by the servant Pru as Queen for the day. This pretended court organised by women, the disputations of love and valour which it hears and the backdrop of the Barnet Inn called 'The Light Heart' have led Julie Sanders to read the play in terms of the politics of female acting, the socially inclusive environment of the inn, sumptuary laws, and the *saloniste* brand of neo-Platonism espoused by the Countess of Carlisle.[4] The play's relationship with the politics and parliamentary activities of 1628 and 1629 has been noted by Martin Butler, although he chooses rather to read the play as a comment on a possible rapprochement of King and Parliament on the death of Buckingham rather than an exploration of the political ideas of the Petition. Indeed, he reads the direct reference to the Petition of Right in Act II as a 'disparaging echo of the most important legislative enactment of the 1628 Parliament' (1992b, p.173). I will argue here that *The New Inn*'s engagement with the Petition of Right is more detailed and more positive than Butler allows, suggesting that the play advocates the balance of subjects' rights against a moderated, if not curtailed, royal prerogative. As the main plot focuses on the position of the prerogative, the sub plot addresses specific grievances of the Petition of Right such as billeting and martial law.

From very early in the play, it is clear that *The New Inn* participates in the discourses of rights, liberties and the appropriate use of prerogative that the Petition of Right raised. Goodstocke, the Host of The Light Heart Inn, declares to Lovel, his melancholy guest, in Act I, scene ii: 'It is against my free-hold, my inheritance, / My *Magna charta*, *Cor laetificat*, / To drinke such balder dash, or bonny clabbee!' (*New Inn*, sigs. B2r-B2v). Although the Host is here ostensibly doing nothing more than commenting on the quality of particular drinks, his terms of reference are political, and particularly relevant to subjects' freedom from arbitrary imprisonment and to their right to hold their own property inviolate to the prerogative claims of forced loans and extra parliamentary taxation. Moreover, his appropriation of these terms is not allowed to pass without comment:

Lov[el]:   Humerous Host.

Host: I care not if I be.

Lov: But airy also.
        Not to defraud you of your rights, or trench
        Upo' your priviledges, or great charter,
        (For those are every hostlers language now)
        Say, you were borne beneath those smiling starres,
        Have made you Lord, and owner of the Heart,
        Of the Light Heart in *Barnet*; suffer us
        Who are more *Saturnine*, t'enjoy the shade
        Of your round roofe yet.
        (*New Inn*, sig. B2v)

---

4   See Sanders's 'The Day's Sports Devised in the Inn'; *Theatrical Republics* (1998, pp.144–63); 'Wardrobe Stuffe' and 'Caroline Salon Culture', respectively.

Although the discussion is framed in light-hearted terms surrounding the humours of the host and his guests, thus connecting this play with Jonson's earlier drama and drawing attention to the play as a theatrical event, Lovel's comments that 'rights', 'priviledges' and the 'great charter' 'are every hostlers language now' suggest a public familiarity with these terms and their meaning. Inns and taverns were potentially places of political discussion in the seventeenth century; that the host of an inn should be familiar with these terms is not unlikely. Adam Smyth notes that inns became increasingly important as locations for meetings between town merchants, county justices and landowners (2004, p.xx), and Michelle O'Callaghan discusses taverns (slightly different spaces in terms of the social hierarchy of drinking establishments but similar in providing a space for lawyers and gentlemen to meet socially) as the location to foster 'new forms of sociability among an urban elite' (2004, p.37) providing a space for educated men to meet for literary and political discussion. Particularly interesting in terms of the political significance of tavern societies, she notes a coincidence in the early seventeenth century in the members of a particular tavern fraternity supporting each other's activities in parliament (2004, p.49). Butler's assertion that Lovel 'sadly acknowledges that every innkeeper with a grudge against the great has started to pick up such loose constitutional terms' (1992b, p.173) assumes an irritation in Lovel's response which is not merited by the rest of their conversation: Goodstocke is the Host of the Inn, this is a good-natured conversation and Lovel remains polite even in his melancholy. There is no reason that his comment should not be a reply to the Host in his own terms. That Goodstocke is, as is later revealed, actually the missing Lord Frampul, and is therefore, as his name suggests, of the 'good stock' of aristocratic descent, may also contribute to his concern with inheritance and familiarity with these terms.[5]

It is against this discourse of Magna Charta, and backdrop of rights, inheritance and liberties that Pru and Lady Frampul set up their mock court where Pru is Queen for the day and in which, with Goodstocke's permission, all at the Light Heart become subject to her rule. The inclusion of all the play's characters in this performance is emphasised in the ladies' disappointment that Stuff, the tailor, has not delivered Pru's monarchical gown: 'If he had but broke with me, I had not car'd, /But with the company, the body politique' (*New Inn*, sig. C2v). Stuff has failed to play his part in the illusion, breaking faith with the newly constituted State under Pru, and with the 'company', both social and dramatic (acting company). This dramatic metaphor is continued in the conversation over the dress Lady Frampul lends to Pru instead:

---

[5]   Inheritance and heraldry are significant themes in this play. See Sheila Walsh, '"But yet the lady, th'heir, enjoys the land": Heraldry, Inheritance and Nat(ion)al Households in Jonson's *The New Inn*', for a discussion of the ways in which the play advocates inheritance by daughters and explores contemporary English colonial activity in Ireland through Shelee-nien who is also the missing Lady Frampul.

Lad[y]:   'Twill fit the *Players* yet,
          When thou hast done with it, and yield thee somewhat.

Pru: That were illiberal, madam, and mere sordid
       In me, to let a sute of yours come there.

Lad[y]: Tut all are *Players*, and but serve the *Scene*.
        (*New Inn*, sig. C3r)

In terms of the acting of this play, most of the main characters are, at some point, acting a role: Lord Frampul as Goodstock, the Host; Laetitia Frampul as Frank (Goodstocke's son) as Laetitia (a relative and companion of Lady Frampul); Pru as the Sovereign; Pinnacia Stuff as a Lady and Stuff as her footman. The deliberate, self-conscious recognition that 'all are Players', that everyone in the play is acting a part (both as actors on the stage, and as disguised or costumed characters) also draws attention to the idea that all of the characters serve a purpose, they 'but serve the scene'. Michael Hattaway notes the significance of the setting of the play in terms of its self-conscious theatricality:

> We know that actors imitate real people, but setting the action in a place of resort
> or revelry reminds us that imitation or acting is characteristic of life as well as of
> art, that men and women as actors perform and play games, maintain illusions,
> ape and reflect one another's roles. (1984, p.17)

This suggests a licence for social experiment and inversion at the Inn which is elaborated on at the mock court with its servant-sovereign, described as the 'dayes sports devised i'the Inne' (*New Inn*, sig. B8r). Whilst 'sport' suggests that this will be the day's entertainment, it also hints towards the amorous encounters to be had at this court, and once again is an indication of the theatricality of the occasion: these proceedings are all, supposedly at least, in jest. The inversion of the usual order in the servant-sovereign and mock court has elements of carnival, and all will be put in its correct order – including the reunion of Lord and Lady Frampul in their proper roles – at the end of the play.

Set in the discourse of rights and prerogatives which pervades the play, the inversions of the 'dayes sports', along with the extensive role playing throughout, provide a framework in which to explore the roles which parliament and monarch should play in relation to subjects' rights and liberties. Indeed, the contemporary political relevance of the play is asserted when Goodstocke comments, again in dramatic terms, on how he sees activities at The Light Heart:

> *If* I be honest, and that all the cheat
> Be, of my selfe, in keeping this Light Heart,
> Where, *I* imagine all the world's a Play;
> The state, and mens affaires, all passages
> Of life, to spring new, *scenes* come in, goe out
> And shift, and vanish, and if *I* have got
> A seat, to sit at ease here, i'mine *I*nne,

> To see the *Comedy*; and laugh, and chuck
> At the variety, and throng of humors,
> And dispositions, that come justling in,
> And out still, as they one drove hence another.
> (*New Inn*, sig. B5r)

This, as earlier, aligns *The New Inn* with Jonson's humours plays, but is also an explicit iteration of the *theatrum mundi* topos (Hattaway, 1984, pp.19, 17). Not only is the audience reminded that the actors *are* actors in this play, but also that the Light Heart Inn, and by extension the theatre in which it is played, is representative of the world outside the theatre.

As sovereign of the day's sports, Pru presides over a court which hears both a petition and a bill of complaint. Lovel's complaint that he has received 'a disrespect' (*New Inn*, sig. D3r) from Lady Frampul results in two sessions of a Court of Love in which he speaks first of love and then of valour.[6] His discourse on valour which 'springs out of reason', 'the scope' of which is 'alwayes honour, and the publique good' (*New Inn*, sig. F4r) appeals for a revival of the gentlemanly sensibilities which led him earlier to make the (subsequently denied) request that the Host give his son to him as a page. His discourse of love follows the arguments of neo-Platonism which were increasingly popular at court, and takes the form of the arguments of Platonic symposia.[7] However, as Julie Sanders argues, the 'neo-Platonic strains in the text have been concentrated upon to the detriment of more politicized and potentially parliamentary strains' (1996, p.559), and here, I am particularly interested in these aspects of Pru's court. When it first convenes, Queen Pru is approached by Colonel Tipto:

Hos[t]:   Ask what you can S^{r.}
            So't be i'the house.

Tip[to]: I ask my rights and priviledges,
         And though for forme I please to cal't a suit,
         I have not beene accustomed to repulse.

Pru: No sweet Sir *Glorious*, you may still command –

Hos: And go without.

---

⁶   For a discussion of the tradition of the court of love, see Hattaway (1984, pp.30–31) and Mukherji (2006b, *passim*).

⁷   See Hattaway (1984, p.32) and Sanders (1996, p.559) for a discussion of the traditions on which Lovel's speeches rely. Whilst Hattaway notes it is unlikely that Platonism was as fashionable as it would be in the mid-1630s (1984, p.32), Sanders argues that the neo-Platonism exhibited in *The New Inn*, with Frances Frampul at its centre, follows that of the *salonistes*, which would have been easily recognisable in London in the late 1620s, and that Lady Frampul can be seen as a partial and satiric portrait of the Countess of Carlisle with whom this movement was associated (2000, pp.458, 456). Karen Britland, however, argues that a clear cut distinction between Henrietta Maria's brand of Platonism and that of the Countess of Carlisle is problematic (2006, pp.9–11).

Pru: But yet Sir being the first,
      And call'd a suit, you'll looke it shall be such
      As we may grant.

Lad[y Frampul]: *It* else denies it selfe.

Pru: You heare the opinion of the Court.

Tip: I mind

      No Court opinions.

Pru: 'Tis my Ladies, though.

Tip: My Lady is a Spinster, at the Law,
      And my petition is of right.

Pru: What is it?

Tip: *It* is for this poore learned bird.
      (*New Inn*, sig. D1v)

This interchange between the mock sovereign and petitioner draws attention explicitly to the Petition of Right, and Tipto's comment on Lady Frampul's position as a spinster emphasises his assertion of what he perceives as his own rights.[8] What he asks for, however, is not a redress of grievances, but the (unmerited) advancement of his man, Fly, at Pru's court. As such, his reference to the Petition is actually an abuse of the discourse of rights prevalent in the 1628 Parliament, serving to highlight the impropriety of undeserving court favourites and, by inference, the propriety of the real Petition of Right. The political significance of a comment on undeserving court favourites in a play written after the assassination of Buckingham and just before the meeting of the new 1629 Parliament should not be underestimated.

For their abuse of the rhetoric of rights and privileges Tipto and Fly are, deservedly, ejected from Pru's sensible court. Nevertheless, although this passage presents the Petition of Right in a favourable light, it does also set limits to appropriate petitioning. Whilst Pru indicates that Tipto may 'command' of her, Goodstocke's comment that in doing so he will 'go without' suggests that making demands of the monarch will result in a poor reception; Tipto's 'sute' must truly be a suit.[9] Moreover, it must be a suit which is 'i'the house' to answer,

---

[8]   Glossing this line, Michael Hattaway notes that 'Tipto suggests Lady Frampul was entitled to no special privilege in a court of law' (Brome, 1984, p.116, note to II.vi.57). Tipto might then be claiming an equal standing under the law with Lady Frampul.

[9]   Charles I later commented on the inappropriateness of couching demands in the form of a petition: discussing the 19 Propositions sent to the King he argued that 'Certainly, to exclude all power of denial, seemes an arrogancy, least of all becomming those who pretend to make their address in an humble and loyall way of petitioning' (1648, sig. F7r).

and 'such / As [Pru] may grant'. Any such petition, the play suggests, must be reasonable, through proper channels, and something that the monarch is able to grant, or it 'denies it selfe' even before it is asked. Pru's deference to the members of her court here suggests something of the importance of advisers giving – and monarchs receiving – advice, and her reference to the 'opinion of the court' invites a comparison between Pru's and the Caroline court, suggesting that there, too, any unreasonable demands will be denied/deny themselves.

Tipto's refusal to accept the court's opinion leads Pru to invoke her mistress as an authority seemingly higher than that of the court, insisting ''Tis my Ladies [opinion], though'. This places Lady Frampul in an ambiguous position regarding the court and laws of the day's sports; she becomes both a spinster *under* the law, and *of* the law in making the rules of the game. However, it is not Lady Frampul who is Queen of this court, but Pru, and her subsequent assertion of authority over Lady Frampul leads to a discussion of the extent of what Pru can legitimately command:

> Pru: Goe and kisse him,
>   I doe command it.
>
> Lad[y Frampul]:   Th'art not wilde, wench!
>
> Pru: Tame, and exceeding tame, but still your Sov'raigne.
>
> Lad: Hath too much bravery made thee mad?
>
> Pru: Nor proud.
>   Doe, what *I* doe enjoyne you. No disputing
>   Of my prerogative, with a front, or frowne;
>   Doe not detrect: you know th'authority
>   *Is* mine, and *I* will exercise it swiftly,
>   *If* you provoke me.
>   (*New Inn*, sig. D2v)

Whilst Lady Frampul is concerned that Pru has taken her authority too far – after all, her power and her 'bravery' are only loaned to her for 'the dayes sports' (sig. B8r) – Pru is absolutely assured of her sovereign power and authority in this matter, and there is no question for the audience that Pru is far from mad ('wilde'). Nor is this an abuse of her 'prerogative'; the on and off stage audiences sympathise with Lovel and with Pru's rules, not with her Lady's objections. Lady Frampul's choice of words here is, however, significant; in many Caroline plays madness is associated with tyranny and arbitrary, absolute monarchy.[10] That this play anticipates, if not participates in, this discourse is clear in the terms Lady Frampul uses in continuing to question Pru's command:

---

[10]   See, for example, Richard Brome's *The Queen and Concubine* and *The Queenes Exchange*, and John Ford's *The Ladies Triall*. I explore these texts in more detail in subsequent chapters.

Pru: The royall assent is past, and cannot alter.

Lad: You'l turne a Tyran.

Pru: Be not you a Rebell,
    It is a name alike odious.
    (*New Inn*, sig. D3r)

In equating tyranny and rebellion, this interchange seeks to present a harmonious, middle way, advocating co-operation between monarch and subjects and, perhaps, appealing to the Caroline audience for a peaceful session of the upcoming Parliament. It cannot be insignificant in the play's parliamentary context that this rejection of both tyranny and rebellion comes so close to the play's delineation of appropriate petitioning and royal response.

Despite Lady Frampul's protestations of tyranny, Pru's refusal to hear her complaint is not presented as the tyrannous act of an arbitrary monarch, but rather couched once again in the terms of contemporary legal argument: 'Would you make lawes, and be the first that break 'hem? / The example is pernicious in a subject, / And of your quality, most' (*New Inn*, sig. D3r). Lady Frampul has assumed that, because under other circumstances she holds authority over Pru, she is able to circumvent the 'laws' of the game she has set up. It is clear that this is not so, and Pru's argument echoes Caroline concerns, evident in several plays, that in his manipulations of the law Charles I broke his own (in being the laws of his kingdom) laws.[11] In placing this argument in the mouth of his stage monarch, Jonson criticises his own King in the presentation of a monarch with an exemplary attitude to law and justice. Contemporary confusion over what should be held as the highest authority, the king's will or the law, is echoed in the difficulty of deciphering who has authority at this point in the play: Lady Frampul's concern that she has 'woven a net / To snare [her] selfe in!' (*New Inn*, sig. D2v), suggests that as the instigator of the 'dayes sports', she holds ultimate authority, but Pru's position as sovereign of these sports gives her the power to enforce her own commands. Latimer's and the Host's interjections of 'Just Queene!', 'Brave Sovraigne!', 'A She-Trajan!' (*New Inn*, sig. D3r) emphasise not only Pru's position of authority, but also the justice of her comments, highlighting the need for obedience to laws from all levels of society. Although Lady Frampul attempts to attribute the popularity of Pru's decision to the fact that 'Prince *Power* will never want her *Parasites*', the play does not endorse this judgement of the mock-sovereign's supporters. Indeed, Pru's statement that justice is the primary concern of her reign ('We that doe love our justice, above all / Our other Attributes' (*New Inn*, sig. D3r)) is no mere posturing; she does attempt to uphold the justice attributed to her.

Although it is clear that moral authority lies with Pru, the confusion over who holds ultimate legal authority is continued throughout the play. Lady Frampul's concern that Pru will overstep her carnival authority is, after Lovel's two hours

---

[11]   Other examples include James Shirley's *The Doubtful Heir*, Richard Brome's *The Queen and Concubine* and Ford's *The Ladies Triall*.

and two kisses in the Court of Love, reversed in a complaint that Pru does not use her authority to make him stay:

Lad[y Frampul]: Why would you let him goe thus?

Pru: In whose power
         Was it to stay him, prop'rer then my Ladies!

Lad: Why in her Ladies? Are not you the Soveraigne?

…

Lad: But had not you the authority, absolute?
         (*New Inn*, sig. F8r)

Lady Frampul again wishes to change the terms of the 'dayes sports' to suit her own wishes. However, whilst she insists it was Pru's prerogative through her absolute sovereignty (which she had earlier denied her) to make Lovel stay, Pru acknowledges the limits to this authority: particularly in matters of love, sovereigns have no authority. She can, as sovereign for the day, command a kiss for Lovel from her Lady, but it would have been an overstepping of her authority to go beyond this.

In her peevishness, Lady Frampul soon highlights to Pru how temporary her powers are, calling her an 'idiot Chambermayd!' (*New Inn*, sig. F8v). In defence of her actions, Pru reminds Lady Frampul of her previous 'frowardnesse' regarding Lovel:

Pru: And were not you i'rebellion, Lady *Frampal*,
         From the beginning?

Lad: I was somewhat froward,
         I must confesse, but frowardnesse sometime
         Becomes a beauty, being but a visor
         Put on. You'l let a Lady weare her masque, *Pru.*

Pru: But how do I know, when her Ladiship is pleas'd
         To leave it off, except she tell me so?
         (*New Inn*, sig. F8r)

That Lovel, like Pru, leaves the mock court not understanding Lady Frampul's true feelings, to her disadvantage as well as his, suggests the importance of clarity in relationships between sovereigns and their 'servants' (*New Inn*, sig. B7r). The 'frowardnesse' Lady Frampul admits indicates a deliberate perverseness in her actions towards Lovel, and perhaps also towards Pru's authority. Lady Frampul responds that Pru would have understood had she been attentive or observant. But the problem Pru has with understanding when and where her authority applies feeds into a wider problem in *The New Inn* regarding what is meant by what is said, and what could not or should not be misunderstood, which James Loxley describes as a 'problem of seriousness' in the play. He suggests that Lady Frampul's response asserts:

> that this is a distinction that an utterance makes for the attentive reader, despite the circumstances which have called forth such an assertion. Language, they claim, ultimately reveals the intentions it embodies – only contingent factors such as ignorance, weakness or deliberate fault can in the last analysis impede such communication. (2002, p.96)

In a play concerned with the Petition of Right and the powers of the monarch, this problem of transparency is not insignificant; this same emphasis on clarity could be marshalled to support either the King's or Parliament's arguments over the law in the Petition of Right. Whilst Charles refused an explanation, maintaining that the law and his prerogative needed no further clarification, parliamentary calls for explanation and clarification of Charles's understanding of the law in the Petition of Right (to avoid such contingent factors as Loxley mentions with regard to authority in the play) could just as well be represented by Pru's question 'but how do I know…?' (*New Inn*, sig. F8r).

    These questions of interpretations and authority are punctuated throughout the play by the activities of the inn's staff and lower class inhabitants. Sir Glorious Tipto's pro-Spanish attitude leads Butler to argue that he is 'some sort of reflection on the world according to Buckingham…a flashy, hispanophile courtier', who, with Pinnacia Stuff and her pretences at gentility, presents antitypes which prove the validity of Lovel's ethical treatises during the Court of Love on love and valour (1992b, p.175). However, along with Fly, Tipto also serves to draw attention to military matters. Although Tipto's military connections are obvious from his title of Colonel, Fly too is associated with military activity:

Lat[imer]: What calling has' he?

Hos[t]:   Only to call in, still.
    Enflame the reckoning, bold to charge a bill,
    Bring up the shot i'the reare, as his owne word is,

Bea[ufort]: And do's it in the discipline of the house?
    As Corporall o' the field, *Maestro del Campo*,

Hos: And visiter generall, of all the roome,
    He has' form'd a fine *militia* for the Inne too.

Bea: And meanes to publish it?

Hos: With all his titles.
    Some call him Deacon *Fly*, some Doctor *Fly.*
    Some Captaine, some Leiutenant, But my folks
    Doe call him Quarter-master, *Fly*, which he is.
    (*New Inn*, sig. C6r)

As well as being a presentation of the dishonest inn-worker who inflates the customers' bills, Fly's position as corporal, lieutenant and Quartermaster (in military terms, usually a lieutenant responsible for finding quarters for the soldiers) raises the issue of billeting in this play already concerned with rights, prerogatives and petitioning. Named as the person responsible for billeting, his home at an Inn presents proper billeting practices: according to Coke and Phelips, 'no one could be compelled to take soldiers but inns, and they were to be paid for them' (Russell, 1979, p.336).

Fly's militia is highlighted as a specifically Caroline enterprise when Tipto describes it as 'an exact *Militia*' (*New Inn*, sig. D6r). His comment that it is 'a fine *Militia*, and well order'd' (sig. D5v) reflects Charles's concerns early in his reign to improve England's military preparation and build an exact militia, which he later could barely afford to maintain. Indeed, the inn is also an appropriate place for the establishment of a militia as much recruiting for Charles's new militia was done at drinking establishments (Sanders, 1996, p.555). The Host's description of Fly's activities at the inn is a series of military puns and the reference to his militia and his enforcement of discipline recalls the imposition of martial law to keep unruly (and unpaid) troops in order. There was some debate over whether the army was subject to civil jurisdiction. Lindsay Boynton notes that officers frequently claimed an exemption from this for the army in disputes with country magistrates, and that 'By doing so they afforded yet another cogent argument to those who maintained that martial, or military law was essential to govern an army, and against those who venerated the common law as a panacea' (1964, p.258). The concern over martial law also presented in the Petition of Right was closely related to billeting, so it is unsurprising that quarter-master Fly is also used to explore military law. Indeed, Fly and his militia are called upon to carry out the punishments decided on for Pinnacia and Nick Stuff: 'Let him be blanketted. Call up the Quarter-master / Deliver him ore, to Flie'. That the sensible, just and 'Mercifull queene Pru' to whom Stuff appeals tells him 'I cannot help you' (*New Inn*, sigs. F2v-F3r) suggests that requests to established judicial authorities outside martial law are or have been ineffective. It is, in this respect, relevant that the punishments decided on for Pinnacia and Stuff are put forward not by Pru but by the Host and Lady Frampul (whose desire to exercise her authority, as we have seen, is only for her own ends).

Nick and Pinnacia Stuff are, ostensibly, punished for delaying the delivery of Pru's gown whilst they enact Stuff's sexual fantasies (Pinnacia dresses as a countess and Stuff as her footman). However, it is clear that they are punished for more serious matters than this delay:

> Lat[imer]: This gown was then bespoken, for the Soveraigne?
>
> Bea[ufort]: *I* marry was it.
>
> Lad[y Frampul]:   And a maine offence,
>   Committed 'gainst the *soveraignty*: being not brought
>   Home i'the time. Beside, the prophanation,
>   Which may call on the censure of the Court.
>   (*New Inn*, sig. F2v)

Pru has already forgiven Stuff for the missing gown since she put on her mistress's dress (*New Inn*, sig. C3r); more important is the 'prophanation' their fantasy brings with it. Unlike Pru, Pinnacia has no authority to dress above her station, and her punishment is that of a common prostitute – 'send her home, / Divested to her flanell, in a cart' (*New Inn*, sig. F3r) – reflecting both her low status and the Stuffs' intended use of the gown. Latimer adds to this, 'And let her Footman beat the bason afore her' which continues the reference to the punishment of prostitutes, but may also be a reference also to the charivari, an unofficial, community-imposed punishment for unpopular marriages or married couples who do not fulfil their appropriate roles. Nick and Pinnacia Stuff are punished at all levels of authority and society for acting outside their proper sphere.

That the main concern over the behaviour of the tailor and his wife is their unfounded and unlicensed claim to authority and high position is made clear in the direct comparison made between Pru and Pinnacia Stuff:

> Lad: Well! go thy wayes,
>   Were not the Tailors wife, to be demolish'd,
>   Ruin'd uncas'd, thou shouldst be she, *I* vow.
>
> ...
>
> Pru: *I* will not buy this play-boyes bravery,
>   At such a price, to be upbraided for it,
>   Thus, every minute.
>   (*New Inn*, sig. F8v)

This is once again self-consciously theatrical (the actor playing Pru playing the sovereign is indeed a play-boy in the Caroline theatre), and it recalls Pru and Lady Frampul's earlier conversation about giving the dress Pru has borrowed from Lady Frampul to an acting company. At that point, Lady Frampul was unconcerned about who might later be wearing her dress, thus emphasising that Pinnacia's crime was to act the Lady, assume a certain authority, without permission. In this respect, it is significant that this interchange arises from Lady Frampul's anger that Pru had not used her sovereign authority as she wanted her to use it.

The assumption of unusual levels of authority is acceptable under particular circumstances, *The New Inn* argues, but not all. The rewards granted to Pru at the end of the play (her marriage to Latimer and a substantial dowry from Lord Frampul) are for her good sense, and acting appropriately with the power she was given. When all characters stop 'acting' at the end of the day's sports and all return to their appropriate social roles, Pru is no longer a servant but Latimer's equal. And whilst Lovel's speeches, the ridiculousness of Colonel Tipto and the cautionary punishments of Stuff and his wife do, as Butler argues, suggest an attempt to 'reconstruct an aristocratic ideology after the removal of Buckingham' from Charles's court (1992b, p.175), the play's concerns are politically broader than the construction of the Caroline court. I would argue that through the discourse of rights, prerogatives and parliaments established from the beginning of the play, *The New Inn* suggests that parliaments too may assert their authority for the good of the 'body politique' (*New Inn*, sig. C2v), questioning higher authorities with parliamentary authority when monarchs break their own laws. Whilst upholding the authority of the true monarch, the play also suggests the need for parliamentary advice:

Pru: Your Ladyship will pardon me, my fault,
      If I have over-shot, I'le shoote no more.

Lad: Yes shoot againe, good *Pru*, Ile ha' thee shoot,
      And aime, and hit: I know 'tis love in thee,
      And so I doe interpret it.
      (*New Inn*, sig. C3v)

If presented appropriately, with the right intentions (not for personal advancement like Tipto and Fly) and proper acknowledgement of position, parliamentary advice should be given and heeded.

Petitioning the King: *The Love-sick Court*

While Jonson's play uses the Petition of Right to examine the relationship between subjects and sovereigns, and the appropriate assumption, use and abuse of position and authority, Brome's play *The Love-sick Court, or The Ambitious Politique* uses the Petition as an example of good government to advocate co-operation between the people, parliament and monarch, and emphasise the common good over individual concerns for power and privilege. Readings of *The Love-sick Court* have tended to focus on the courtly activities of the play, discussing the possible husbands for Princess Eudyna, whose marriage is thought to be, for most of the play, the only way to secure the succession and therefore the stability of the State. *The Love-sick Court*'s emphasis on love and friendship led Harbage to argue that it was a poor imitation of contemporary courtly plays of neo-Platonic love (Harbage cited in Steggle, 2004, p.138), but R. J. Kaufmann argues that rather than an imitation of the plays popular at court in the 1630s, *The Love-sick Court* is a parody or burlesque of this dramatic genre (1981, pp.126–7). Butler, following Kaufmann, then interprets the play as a comment upon the seriousness with which Caroline courtiers approached political issues. If courtly drama is representative of courtly thought on politics, then '[c]ourt life, as seen through the drama the court prefers, is a ludicrous farrago of extravagant, conflicting intrigues, remote sensibilities and impossible fastidiousness. In this court, making love has become more important than matters of state' (Butler, 1984, p.267). Courtly, neo-Platonic love, this suggests, has indeed made the court (dramatic and Caroline) politically 'sick'. I will argue that between its representation of the two (unsatisfactory) alternatives of its title – 'the love-sick court', and 'the ambitious politique' – the play posits a third, parliamentary, way of governing in its references to the Petition of Right and representation of the country swains, whose importance to an understanding of the political engagement of the play has been much underestimated.

The Love-sick Court opens with a comment on the King's health, which is indicative not only of the state of the court but of the state of the commonwealth: when the head of the body politic is sick, so is its body. Indeed, Disanius's suspicions as to the cause of the King's sickness suggest disorder in the country:

> I that have not seen him
> Since he was sick, can guess, then at the cause
> Of his distemper. He is sick o' th' subject;
> Th'unquiet Commons fill his head and breast
> With their impertinent discontents and strife.
> The peace that his good care has kept'hem in
> For many years, still feeding them with plenty,
> Hath, like ore pampered steeds that throw their Masters,
> Set them at war with him.
> (*Love-sick Court*, sig. F8r)

At the beginning of the play, Disanius sets up a conflict between the King and his people, and his sickness 'o'th'subject' can be read as weariness with a *particular subject* (the marriage of his daughter) or as caused by his *subjects*. Whilst it is possible that here Commons means 'the common people ... as distinguished from those of noble or knightly or gentle rank' (*OED*, 'commons', 1a), that the 'swain heads of Thessaly' (*Love-sick Court*, sig. K3r) are representatives of the commoners suggests that Commons should also be taken to mean the House of Commons (*OED*, 'commons', 2c), thus raising the issue of Parliament. Of course, in the 1630s, the House of Commons in England was very quiet indeed, but in the play's kingdom of Thessaly both the common people and their representatives are 'unquiet' regarding the future government of the country. To Disanius, the Commons' discontents are 'impertinent', suggesting both that he believes they overstep their authority in what they ask and that their opinions are irrelevant to him, if not to the King – an early indication, perhaps, that the courtiers disrupt relations between King and Commons. Although his criticism is directed primarily towards the Commons in their complaints despite living in years of peace and plenty that the King has provided, Disanius's horse-riding analogy is not uncritical of the King, both in that he believes that he has 'oer pampered' his subjects, and in the suggestion that the King is no longer in control.[12] It was a particularly appropriate image for a Caroline audience, as Charles himself was repeatedly pictured on horseback.[13]

---

[12]   An analogy was made between accomplished horse riding and keeping control of both a man's own passions and those over whom he governed: 'Taming a great beast was a taming of nature's wildness and so, like the Caroline masques and paintings in which disordered nature is calmed, represented an act of government' (Sharpe, 2000, p.100).

[13]   In the 1630s two paintings by Van Dyck and a statue by Hubert Le Sueur presented Charles I on horseback. For a discussion of the paintings in relation to Caroline court and political activities, see Roy Strong's *Van Dyck – 'Charles I on Horseback'*.

Whilst Disanius emphasises conflict, and suggests the way to restore the King to health is to execute the 'leading heads' of the Commons (*Love-sick Court*, sig. F8v), the King himself is much more aware of the need to listen to their concerns and appease them:

> To determine
> Of you *Eudyna*, is by heaven committed
> In present unto me. On you depends
> The future glory and prosperity,
> Both of my house and Kingdom. Tis besides,
> Exacted of me by my near Allies,
> And by my Subjects (whom I must secure)
> To constitute a Successor: And no longer
> Will I expect your answer, then five dayes.
> By then you must declare who is your husband;
> Or else expect one from my self; the man
> Whose name I am as loth to mention
> As you to hear, even *Stratocles*.
> (*Love-sick Court*, sig. H5v)

The centrality of Eudyna's marriage for the future stability and prosperity to the state is clear, and it is the King's prerogative, here a divinely given right as monarch and father, to determine her future. However, he does allow her a choice, providing that this choice is made sufficiently quickly to calm the fears of his allies and his people. The unpopular action he threatens, using his power to impose a husband upon her who might be distasteful to them both, is defended in terms of political necessity: he 'must' secure his allies and his subjects.[14] In pressing for a marriage to Stratocles, he is willing to put his subjects' wishes and his allies' concerns before his own desires; the play thus highlights the King's concern for his people and his country.

The King's reception of the Commons emphasises his availability to his people and willingness to hear their grievances:

> Dis[anius]: O here they come. These be the principals
> The heads, the heads, forsooth they call themselves.
> Head-carpenter, head-smith, head-plowman, & head-shepherd.

---

[14]   This might be related to the arguments of 'necessity' Charles advanced for the exercise of his prerogative powers. Although this particular instance is an admirable use of necessity, many thought that Charles's use of such arguments allowed him too much freedom to act outside the law. There were those in the Parliament of 1628 who believed that Charles resorted to the Forced Loan out of necessity to fund the war and that voting sufficient parliamentary supply would relieve the necessity and therefore Charles would return to parliamentary taxation for funding. Lord Keeper Coventry noted in his speech to open the 1628 Parliament, that 'just and good kings finding the love of their people and the readiness of their supplies may the better forbear the use of their prerogatives and moderate the rigour of their laws towards their subjects' (quoted in Russell, 1979, p.339).

>Kin[g]: Nay, pray approach; & seem no more abash'd
>   Here then amongst your giddy-headed rowts,
>   Where every man's a King, and wage your powers
>   Gainst mine in foul defiance. Freely speak
>   Your grievance, and your full demand.
>
>1 Rus: Tis humbly all exprest in this petition.
>   (*Love-sick Court*, sig. G2r)

Disanius's dismissal of them as self-titled 'heads' followed by a list of their occupations shows his contempt for their low status, particularly in comparison with the King who is the 'head' of the body politic. The King too criticises their actions away from court, suggesting that there, 'amongst [their] giddy headed rowts', they act as if they are kings, and pit their power against his as if they were equal. The reference to 'foul defiance' has political connotations regarding the Petition of Right, as Parliament refused to pass the requested subsidy bill until Charles assented to the Petition confirming subjects' rights and limiting the use of his prerogative in particular areas. Although he accuses the 'heads' of overstepping their authority amongst their peers, Brome's King is prepared to give them fair and free hearing when they present themselves to him in the proper manner as representatives of his subjects. The combination of demands and grievances the King expects from the country swains is particularly resonant of the Petition of Right; 'grievance' was a heavily loaded word in the context of the 1628 Parliament. The Petition was a means to force the King to address the grievances of the people, and Coke had named the Duke of Buckingham as the 'grievance of grievances' (quoted in Foster, 1974, p.23). In recognising that these men have a grievance, the King, like Charles in his second response to the Petition of Right, acknowledges they have legitimate grounds for complaint. Indeed, that they choose to present these grievances to the King in the form of a petition is made more striking in the Caroline political context, particularly as it follows soon after the King's offer to explain one of Thessaly's laws to the assembled courtiers:

>My lords, altho' our Lawes of *Thessaly*
>To you, as well as to our self, are known,
>And all our customs, yet for orders sake
>I shall lay open one to you.
>(*Love-sick Court*, sig. G1v)

The Caroline Commons' requests that Charles explain what was meant by certain laws, rights and prerogatives, and the perceived need for this kind of laying open the law, was in part what led to the Petition of Right. The King's comment that the laws are as well known to these 'heads' as to himself may reflect Charles's refusal to give an explanation, but Thessaly's King, in a demonstration of good kingship, and 'to keep order', agrees to an explanation. In relation to parliamentary activity regarding Charles's first reply to the Petition of Right, it is interesting to note that the Commons later re-petition the King through Placilla to adjust his initial response to their petition (*Love-sick Court*, sig. L2v).

Disanius's proposal to execute the ringleaders is one of the first suggestions in this play that it is courtiers who prevent a peaceful accommodation between the King and the Commons, and reflects a similar attitude current in the Caroline period. During the 1620s, the courtier in question was the Duke of Buckingham; in terms of courtiers of the 1630s, Kaufmann suggests that Stratocles might relate to the 'potent figure of Strafford' at the Caroline court (1981, p.111, fn.6). In this play, Stratocles, 'the ambitious politique' of the subtitle, is explicitly noted as the cause of trouble. His disruptive presence is emphasised by his first appearance:

> Jus: You are too sharp *Disanius*. There's a means,
>   As milde as other of the Kings clear Acts,
>   In agitation now, shall reconcile
>   All to a common peace, no doubt.
>
> Dis: What's that *Justinius*?
>
> Jus: Stay: here comes *Stratocles*.   *Ent.* Strat.
>
> Dis: I fear, in that
>   Ambitious pate lies the combustable stuff
>   Of all this late commotion.
>   (*Love-sick Court*, sig. F8v)

Stratocles is indeed 'combustible' in being prone to passions, as demonstrated in his later attempts to abduct and rape the Princess. Disanius's suspicions that Stratocles is to blame for the disorder in the country are confirmed by the stage business: Stratocles's entrance quite literally interrupts the explanation of a way to restore peace between the King and Commons. Impeaching Buckingham was not the intention of the 1628 Parliament, but their attempts to do so previously had contributed to Charles dissolving the Parliament of 1626. At the 1628 session, the Commons chose not to antagonise the King in renewing their attempts to bring down Buckingham, but to focus on recent grievances and the maintenance of subjects' rights and liberties. However, after Charles's first unsatisfactory answer to the Petition of Right in which the King willed that 'right be done according to the laws and customs of the realm' but did not acknowledge that wrongs had been done to his subjects or give an indication that he would not abuse his prerogative power in the future, the Commons once again considered impeaching Buckingham, and were only prevented by Buckingham's own engineering of a further request to the King to give an alternative answer to the Petition. In making Stratocles ambitious and the cause of trouble but also distasteful to the King and courtiers, Brome both allows and disallows the association of Buckingham and Stratocles and suggests a more appropriate royal scepticism towards overly ambitious courtiers than Charles had shown in the 1620s.

Stratocles's ambition is based in theories of kingship which ascribe divinity to kings:

> Why is man
> Prescrib'd on earth to imitate the Gods,
> But to come nearest them in power and action?
> That is to be a King! That onely thought
> Fills this capricious breast. A King or nothing!
> (*Love-sick Court*, sig. F8v)

It is this claim for the god-like powers of kings which immediately follows Disanius's suggestion that Stratocles is the cause of the 'commotion'; a desire for personal power, apparently unbounded by law and subject to whim, causes the disruption to the commonwealth in Thessaly.[15] Significantly, it is the undesirable suitor to Eudyna who gives voice to this aspiration to capricious absolutism; this is not, the play suggests, an appropriate way to think about governing. Stratocles makes a striking contrast with the current King, who seems to place his country's good above his own. Indeed, almost immediately before Stratocles declares that all of his power and position 'is as none' without 'majesty' which to him is 'The supream / Estate on earth, and next unto the Gods', the King expresses his disappointment that the Oracle has not helped him to give 'My countrey satisfaction, and my self' (*Love-sick Court*, sigs. I1v, I1r). The King puts satisfying the people before his own satisfaction; indeed, he expects the same solution to satisfy the people and himself, suggesting that the second wish is closely bound to, if not accomplished by the first. In demonstrating his own understanding of his authority, the King only makes reference to his divinely given rights in relation to deciding Eudyna's future. He is aware of his power as is shown in his conversation with the rustics discussed above and in an interchange with Thymele in which he refuses, albeit with her interests at heart, to explain himself ('My will has been above your question. Pray / Let me request you go' (*Love-sick Court*, sig. L2v)). Nevertheless, he uses this power for the good of his country, not to raise his own position to a god-like divinity.

The Commons, too, are aware of the King's power. The 'heads' who present their petition at court are representative of all of the King's subjects, as indicated in their comments when they approach the King:

> 2 Rus: By all means have a care that, to any question, we give the King good words to his face; He is another manner of man here then we took him for at home.
>
> 3 Rus: I sweat for't. I am sure I have scarce a dry thread in my leather lynings.
>
> 4 Rus: They made us heads i' the countrey: But if our head-ships now, with all our countrey care should be hang'd up at court for displeasing of this good King, for the next Kings good our necks will not be set right again in the next Kings raign I take it. (*Love-sick Court*, sig. G2r)

---

15 *OED*, 'caprice', 2, 3. Ideas of the divinity and divine right of kings and its treatment in Caroline drama will be developed in Chapter 2.

The reference to the rustics being 'made heads i' the country' suggests election, or at least nomination, and tightens the connection between these rustics and parliament suggested by their petition of grievances. Nevertheless, although they had been made 'heads i' the country', here they are obviously subject to a higher authority whose power they had much underestimated; he is 'another manner of man here'. Although described as 'good', he does have the power to hang men who displease him, but this power is couched in terms of political legacy, making them an example so that the next king will not have to deal with similar disobedience. Kings, they suggest, must be approached in the proper way, and this is through petitioning and with deference ('good words'). In this way, the play echoes the importance of appropriate petitioning and approaches to the monarch suggested in *The New Inn*. When considered in a parliamentary context, this also adds a further dimension to their concern to give the King 'good words' in that as a governmental body, they must be careful to give the King morally sound advice. The use of the word 'country' here also requires further exploration. The earlier (albeit disparaging) references to their occupations and their title as 'rustics' associate them with the countryside, and Butler understands the rustic 'Swain heads of Thessaly' (*Love-sick Court*, sig. K3r) in relation to other plays of the period such as Brome's *The Queen and Concubine* and *The Queenes Exchange*, positioning them in a framework which contrasts court and country (county) ideologies, making the country morally superior to the court (1984, pp.267–8).[16] In the more specific parliamentary context I have established for these men, however, not only are they from the country(side)/counties, but they are representatives of the whole country (England). Thus their 'countrey care' is not rustic innocence or limited to their county; their concern is for the country as a whole.[17] The idea that these 'rustics' could be hanged for their national concerns is discomfiting in the context of the royal and parliamentary activities of Charles's reign.

The 'country care' of the Thessalian rustics is contrasted throughout the play with an apparent lack of concern for the country by the courtiers. The opening scenes of political seriousness at court develop into a romantic drama revolving around the Princess's choice of husband between two Princes, Philargus and Philocles, and Stratocles's attempts to engineer his own marriage to Eudyna. The Princes are sworn brothers, and each attempts to uphold the other's claim to the Princess to his own cost. The way they behave towards each other, and their courting of Eudyna as an ideal, divine woman ('Can I look on her and ask a Reason? / O the divinity of woman' (*Love-sick Court*, sig. H3r)) rather than

---

[16] See Chapter 3 for my discussion of *The Queen and Concubine* and *The Queenes Exchange* in relation to common law and prerogative.

[17] This interpretation of the term is not anachronistic. Richard Cust and Peter Lake argue that although it has 'become a commonplace of modern scholarship that when a seventeenth-century Englishman spoke of his "country" he was referring to his county', for Richard Grosvenor (1585–1645), MP and local governor, country meant both county and the country as a whole (1981, pp.48–9).

an object of desire, is reminiscent of the cult of neo-Platonic love surrounding Henrietta Maria at Charles's court in the 1630s.[18] The alternatives the play seems to present for Eudyna's possible husband, then, are representatives of grasping capricious absolutism in Stratocles or of ineffective neo-Platonism in Philocles and Philargus. Neither are presented as particularly viable options.

The demands that love and friendship make on the brothers bring them to forget about the point of the marriage: to secure the succession and the stability of Thessaly. Only once, whilst trying to defer to his brother's happiness does Philargus remember the State: 'But how can you forgo that equal interest / You have with me in *Thessaly* and *Eudina*' (*Love-sick Court*, sig. K7v). The collocation of Eudyna and Thessaly here implies a representation of the one in the other which occurs throughout the play. However, Philargus's concern is still for the sacrifices Philocles is offering to make, not for the state or the Princess themselves. This is emphasised in the fact that this conversation occurs whilst the brothers delay answering the King's summons to court to determine the marriage and succession, instead arguing over which of them will abandon his claim in favour of the other. Disanius attempts to be the voice of reason, and encourages them to return to the court: 'I could even swadle'em both for a brace of Babyes. / Your folly makes me mad: will you return / Yet to the presence, both of you?' (*Love-sick Court*, sig. K7r). In commenting on the childishness and folly of this behaviour, Disanius also passes comment on the frivolity or silliness of any court's absorption in this kind of activity. He is aware of what is at stake, and tries to press this upon his nephews:

> Nephew, come, be wise:
> It is a crown that Courts you; and the name
> Of friend, or Brother ought to stand aloof,
> And know a distance, where such dignity
> Is tendred. Take your opportunity.
> (*Love-sick Court*, sig. K7r)

Disanius undermines the posturing of their courtly friendship by bringing their inflated arguments down to a practical reality – what they 'ought to do' – and to political ambition in taking their 'opportunity'. If, as in Butler's argument, the neo-Platonic plays of the court reflect a courtly over-concern with 'love' and lack of concern with politics, this sharp reminder of what ought to take precedence at the Thessalian court is also a rebuke to the Caroline court for its preoccupation with such ideas of neo-Platonism and courtly love. Kaufmann argues that the subplot also serves to undermine this courtly behaviour. In this subplot there are three potential husbands for Doris, the waiting woman, who are specifically paralleled with the Princes and Stratocles. Placing the courtly behaviour amongst the servants illustrates how ridiculous it is. Doris agrees to marry whichever

---

[18]   See Kaufmann (1981, pp.127–9), Lynch (1967, chapters III and IV) and Britland (2006, especially 6–13) for a fuller explanation of neo-Platonic love at court. Lesel Dawson gives a brief over-view of the doctrine of Platonic love (2002, paragraphs 1–10).

of them is servant to the Prince who marries the Princess, or to marry Geron if Stratocles is successful in gaining Eudyna's hand. Disanius's interventions, though, question this courtly posturing from within the main plot too (Kaufmann, 1981, p.122). That their servants neglect their duty to the Princes whilst they court Doris can be likened to the Princes' failure to serve the King/state whilst they court Eudyna. Disanius's potential play on 'Courts' as both 'courting' and 'becoming the centre of a royal court' reminds the audience, if not the Princes, of the purpose of their dispute. Making the Princes the ones who are courted rather than courting feminises them and their indecision.

The Princes' lack of manliness is also associated with a lack of reason. It is not that the twins do not love Eudyna, but that their approach to her is inappropriate, both in their inaction and in the terms in which they describe it. Philocles places his love for her above reason and virtue:

> Fond reason I disclaim thee,
> Love is a strain beyond thee, and approaches
> The Gods estate: Friendship's a moral vertue
> Fitter fr [*sic.*] disputation, then observance.
> *Eudina. O Eudina*! In what price
> Art thou with me, for whom I cast away
> The Souls whole treasury Reason and Vertue?
> (*Love-sick Court*, sig. H2r)

Philocles's contrasting of moral virtue with how love should be treated implies that action should be taken where love is concerned, something the brothers patently fail to do. More important, however, is that Philocles here claims he will voluntarily give up reason and virtue to pursue Eudyna. Philargus, too, couches his love in these terms:

> But, where [love] rules and is predominant,
> It tiranizeth; Reason is imprison'd;
> The will confined; and the memory
> (The treasury of notions) clean exhausted;
> And all the sences slavishly chain'd up
> To act th'injunctions of insulting love,
> Pearch'd on the beauty of a woman.
> (*Love-sick Court*, sig. H2v)

The 'tyranny' Philargus ascribes to love associates irrational desire with arbitrary authority, a trope which is returned to repeatedly in Caroline drama and explored in subsequent chapters. Although Philocles and Philargus do not abandon reason for passion/desire as could be inferred from these speeches, they do in their foolish deference to each other. The abandonment of reason is not, however, entirely consistent with neo-Platonic thought. In his discussion of court masques, Kevin Sharpe argues that:

> The love we read of in the masques is Platonic love. In the masques, as in
> Neo-Platonic theory, beauty, that quality which expresses the virtues, perforce
> attracts them to itself, and so draws those attracted to the love of the good which
> raises them above the plane of sense and appetite (the antimasque) to the sphere
> of reason, the soul. (1987, p.203)

Whilst Philocles and Philargus have clearly raised themselves above the physical,
they have not moved towards, but rather away from reason. As with their (in)
action towards Eudyna, they have missed the point of this love, too. The political
parody implies the same for the Caroline court, despite its self-representation as
the haven of reason and beauty in masques such as *Tempe Restord*.[19]

Whilst the Princes' idolising of Eudyna is criticised as politically ineffective,
Stratocles's attempt to abduct and rape the Princess provides a concrete connection
between sexual desire and political ambition in the play (Steggle, 2004, p.141). This
connection between uncontrolled/uncontrollable desire for a woman and desire for
power is explored in several plays of the period, particularly regarding absolute,
arbitrary rule, and in these terms it is important to remember that Stratocles's
visions of majesty involve absolute divine power.[20] In contrast with Stratocles,
whilst Philocles and Philargus profess to love Eudyna, they do not seem to desire
her. Steggle suggests that they do not love her in 'any meaningful sense' because
'neither brother seems properly aware of the power of heterosexual desire or of the
will to power' (2004, pp.140–41). This apparent lack of desire is consistent with
the play's neo-Platonism; in conventional platonic terms, 'such love transcends
physical attractions, it is the noble attitudes of what is best' (Parry, 1981, p.185).
However, too much of this is dangerous; if it were not, then Stratocles's actions
would not be so strongly condemned in the play, in other courtiers' condemnation
of him, in the distaste for his potential marriage to Eudyna, and in his ultimate
repentance. Indeed, his uncontrolled desire costs him the support of the Thessalian
rustics:

>   Those are enough
> To hang the man [Matho], and turn his Lord out of
> Our Countrey favour: If we find he has
> That plot upon the body of the Princess
> Of Rape and Murder. He can be no King
> For us: for, sirrah, we have wives and daughters.
> (*Love-sick Court*, sig. K3r)

Again, their 'countrey favour' suggests local and national concerns; an ambition
for too much power would put courtiers (and kings) out of favour with the

---

[19]   This criticism of Caroline government in terms of rationality also feeds into a
discourse of reason and law, passion and absolutism current throughout the period, which I
discuss in detail in Chapter 3.

[20]   The connection between desire and absolutism will be explored in more detail in
Chapters 2 and 3.

country. While Steggle suggests that the swains' concern over Stratocles from this point on is not so much in relation to his ruthlessness *per se*, but his sexual untrustworthiness (2004, p.141), the connection between sexual desire and political power in this play makes it difficult to suggest that their political concerns are not equally prevalent. Greedy courtiers (or kings with aspirations to god-like absolutism) cannot be allowed to take what rightfully belongs to others, be it their 'wives and daughters' or material property. In preventing a power-hungry courtier from seizing what is not rightfully his, the swains' actions may also be related to their earlier association with the Petition of Right, which prevented the improper seizure of persons and property at the King's will.

The Princes' irrationality and consequent failure to respond to the King's summons through their courtly attempts to defer to each other's happiness almost allows Stratocles into power:

> King: No answer, no return? Must I intreat,
>   Yet have my undeserved favours slighted?
> …
>
> King: … So, call in Stratocles.
>   (*Love-sick Court*, sig. L1v)

The play suggests that it is the courtiers' playing at neo-Platonic love which potentially allows arbitrary, grasping absolutism to thrive at court. It is only Stratocles's refusal to marry the Princess that delays the King's decision long enough for the truth to be revealed that Philocles is actually Eudyna's brother, so the succession falls to him; Philargus then is free to marry the Princess without abandoning the principles of friendship expounded throughout the play. '[A]s *Juno* to her *Jupiter*, / Sister and wife' (*Love-sick Court*, sig. L6v), Placilla can marry Philocles, whom she has loved apparently incestuously throughout the play, and Stratocles, now repentant for his former ambition, fades from the action after refusing the Princess in marriage. The removal from the action of those who assert absolute authority in the happy resolution of the drama is indicative of the need to temper absolutism in order to restore order and harmony in the country.[21]

This idealised conclusion, in which the court is returned to order, almost obscures the potential for disaster caused by the Princes' neglect of duty explored in earlier scenes. Their concern for each other's future makes them completely unaware of Stratocles's scheming to undermine both of them and take power and Eudyna for himself. He arranges that the brothers meet each other in the North Vale Of Tempe to duel. The note his servant Matho composes for each of them is significant in criticising the brothers' courtly behaviour: '*Brother* Philocles*, we are the laughing stock of the Nation; and injurious both to the King, our Countrey, the divine* Eudina*, and our selves, by our childish love*' (*Love-sick Court*, sig. I5v). Kaufmann argues that the note reminds the audience of the comic appearance and

---

21   See further my discussion of *The Queen and Concubine* in Chapter 3.

childishness of their conduct (1981, p.119), something emphasised by the comedy of their duel: 'They espie one another draw, and pass at each other, instantly both spread their arms to receive the wound'. When this ploy fails, '[Philocles] offers to kill himself, *Philargus* closes with him. They strugle, and both fall down, still striving to hold each others sword. &c.' (*Love-sick Court*, sigs. K1r, K1v). More important in the challenge to a duel, however, is the threatened injury to the King, country and Princess which their courtly inaction causes. Their folly will cause damage to the King (of Thessaly and, by analogy, of England) in terms of reputation and in answering the petition of the Commons, and their disregard for the country will, of course, damage the state. Whilst the brothers fight over which one will kill himself so the other can marry Eudyna, Stratocles abducts the Princess, planning to rape her, so their delay is indeed potentially injurious to the court and the Princess. 'The main critique', as Matthew Steggle argues, 'that the play makes of the cult of courtly romance is that it makes effective civic government impossible' (2004, p.139).

However, *The Love-sick Court* offers an alternative form of government from the court in the 'chief / Swain heads of Thessaly' whose meeting together at Tempe 'to lay [their] heads together / For good of commonwealth' (*Love-sick Court,* sig. K3r) allows them to overhear Mathos's confession to the Princes of Stratocles's plot, and to intervene to save the Princess.[22] In the context of the 'Swain heads' as petitioning, parliamentary figures, this gathering at Tempe could be understood as a parliamentary session. It could, however, also make reference to the 'middling sort' (Hindle, 2000, p.229) officials who worked to maintain order in the provinces: 'Court, Privy Council and parliament were only the highest institutional expressions of state authority. Governmental realities dictated that the state relied upon inferior officers for a palpable presence in the localities' (Hindle, 2000, p.21). Moreover, it has already been suggested that these swains were not given authority by the royal court, so they may also be seen as representative of the increasing number of parish vestries consisting of self-appointed local men who sought to maintain order and stability in their area.[23] In the swains' claim that 'the King has known us', their election to petition the King, and their independent gathering at Tempe 'regardful / Ever with eye and ear for common good' (*Love-*

---

[22]   The reference to Tempe here may be an allusion to Aurelian Townshend's masque *Tempe Restord*, performed at court in 1632, in which the valley of Tempe which has been under the control of Circe (uncontrolled desire) is returned to reason by Charles and his Queen in the forms of Heroic Virtue and Divine Beauty. In this way, the play not only parodies neo-Platonic courtly drama, but questions the ideologies presented in the court masque. In turning the masque's reason of Tempe (where these courtiers only visit occasionally either to indulge in foolish duels or commit acts of sexual violence) over to parliament or local governors, Brome appropriates royal discourses of reasoned behaviour and associates neo-Platonic love (with its cult of divine beauty) with ineffective government and lack of concern for the state. It is not enough to present a theatrical discourse of reasonable behaviour; the court must also behave reasonably, and to do so, the King must call a parliament.

[23]   See Steve Hindle, *The State and Social Change in Early Modern England, 1550–1640,* (2000, chapter 8).

sick Court, sig. K3r), Brome widens the idea of parliamentary participation in good governance already established in the idea of Petitioning to one of a more general, local participation in the maintenance of law and good order.

Moreover, such devolution of authority does not necessarily constitute a separation of local and central authorities if the court is willing to listen to the local authorities. Indeed, although it meets without royal permission, the assembly of swains is wholly loyal to the King and the Princess. Having captured Matho and Stratocles in their attempts to kill the Princes and rape the Princess, they debate what to do with them:

> Now it remains, that we advise our selves,
> Brethren of *Tempe*, that since these delinquents
> Are fallen into our hands, that we discharge
> Our Countrey loyalty with discretion,
> And not release him from our power, but by
> The power above us. (that's the kings) wee'l wait
> On you to court.
> (*Love-sick Court*, sig. K4r)

They clearly acknowledge the King's superior authority, although it should be noted that they are aware that they, too, have power, from which Stratocles will not be released until theirs is superseded at court. Whereas previously their 'countrey care' required that they petition the King, it seems here that discharging their 'countrey loyalty' involves not only apprehending the criminals, but taking them to the appropriate place and person for judgement; 'Participation was "inspired not merely by obedience but by the acknowledgement of a shared public duty", often articulated with a kind of "rhetorical patriotism" which might find both national and intensely localised expression' (Hindle, 2000, p.216). Although the swains have previously questioned the King, they can still be loyal in carrying out their duties under him. The Caroline Parliament, by extension, can remain loyal to the King despite their Petition in 1628, and could be both loyal and useful if called in the 1630s. Government focussed less closely on the court alone is shown to be much more effective.

When caught by the country swains, Stratocles realises that he is out numbered – 'You have ods o' me' (*Love-sick Court*, sig. K3v) – and this too is Matho's excuse for revealing their plot:

> Str.   Coward, slave,
>   Thy faintness hath betray'd me.
>
> Math: No, 'twas ods,
>   Such as men meet that fight against the Gods.
>   (*Love-sick Court*, sig. K3v)

While his reference to the gods may be related to the Delphian oracle which stated that Philocles and Philargus would both win the prize of crown and Princess, there is an interesting transference of the god-like power from those with a claim to absolute rule (here represented by Stratocles) to the parliamentary swains. The greater number of them is significant; only with a parliament can the court take care of the State, embodied here in Eudyna. The usefulness of the Swain-Parliament both in their earlier petition and in their immediate action for the Princess is highlighted when the King draws attention to the uselessness of the courtiers regarding Eudyna's disappearance:

> Bereft of all my joyes and hopes at once!
> Is there no comfort, nor no counsel left me?
> Why stand you gazing thus with sealed lips?
> Where is your counsell now, which you were wont
> In trifling matters to pour out in plenty?
> Now, in the peril of my life and state
> I cannot get a word.
> (*Love-sick Court*, sig. K4r)

In the context of the 1630s, when neo-Platonism held sway at court and Charles ruled without a parliament, the play's emphasis on the usefulness of parliaments 'For good of common wealth' (*Love-sick Court*, sig. K3r) and for the protection of the king, his subjects and the State must be seen as a pointed political statement. Steggle, Butler and Kaufmann, concentrating on the potential for political commentary in the parody of courtly drama, do not take the political implications of petitioning or parliaments raised by the country swains sufficiently into account. Steggle's commentary describes the Swain heads as 'good-hearted though stupid' and 'unsophisticated but sincere' rustics, but does acknowledge that the play suggests the future of good government in Thessaly remains in their hands and with Disanius (2004, p.141); Butler, however, notes only the contrast of good country counsel and courtly royal favourites (1984, pp.267–8). To do this is to miss the centrality of the swains' parliamentary discourse, action and concern for the commonwealth to the movement and political impact of the play.

The *Love-sick Court*'s emphasis on parliamentary effectiveness notwithstanding, it should be noted that the play's King is not often criticised. He deals fairly with the country swains despite their 'foul defiance'; he tries to act on their petition, and uphold his vow to secure the succession, and he agrees, mercifully, to Eudyna's request to pardon Stratocles for his offences. It is clear that it is his court and courtiers, not the King, who are presented as hindering the good of the commonwealth in *The Love-sick Court*. Brome's King, like Jonson's Pru, is an example of good monarchical rule, but this rule is not effective without the co-operation of, and his collaboration with, the country swains, either as local officials – to be the King's authority where he cannot reach – or as parliamentary advisers. Performed in the 1630s, the play comments on the need to call a parliament, which has already demonstrated its care for the country, and which can do so again with loyalty to the crown. The alternatives – the absolute rule of ambitious, rapacious men or the ineffectiveness of neo-Platonic courtiers – do not provide a satisfactory or secure method of government. The King's rule in consultation with the country swains provides a reasonable middle way between absolutism and inaction.

* * *

In 1628, the Petition of Right brought the relationship between the royal prerogative, the common law and the rights of Charles's subjects into sharp focus, and highlighted Parliament's role in defending the rights and liberties of English people. Whilst Jonson's *The New Inn* picks up on this immediate political context, debating its potential adjustment of powers, privileges and appropriate roles, including a close engagement with the terms and grievances presented in the Petition, Brome's *The Love-sick Court* takes a broader perspective, using a dramatic presentation of the Petition to illustrate good kingship and to advocate, through the 'countrey care' of the swains and the ineffective neo-Platonic actions of the courtiers, wider participation in government for the good of the commonwealth. Both plays emphasise the need for co-operation between the King and Parliament. *The New Inn* warns subjects not to assume more authority than they should but praises their appropriate use of authority and influence, and *The Love-sick Court* presents the dangers to the King, the state and the people when there is no parliament, and illustrates parliamentary effectiveness, particularly in safeguarding liberty and property. Almost at the border between Charles's parliamentary rule of the 1620s and personal rule of the 1630s, the Petition of Right and these plays which depend on it for their political impact provide a valuable summary of the political and legal concerns of the Caroline period. The issues they raise regarding the divine right of monarchy, the relative positions of prerogative and law and the appropriate use of authority will be taken up in subsequent plays and subsequent chapters.

Chapter 2
Shaking the Foundations of Royal Authority: From Divine Right to the King's Will

'The King is above the Law, as both the author, and giver of strength thereto', argues James VI and I in *The True Lawe of Free Monarchies* (1603, sig. D1v). For Henry of Bracton, writing much earlier in c1235, but often cited as a legal authority in the early Stuart period, 'The King must not be under man but under God and under the law, because the law makes the king /Let him therefore bestow upon the law what the law bestows upon him, namely, rule and power/ for there is no *rex* where will rules rather than *lex*' (1968–77, p.33).[1] Theories of the foundations of royal authority such as rule by divine right, patriarchalism, contract and designation led to different arguments over the relative positions of the king, the people and the law. Having first laid out the claims these theories make for the basis and extent of the authority of the king, this chapter will explore the changes in the representation of the foundations of monarchical authority on the Caroline stage in Massinger's *The Roman Actor* (1626), *The Emperour of the East* (1631) and *The Guardian* (1633), and the effect these changes have on an understanding of the relationship presented between the king and the law. It will argue that from presenting a stage monarch whose word is law, and who justifies all his actions by his quasi-divine status in *The Roman Actor*'s Domitian, Massinger's rulers gradually come to be seen as powerful, wilful and, significantly, merely mortal men, whose authority and motives for their actions can be questioned. Such a demystification of monarchy conflates the king's two bodies into one charismatic and powerful, but ultimately flawed, human being.[2]

The Foundations of Authority

Arguments regarding royal sovereignty, how it is gained and whether it can be revoked, play a fundamental part in the understanding of legitimate legal authority, and the relationship between the king and the law. There were several theories which asserted or contested the absolute, unquestionable, irrevocable authority of the monarch. This section will lay out the understood foundations of royal authority in theories of divine right, including patriarchalism and designation, which held that the king was accountable only to God, and was thus above the

---

[1] For example, Edward Coke quotes this passage of Bracton in *Reports 4* (1635c, sig. B5r).

[2] For a lively discussion of the gradual decline from sacredness of European monarchs in the early modern period, see Paul Kleber Monod's monograph, *The Power of Kings: Monarchy and Religion in Europe 1589–1715*.

law. Then, it will briefly sketch out some of the ways in which this assertion was contested, before examining the main points of argument concerning the relative positions of the king and the law.

The doctrine of divine right rule argued that the king received his authority directly from God, and was answerable only to God:

> There are two speciall grounds, or foundations of true Soveraignty in our gratious Lord the King. The one that receiving his Authority only from God, hee hath no superiour to punish or chastice him but God alone. The other, that the bond of his subjects in obedience unto his sacred Majesty is inviolable, and cannot bee dissolved. (Mocket, 1615, sig. C8r)

According to this argument, the king cannot be subject to earthly law, as this would place an authority which was below God above the monarch. Such arguments for the foundation of royal authority meant that even if a king acted tyrannously, there was no redress for his subjects. James VI and I, in his commentary on I Samuel 8:1–22 in which the Israelites ask for a king to rule them, points out that the people were warned that a monarch might rule tyrannically:

> 18 And yee shall cry out at that day, because of your King, whom yee have chosen you: and the Lord God will not heare you at that day.
> 19 But the people would not heare the voice of Samuel, but did say: Nay, but there shalbe a King over us. (1603, sig. B6r)

Having been thus warned, the people have no grounds for complaint if their king is tyrannous, nor can they depose or remove him themselves, because sovereignty is given and maintained by God:

> For as yee could not have obteined [a king] without the permission and ordinance of God: so may yee no more, for he be once set over you, shake him off without the same warrant. And therefore in time arme your selves with patience and humility, since he, that hath the only power to make him, hath the only power to unmake him; and yee only to obey, bearing with these straits that I now fore-shewe you, as with the finger of God, which lyeth not in you to take off. (1603, sigs. B7v-B8r)

Only if a king acts against the laws of God can people disobey him, but even in this, they may only fly from his fury, 'without resistance, but by sobes and teares to GOD' (James VI and I, 1603, sig. C5v).

The most commonly asserted Biblical evidence for the divine status, absolute power and irresistibility of kings, however, was St Paul's command in Romans 13:

> Let every soul be subject unto the higher powers. For there is no power but of God: the powers that be, are ordained of God. Whosoever therefore resisteth the power, resisteth the ordinance of God: and they that resist shall receive to themselves damnation. (Romans 13:1–2)

The importance of this text to John Maxwell's argument for the authority of kings in his *Sacro-sancta Regum Majestas* is indicated in the decision to reproduce it on the title page. More specifically, however, Maxwell relates this passage to the idea of monarchy founded in paternal sovereignty as, he argues, God created it in Adam (1644, pp.84–5):

> we may be led on to consider how *Monarchia fundatior in paterno jure*. How Monarchie is founded in paternall Soveraignty; and the best way to finde out *jura Majestatis*, the Soveraign's prerogative, is to consider well what in Scripture, what in nature, we finde to be the true and naturall right of a father; onely probably, because of mans corruption and untowardnesse by reason of sinne, it is like that God hath allowed more to Soveraigne power to enable and secure it. (1644, p.85)

Biblical precedent authorised fatherly power, and the Fifth Commandment was made to serve political purposes:

> Somewhat I heard this evening Praier from our Pastor in his Catechisticall Expositions upon the fifth Commaundement, *Honour thy Father and thy Mother*: who taught, that under these pious and reverend appellations of *Father* and *Mother*, are comprised not onely our naturall Parents, but likewise all higher powers; and especially such as have Soveraigne authoritie, as the Kings and Princes of the earth … And the evidence of reason teacheth, that there is a stronger and higher bond of duetie betweene children and the Father of their Countrie, then the Fathers of private families. These procure the good only of a few, and not without the assistance and protection of the other, who are the common foster-fathers of thousands of families, of whole Nations and Kingdomes, that they may live under them an honest and peaceable life. (Mocket, 1615, sigs. B1v-B2r)

Thus the respect due to fathers was extended and increased to the king, the 'father' of the country. Indeed, Sommerville argues that the strength of patriarchalism lay in its appeal to contemporary social assumptions and structures of the patriarchal early modern society (1999, 29). This kind of catechistical argument was widespread and taught from an early age, although Mocket's reasoning from the Commandment gives a more logical expression to the analogy than other tracts.[3]

Sir Robert Filmer rationalised and codified this analogy between fathers and kings in his *Patriarcha* (1628–42).[4] Filmer argued a 'genetic' history of patriarchal

---

[3] See, for example, the anonymous, *The A B C with the catechism that is to saie, the instruction ... to be learned of everie childe* (1601, sigs. A6r-A6v), which details all those figures of authority who should be considered under this Commandment. Mocket's text was authorised by King James as a textbook for the instruction of the young in their political duties (Sommerville, 1999, p.13; see also James VI and I's *A Proclamation for the Confirmation of all Authorised Orders*, 1615).

[4] There is some debate over the date of composition of *Patriarcha* because it first appeared in manuscript and was meant only for circulation amongst a group of Filmer's

politics, in which the political authority of the king developed from the social authority of fathers in times when the father literally was the ruler of his (extended) family.[5] This paternal power, Filmer argued throughout *Patriarcha*, was inherited from Adam, to whom it was given by God, was re-affirmed in Noah and descended down to Filmer's time of writing.[6] Therefore kingly power was given by God and, because of this, unlimited except by God's laws (Filmer, 1680, sig. F7v). Patriarchalism did, however, imply a responsibility on the king's part to govern in the best interests of his subjects:

> By the lawe of Nature the King becomes a naturall Father to all his Leiges at his Coronation. And as the Father of his fatherly dutie is bound to care for the nourishing, education, and vertuous government of his children: even so is the King bound to care for all his subjects. (James VI and I, 1603, sig. B4v)

He is not, though, bound by anything other than his conscience to do so. Samuel Rutherford disputes such claims, arguing that the king must be responsible to his people as well as to God, because he cannot fail in his obligation to God to care for his people, unless he fails in his obligation to his people to care for them (1644, p.107).

There were, however, other objections to patriarchalist arguments. Filmer himself acknowledged the objection that 'It may seem absurd to maintain that Kings now are the Fathers of their People, since Experience shews the contrary'. Whilst he attempts to overcome this objection by arguing that kings 'all either are, or are to be reputed the next Heirs to those first Progenitors, who were at first the Natural Parents of the whole people' (1680, sig. C2r), Maxwell offers an alternative. He argues that when nations are disordered and without a patriarchal ruler, 'they condescend that one shall have Soveraigne power over all, and so by consent shall be surrogated in the place of the common father' (1644, sig.

---

friends and acquaintances. It is believed that the Chicago manuscript was written before 1631, and the Cambridge manuscript between 1635 and 1642. What is noteworthy, however, is that all of the possible dates for composition fall within Charles I's rule. *Patriarcha* was printed posthumously in 1680.

  [5]   I have taken the term 'genetic history' from Gordon Schochet. According to genetic history, the essence of a state is explained by the manner of its origin; there can be no change or development (Daly, 1979, p.57). Thus, the authority of the king is thought to descend directly from the authority of the original fathers of families beginning with Adam which, through joining together, evolved into a society governed by the father of the now 'extended' family. Although society may have lost track of the genetic lineage between the king and the original fathers, that does not, according to *Patriarcha*, mean there is no connection (Filmer, 1680, sigs. C2v-C3r). Compare Maxwell (1644, pp.80–88).

  [6]   Samuel Rutherford denies this genetic argument in *Lex, Rex*, although he does not deny a rule by fathers before rule by kings: 'It is a lie, that people were necessitated, at the beginning, to commit themselves to a *King*: for we read of no King, while *Nimrod* arose: Fathers of families (who were not Kings) and others, did governe till then' (1644, p.221). Bodin also argues there were no kings before Nimrod (1606, p.200).

M3v). This argument, however, leaves open the possibility that authority is given to the king by a sovereign people, and thus can be revoked. Maxwell denies this possibility, arguing that in choosing a ruler, 'all their part is onely *to designe or declare the man*, which is onely *potestas designativa, potestas deputativa*, but the power is onely from Almighty God, the *potestas collativa*, the Authority, the Soveraignty, is of God, from God, Gods' (1644, p.86). This is the argument of designation theory. Although the people may designate the man who is to be their ruler, the authority with which he rules comes not from them, but from God, in another form of the divine right doctrine. Maxwell's emphatic repetition of 'God' here leaves his reader in no doubt of the origin of the king's power; it is not only given by God, but it is God's own power. There can be no return of sovereignty to the people because they were never sovereign.

However, there were those who claimed that the people collectively were sovereign and had decided to confer this power onto a single ruler. In what is a kind of 'designation theory in reverse' Samuel Rutherford argues, with Biblical precedents to match those of the absolutists, that rather than the people choosing a king and God granting him the authority to rule, God instead designates a man in guiding the people in their choice, and then it is the people who confer authority upon him:

> no man can be formally a lawfull *King*, without the suffrages of the people: for *Saul*, after *Samuel* from the *Lord* anointed him, remained a private man, and no *King*, till the people made him King and elected him. And *David*, anointed by that same divine authoritie, remained formally a Subject, and not a King, till all *Israel* made him *King at Hebron*. And *Saloman*, though by God designed and ordained to be *King*, yet was never *King*, till the people made him *King*; ... *ergo*, there floweth something from the power of the people, by which he who is no *King*, now becommeth a *King*, formally, and by *Gods* lawfull call; whereas before the man was no *King*, but as touching all royall power a mere private man. (1644, sig. C4r)

Rutherford's *Lex, Rex* was written in answer to John Maxwell's *Sacro-sancta Regum Majestas: The Sacred and Royal Prerogative of Christian Kings*, to assert the prerogative of a sovereign people in comparison with that of the king.[7] Unlike Maxwell's uncompromising assertion that the authority is 'of God, from God, Gods', here the authority is conferred entirely by the people with the guidance of God. In this way, Rutherford maintains a careful balance between the 'just prerogative of the king and people' of the extended title of his *Lex, Rex*.

When conferring authority upon the king, contract theorists argued, the people were able to set the conditions of its tenure. In his *De Jure Regni Apud Scotos Dialogus* (1579), George Buchanan argues that if a king breaks the terms of

---

[7]   John D. Ford (1994, *passim*) provides a detailed discussion of the ways in which Rutherford's text responds to Maxwell's.

the contract by which he rules, the people can revoke his power (2004, p.125).[8] His argument, based on an assumption of innate reason in a people, states, 'it is incredible that, in return for bestowing such a great privilege on their kings, the people should allow themselves to have less favourable rights than they had before' (2004, p.101). Rutherford takes his argument further, stating that not only is it incredible that the people would do this, but they do not have the power to do so:

> It is false that the people doth, or can by the Law of nature resigne their whole liberty in the hand of a King, 1. they cannot resigne to others that which they have not in themselves, *Nemo potest dare quod non habet*, but the people hath not an absolute power in themselves to destroy themselves. ... for neither God, nor Natures Law hath given any such power. (1644, p.147)

His reference to Natural Law raises the idea of a natural instinct for self preservation, which political theorists argued first led people to form communities and governments.[9] Such a law of self preservation would not allow a naturally sovereign people to subject themselves irreversibly to rule by a tyrannous man.

Like Buchanan, Rutherford, too, argues that it is against reason that a sovereign people would allow a tyrant the absolute right to rule:

> The people either maketh the man their Prince *conditionally*, that he rule according to Law; or *absolutely*, so that he rule according to will or lust: ... He is not *Deut.* 17.15, 16. made *absolutely* a King to rule according to his will and lust; for, [*Reigne thou over us*] should have this meaning; *Come thou and play the Tyrant over us, and let thy lust and will be a law to us*: which is against naturall sense. (1644, pp.105–6)

In suggesting that to allow a monarch the opportunity to tyrannise over a people, they invite him to make his will law, Rutherford implicitly denies that the king's will should be law. More than this, if a king does not act in accordance with established law, he breaks one of the conditions of his kingship, and can then be challenged or removed. The terms of his argument are particularly interesting in relation to the exploration of absolute authority on the Caroline stage; the uncontrolled desire or lust of the king is often a marker of a stage king's submission to will alone and a descent into tyranny. This, of course, is not unique to Caroline drama; lustful and corrupt monarchs had appeared throughout Jacobean tragedy, too. What is different for Caroline plays, as this book will go on to discuss in later chapters, is that, as in the terms of Rutherford's argument, *law* comes to be set up as an opposing or moderating force over the wilful, powerful man.

---

[8]   Buchanan's text is a discussion on the difference between monarchy and tyranny, and attempts to justify the enforced abdication of Mary Queen of Scots in 1567.

[9]   This is based on arguments concerning the original institution of governments through a natural law or instinct which led individual people to gather together in societies for protection, safety and better government. To Aristotle, political society was natural. For a detailed explanation, see Sommerville (1999, pp.14, 18–23).

Law, Kingship and Tyranny

The relationship between the king and the law as to which held the highest authority was closely connected to these arguments over the foundation of royal authority. For James VI and I, the king is the point of origin for the law: 'Kings were the authors and makers of the lawes, and not the lawes of the Kings' (1603, sig. C7r). Even when acting in accordance with law, the king remains absolute:

> For althogh a just Prince will not take the life of any of his subjects without a cleare law: Yet the same lawes, whereby he taketh them, are made by himselfe, or his predecessors. And so the power flowes allwayes from himselfe. (James VI and I, 1603, sig. D1r)

If this is the case, a king cannot act against the law, as he is the point of its authority. However, for Rutherford who places the origin of the king's sovereignty in the people, the origin of law is also in the people:

> Obj. *The King is the fountaine of the law, and Subjects cannot make Lawes to themselves, more than they can punish themselves. He is only the Supreme.*
>
> Answ: The people being the fountaine of the King, must rather be the fountaine of the Lawes....
> The civil Law is cleare, that the laws of the Emperor have force only from this fountaine, because the People have transferred their power to the King. (1644, 208)

The point of administration of the law (that is, the king) remains the same in this argument, as the king exercises legal justice through the law-making powers vested in him by the people; for Rutherford, however, it is the people who maintain the ultimate legal authority.

Whilst he argues that the king is the origin of law, James VI and I does concede that he should rule, wherever possible in conjunction with the law:

> [T]he King is above the Law, as both the author, and giver of strength thereto: yet a good King will, not onely delight to rule his subjectes by the Law; but even will conforme himselfe in his owne actions there unto, alwayes keeping that ground, that the health of the common-wealth be his chiefe law. And where he sees the law doubt-some or rigorous, he may interpret or mitigate the same. (1603, sig. D1v)

James states that the good of the commonwealth should override any concern for maintaining established law, and the use of prerogative power to act outside the law allows him then to rule equitably. Bodin, too, maintains that a good king should uphold established law in so far as it is equitable:

> And yet neverthelesse the maxime of right still standeth in force, That the soveraigne prince may derogat unto the lawes that hee hath promised and sworne to keepe, if the equitie thereof ceased, and that of himself without consent of his subjects: ... But if there bee no probable cause of abrogating the law he hath

promised to keepe, he shall do against the dutie of a good prince, if he shall go about to abrogat such a law: and yet for al that is he not bound vnto the covenants and oathes of his predecessours, further than standeth with his profit, except he be their heire. (1606, p.93)

Both of these arguments set forward the notion maintained by absolutists that the king's ability to abrogate laws which were no longer equitable was a necessary part of his role as the fountain of Justice. However, it is also made clear that a king is under no obligation to obey established law.[10]

Rutherford agrees that the king's prerogative should allow him to use discretion in interpreting the law for the sake of equity; this he calls a 'prerogative by way of dispensation of justice', and it is a legitimate exercise of royal power outwith the law.[11] He does, however, reject entirely the idea of an absolute prerogative for a king to act entirely above the law at his own will and pleasure. According to *Lex, Rex*: 'A Prerogative Royall must be a power of doing good to the people, and grounded upon some reason or law: but this is but a branch of an ordinarie limited power, and no prerogative above or beside law' (Rutherford, 1644, 192–4, quotation at 193). Whilst this may seem similar to King James's argument above, for James there is no doubt that the king is not compelled to obey the law by anything other than his own wishes: 'a good King will frame all his actions to be according to the law: yet he is not bound thereto but of his good wil, and for good example-giving to his Subjectes' (1603, sig. D1v). For Rutherford, the king has no dispensation to act outside the law.

Indeed, the way in which a king acts in relation to the law is that which becomes a marker of the difference between kings and tyrants. This is suggested somewhat tentatively by King James:

The one acknowlegeth himself ordeined for his people, having received from God a burthen of governement whereof he must be countable: The other thinketh his people ordeyned for him, a praye to his appetites ... A good King (thinking his highest honour to consist in the due discharge of his calling) employeth all his studie and paines, to procure and mainteine (by the making and execution of good lawes) the well-fare and peace of his people, and (as their naturall father and kindly maister) thinketh his greatest contentment standeth in their prosperitie

---

[10] Indeed, Bodin goes so far as to argue that a king who is obliged to maintain and obey the laws of his predecessors cannot be sovereign; all earthly laws, in fact, according to Bodin, depend upon nothing but the sovereign's 'meere and franke good will' and the right and ability to make law without his subjects' consent is the 'principall point of soveraigne majestie, and absolute power', and 'unto Maiestie, or Soveraigntie belongeth an absolute power, not subject to any law' (1606, pp.93, 92, 98, 88).

[11] There are two other dispensations: of power and of grace. The one of power is not, according to Rutherford, a legitimate use of royal power because it would excuse an action which would be 'sin' without the royal will to deny this. The dispensation of grace is similar to the dispensation of justice; it allows the king to lift the 'custome' for a poor man who cannot afford to pay (Rutherford, 1644, p.194).

> .... An usurping Tyrant ... will then (by inverting all good lawes to serve onely for his unrulie private affectiones) frame the common-weale ever to advance his particular: buylding his suretie upon his peoples miserie. (1599, sigs, E2v-E3v)

The duties of a king suggested, however, are not enforceable; rebellion is 'ever unlawful' (James VI and I, 1599, sig. E4r) and performance or otherwise of these duties is to be left to the king's conscience. It is noteworthy here that the 'good king's' position in relation to earthly laws remains ambiguous. Whilst he argues that a king should make and execute good laws, James does not state whether the laws to be upheld are statute laws, the common law or those made by the king's prerogative decree, nor does he state how to decide which laws are good. It is emphasised only that a good king will rule in the interest of his people, and is accountable to God for his actions. Other writers, however, make the connection between rule without law and tyranny much more starkly. Rutherford notes that a tyrant is a man who 'habitually sinneth against the Catholike good of the Subjects and State, and subverteth the Law' (1644, p.217), and Bodin, too, marks the difference between kings and tyrants in this way: 'the one measureth his manners, according unto his lawes; the other measureth his lawes, according to his owne disposition and pleasure' (1606, p.212). It should be noted that Bodin places a greater emphasis on the tyrant's habit of breaking God's laws and the law of nature rather than earthly laws (1606, pp.210–12), but nevertheless, earthly law is not overlooked. Whereas for Rutherford, tyranny removes the authority of the king's office because a king acting outside the law acts outside his office and is therefore no longer king (1644, pp.186, 243), for Bodin, a tyrant cannot be resisted as long as he is sovereign:

> I cannot use a better example, than of the dutie of a sonne towards his father ...
> Now if the father shall be a theefe, a murtherer, a traytor to his countrey, ... or what you will else; I confesse that all the punishments that can be devised are not sufficient to punish him: yet I say, it is not for the sonne to put his hand thereunto ... I say therfore that the subject is never to be suffered to attempt anything against his soveraign prince, how naughty & cruel soever he be: lawful it is, not to obey him in things contrarie to the laws of God and nature: to flie and hide our selves from him; but yet to suffer stripes, yea and death also rather than to attempt anything against his life or honour. (1606, p.225)

Divine Status and Absolute Power: *The Roman Actor*

The Roman Actor is, perhaps, the best known of the plays to be discussed in this chapter. It is often read as a theatrical response to contemporary anti-theatrical tracts, and criticism of the play tends to focus on the plays-within-the-play and their interpretation.[12] In what follows, I will discuss a different aspect of Massinger's

---

[12]   For example, David Reinheimer (1998) and Andrew Hartley (2001) read the play in relation to censorship; Jonathan Goldberg discusses the way that the senate courtroom becomes a theatre, the plays within the play and finally Domitian's 'theatre of conscience'

play which is often overlooked, arguing that *The Roman Actor* is deeply concerned with issues of the foundation and exercise of monarchical authority, engaging with the ideas of the divinity of kings, the relationship between the ruler and the law and resistance to the king which I have set out above.

The Roman Emperor, Domitian, rules by divine right, claiming protection from the goddess Minerva (*Roman Actor*, sig. H4v). More than this, however, Domitian behaves and speaks as if he were a god:

> In the *Vitellian* warre he rais'd a Temple,
> To *Jupiter*, and proudly plac'd his figure
> In the bosome of the God. And in his edicts
> He does not blush, or start to stile himselfe
> (As if the name of Emperour were base)
> Great Lord, and God *Domitian*.
> (*Roman Actor*, sig. B2v)

Already in Act I, Domitian is shown to be over ambitious, being discontent with his high position as Emperor, and preferring to be a god. In describing himself as God in his edicts, Domitian also gives these (the direct commands of the Emperor, not the established laws of Rome) the unquestionable authority of divine law. The attribution of a divine status to a monarch is not unusual; James VI and I made similar claims for kingship, writing in *Basilikon Doron*, '[L]earne to know and love that God, whomto ye have a double obligation; first, for that he made you a man; and next, for that he made you a little God to sit on his Throne, & rule over other men' (1599, sig. B2v). What is unusual is the extent to which the Emperor insists on, and Massinger emphasises, Domitian's divinity throughout the play. Not content with being a '*little* God' (my emphasis), Domitian sees himself as equal to, and in the heart of, the king of the gods, placing himself in the centre of Jupiter's statue. He also claims Jupiter's prerogative of thunder as his own, offering some of his subjects the opportunity to 'receive the honour / To kisse the hand, which rear'd up thus, holds thunder / To you 'tis an assurance of calme' (*Roman Actor*, sig. C4r).[13]

That Domitian's emphasis on his divinity was a significant aspect of the play to contemporary audiences is evident from Thomas Jay's commendatory poem:[14]

(1989, pp.203–9). Joanne Rochester's recent book (2010) takes plays within the plays as its focus, engaging with how Massinger's on stage audiences reflect and mediate the responses of the off stage theatre audience. Butler is a notable exception to this trend in reading the play politically, and in relation to other plays with a classical setting (1985, *passim*; pp.150–62 focus on *The Roman Actor*). I will discuss *The Roman Actor*'s trial scene and relationship with anti-theatrical tracts in Chapter 5.

[13]   'Prerogative' is the term used by Edwards and Gibson here (*Plays and Poems*, V. p.185). In claiming this they apply particularly appropriate contemporary political terminology. In being a prerogative, it is a right reserved only to the ruler, and this suggests that Domitian is over-stepping his authority in claiming a power reserved for Jupiter.

[14]   Thomas Jay was one of the play's dedicatees. He was one of Massinger's close associates and attended Lincoln's Inn. He was knighted in 1625.

> Each line thou hast taught CEASAR is, as high
>   As Hee could speake, when grovelling Flatterie,
> And His owne pride (forgetting Heavens rod)
>   By His Edicts stil'd himselfe great Lord and God.
> By thee againe the Lawrell crownes His Head;
>   And thus reviv'd, who can affirm him dead?
> Such power lyes in this loftie straine as can
>   Give Swords, and legions to DOMITIAN.
> (*Roman Actor*, sig. A3r)

Jay's poem commends the effectiveness of Massinger's choice in Domitian's language, through which he claims the playwright (and the actor) make Domitian live again. However, in praising the liveliness of Massinger's words, there is also a hint of the power of the word of the Emperor in the ambiguity over whose 'loftie straine' Jay refers to. Massinger's poetry brings Caesar and his acts to life, but perhaps it is the power of Domitian's words that gives him 'Swords, and legions'; his personal power and resort to physical force give him authority.

It is not only in direct references that Domitian becomes identified as a god. Domitia's response to Domitian's advances ironically echoes Mary's song of praise at the annunciation, 'And my spirit hath rejoiced in God my Saviour. For he hath regarded the low estate of his handmaiden' (Luke 1:48):[15]

> I am transported,
> And hardly dare beleeve what is assur'd here.
> The meanes, my good *Parthenius*, that wrought *Caesar*
> (Our God on earth) to cast an eye of favour
> Upon his humble handmaide!
> (*Roman Actor*, sig. B3r)

This adoption of Biblical register and phrasing is maintained throughout the scene, emphasising Domitian's position as 'God on earth'. There is, for example, a credic resonance to Parthenius's statement of Domitian's widespread political power, 'The world confesses one *Rome*, and one *Caesar*' (*Roman Actor*, sig. B3v). The disjunction between the religious echoes and the use Domitian makes of his power – here it is to enforce a divorce between Domitia and her husband Lamia so that she is free to become his wife – also serves to highlight Domitian's abuse of his position as ruler, and his usurpation of heavenly privileges. These religious allusions shift the frame of reference of the play from classical, pagan Rome to a Christian construction of society, facilitating a comparison between the Roman Emperor and the English King which is suggested in Paris's earlier emphatic reference to Domitian as '*Caesar*, in whose great name / All Kings are comprehended' (*Roman Actor*, sig. C1v). Both James VI and I and Charles I employed Roman imperial iconography at court, and whilst it would be pushing the political engagement of the play much too far to suggest that Massinger represents either of these monarchs

---

[15]   cf. *Plays and Poems*, V. p.183, note to I.ii.19–21.

in Domitian, the play does suggest an alternative, much less positive interpretation of ancient Rome than James had done or Charles was to do.[16] The step from glorious imperial Rome to tyrannous emperor is not a large one.

Parthenius's persuasions to seduce Domitia from her husband also make claims for Domitian's relationship with the law:

> Domit[ia]: You know I have a husband, for my honour
>   I would not be his strumpet, and how lawe
>   Can bee dispenc'd with to become his wife.
>   To mee's a riddle.
>
> Parth[enius]:   I can soone resolve it.
>   When power puts in his Plea the lawes are silenc'd.
>   The world confesses one *Rome*, and one *Caesar*,
>   And as his rules is infinite, his pleasures
>   Are unconfin'd; this sillable his will,
>   Stands for a thousand reasons.
>   (*Roman Actor*, sig. B3v)

The personification of power here ('*his* Plea') implies that infinite power and the Emperor are indivisible, which is emphasised in claims for the extent of his power across the world. The language of the law courts in 'Plea' suggests an official legal negotiation, and this maintains a pretence of acting within the law whilst denying its power. In fact, such is the authority that the Emperor exercises, that merely a syllable from him holds more power than the law. What becomes clear is that Domitian rules only in accordance with his own will, and is not bound to give any explanation, morally or legally, for his actions as 'his will, / Stands for a thousand reasons'.

Parthenius's assertions of the Emperor's power in this respect are set alongside Lamia's objections to Domitian's seduction of Domitia:

> This is rare.
> Cannot a man be master of his wife
> Because she's young, and faire, without a pattent.
> I in mine owne house am an Emperour,
> And will defend whats mine.
> (*Roman Actor*, sig. B4r)

In the same way that the analogies of patriarchalism argued that the king gains his power as the father of the kingdom, Lamia, as head of his household, is a king in the domestic sphere. His reference to needing a 'pattent' from the Emperor to

---

[16] In a similar vein, Butler argues that 'Massinger's mirror for tyranny stands in radical opposition to the contemporary court culture both aesthetically and politically' (1985, p.152). For a discussion of James VI and I's employment of imperial iconography, see Kewes (2002, *passim*). In 1633, Van Dyck painted Charles riding through a triumphal arch, and in 1632, Charles danced in the masque *Albion's Triumph*.

keep his wife reflects concerns over monopolies in James I's reign which would become increasingly contentious under Charles. In maintaining his rights to hold his property absolutely, Lamia sets the subjects' rights in direct opposition to the rights the Emperor claims, and in doing so prefigures the claims made later in Charles's reign over individuals' rights to hold property inviolate to prerogative demands. As Martin Butler argues, 'the crucial principle at stake is that [Domitian's] conception of his power exhibits exactly that challenge to the fundamental freedoms of the subject which was feared from Stuart government' (1985, p.154). When Lamia's appeal to his supposedly inalienable rights as a husband fails, he resorts to what should be the safeguard of these rights in the law, asking, 'Is this legall?'. Parthenius's response, 'Monarchs that dare not doe unlawfull things, / Yet bare them out are Constables, not Kings' (*Roman Actor*, sig. B4r), asserts not only that Domitian does not have to act according to the law, but also that if he were to act only according to the law, he would not be a king. This is a sharp contrast with Rutherford's arguments in *Lex, Rex* that only in obeying the law can monarchs be true kings, not tyrants.

Domitian himself makes a direct statement concerning his position in regard to the law:

> Shall we be circumscrib'd? let such as cannot
> By force make good their actions, though wicked,
> Conceale, excuse or qualifie their crimes:
> What our desires grant leave, and priviledge to
> Though contradicting all divine decrees,
> Or lawes confirm'd by *Romulus*, and *Numa*,
> Shall be held sacred.
> (*Roman Actor*, sig. D3r)

For Domitian, his power allows him to do anything, without explanation or excuse. Whilst there was debate in the period over the position of the king in relation to earthly law, there was no debate over the primacy of God's laws. James VI and I maintained throughout his political tracts that kings must remain answerable to God for their deeds, and must therefore uphold His laws.[17] Domitian's denial of their precedence, then, is an arresting comment, and following the Renaissance tragic tradition of the overreacher, Domitian has sealed his fate. The Emperor's opinion of other earthly power too is unusual. Domitian's reference to Romulus and Numa cites the earliest precedent for Roman kingly authority, those in whom his position of authority originates, and then denies any lasting power to their laws. The reference to Numa is particularly significant in the portrayal of Domitian's

---

[17]   See, for example, the first book of *Basilikon Doron*: 'Anent a King's Dutie towards God'. See also Bodin, 'as for the lawes of God and nature, all princes and people of the world are unto them subject' (1606, p.92).

tyranny, as he was associated with justice and the legal power of kings.[18] These claims contrast starkly with most politico-legal argument of the period which bases its truth and force on precedent. Domitian claims instead that it is his desires which give him 'leave, and priviledge' and should be held 'sacred', presenting his will as the highest authority. This collocation of desire and privilege is implicitly critical of the royal prerogative, suggesting that the prerogative is not a royal right, but a more acceptable name for royal wilfulness.

Whilst it is in his divorce of Lamia and Domitia that Domitian is seen to exercise his power above all laws, it is, ironically, in his relationship with Domitia that he is shown to be most weak. Having discovered her attempt to seduce Paris (his favourite actor), he orders her torture and death, but quickly changes his mind:

> O impudence! take her hence.
> And let her make her entrance into hell.
> By leaving life with all the tortures that
> Flesh can be sensible of. Yet stay. What power
> Her beautie still holds o're my soule that wrongs
> Of this unpardonable nature cannot teach me
> To right myselfe and hate her? – Kill her. – Hold.
> (*Roman Actor*, sig. H3r)

The caesuras and uneven metre here illustrate clearly Domitian's confusion and loss of coherence as the short phrases and enjambed lines indicate his conflicting mental processes. This indecision is not characteristic of Domitian, and provides a stark contrast with his earlier command for the public torture of Rusticus and Sura. Even in response to Parthenius's reasonable and deferential cautions in this, Domitian is resolute in his decision, confirming this in the decisive statement, '*Caesar* hath said it' (*Roman Actor*, sig. F2r). His desire for Domitia, however, has undermined his authority to the extent that Stephanos describes his doting on her as 'the *impotence* of his affection' (*Roman Actor*, sig. I2v, my emphasis). Domitia herself knows she has power over him, and in a scene which is reminiscent of Domitian's gloating to Lamia having taken his wife, she taunts him over his weakness:

>   Though thy flatterers
> Perswade thee, that thy murthers, lusts, and rapes
> Are vertues in thee, and what pleases *Caesar*
> Though never so unjust is right, and lawfull;
> Or worke in thee a false beliefe that thou
> Art more then mortall, yet I to thy teeth
> (When circl'd with thy Guards, thy rods, thy axes,
> And all the ensignes of thy boasted power)
> Will say *Domitian*, nay adde to it *Caesar*
> Is a weake feeble man, a bondman to

---

[18]   Numa is one of two ancient figures to appear in the painted arch of James Shirley's *Triumph of Peace* of 1634 (sig. A4r), which negotiates between the royal prerogative and the established law, and is discussed in the Epilogue to this book.

> His violent passions, and in that my slave.
> Nay more my slave, then my affections made me
> To my lov'd Paris.
> (*Roman Actor*, sig. I3r)

In submitting to his desire for her he has shown himself to be not only less than a god, but less than a free man. The comparison between his passion for her and hers for Paris emphasises this in suggesting that his desire makes him weaker than a woman. She undermines both his claims to divinity and his power to make his will into law by dismissing these ideas as those 'false beliefe[s]' with which sycophants flatter him, and stresses his vices by naming his actions as what they really are – murder, lust and rape – and highlighting his guards, rods and axes as empty symbols of his power. For her, to whom he is subject, he is unable to 'By force make good [his] actions, though wicked' (*Roman Actor*, sig. D3r).

At the end of the play, Domitian's 'murthers, lusts and rapes' return to haunt him, literally in the ghosts of Rusticus and Sura (*Roman Actor*, sig. K1r), and metaphorically in his assassination. Until this point, there has been an emphasis on the impossibility of active resistance to the Emperor: in an extended version of Julia's comment 'What we cannot helpe, / We may deplore with silence' (*Roman Actor*, sig. F1v), Lamia states:

> And since we cannot
> With safetie use the active, lets make use of
> The passive fortitude, with this assurance
> That the state sicke in him, the gods to friend,
> Though at the worst will now begin to mend.
> (*Roman Actor*, sig. B3r)

This simultaneously suggests and denies the possibility of resistance. He cannot actively resist the Emperor in plotting or with physical strength for fear of his life, but instead can wait with patience ('passive fortitude') for Providence to rescue the State. Rusticus and Sura, to whom he makes this comment, exercise a different kind of passive resistance at their execution, during which they 'grinne', and assert that 'beyond our bodies / Thou hast no power' (*Roman Actor*, sig. F2v). In their transcendence of the physical, they defeat the tyrannous Emperor who can only exercise his power over them in shows and actions of cruelty. Their reply to Domitian's question, 'Are they not dead?' emphasises their superiority to him:

> Sur[a]:   No, wee live

> Rust[icus]: Live to deride thee, our calme patience treading
>   Upon the necke of tyrannie.
>   (*Roman Actor*, sig. F3r)

In actions they cannot defeat him, but in patience he is conquered. Indeed, their calm and orderly speech, even under torture, provides a stark contrast with Domitian's outbursts to the hangman:

Againe, againe. You trifle. Not a groane,
Is my rage lost? What cursed charmes defend 'em!
Search deeper villaines. Who lookes pale? Or thinkes
That I am cruel?
(*Roman Actor*, sig. F2v)

The short sentences, repetitions, questions and exclamations all indicate that the Emperor, unlike his victims, has lost control.

It is clear in *The Roman Actor* that some kinds of resistance to the Emperor are possible: Rusticus and Sura's acceptance of their punishment, their simultaneous (non-active) resistance to his power, and their threats to haunt Domitian cause him a moment's pause ('By my shaking, / I am the guiltie man, and not the Judge' (*Roman Actor*, sig. F3v)), and later the conspirators do succeed in killing the Emperor. However, the legitimacy of these acts of resistance is yet to be determined. Lamia's advice to trust in Providence to alleviate the sickness of the state is seconded throughout the play in the absolutist notion that a king, however evil, cannot be deposed by his people because of his divine status:[19]

The [im]mortall powers
Protect a Prince though sould to impious acts,
And seeme to slumber till his roaring crimes
Awake their justice: but then looking downe
And with impartiall eyes, on his contempt
Of all religion, and morrall goodnesse,
They in their secrets j[u]dgements doe determine
To leave him to his wickednesse, which sinckes him
When he is most secure.
(*Roman Actor*, sig. E4v)[20]

The description of Domitian's crimes as 'roaring' highlights their immensity, and suggests that his speech as well as his actions have been out of place. In claiming to be above the gods, and in acting tyrannously against the law of the gods, Domitian has committed crimes of action and of words. The reference here to the divine protection of princes is not, as Douglas Howard suggests, a mere exercise in political expedience on Massinger's part (1985, p.126); rather, the emphasis

---

[19] The people cannot act against a king because of their low position in relation to him: 'the person and power of the *King* is alwaies sacred and inviolable. It is not for those whom God hath appointed to obey, to examine titles & pedigrees' (Dickinson, 1619, sig. C2r). Rutherford, however, argues that the people are greater than the king in that there are more of them in number, and therefore in importance (1644, sig. T2r).

[20] In the 1629 edition, the first line of this quotation reads 'The mortall powers', but in context both of this quotation and the wider scene, Edwards and Gibson's change to 'immortall' based on the manuscript makes more sense (*Plays and Poems*, III, p.52). If read as 'mortall powers', the statement is much more radical, claiming an almost divine power for the Emperor's subjects.

throughout the play on Domitian's relationship with the gods makes this idea an integral part of the play. Some political theorists of the period who argued against resisting tyrannous monarchs maintained that kings were divinely protected:

> if there bee any offence committed by him forasmuch as there is no breve to enforce, or constraine him, there may be supplication made that he would correct, and mend his fault: which if he shall not doe: it is abundantly sufficient punishment for him that he is to expect God a revenger: for no man may presume judicially to examine his doings, much lesse oppose them by force and violence. And this is no other kingly Soveraignety than God himselfe has given unto his Maiestie. (Mocket, 1615, sigs. D3r-D3v)[21]

However, there were those who argued that resisting tyrants was a legitimate, indeed praiseworthy activity. George Buchanan, for example, argues that those who are unwilling to live by laws which maintain the stability and prosperity of the community, that is, those who do not behave with reason, are no better than wild animals and it is praiseworthy to rid a community of this kind of danger (2004, p.89).[22]

Rusticus and Sura's passive resistance is vindicated in their peaceful transcendence of the earthly, and in their troubling appearance in Domitian's dream. The assassination of the Emperor, however, is more complicated. In his presentation of the conspirators' murder of Domitian, Massinger differs from his sources.[23] In Suetonius, Stephanos's part in the action is brought on by fears for his own life; he was 'in trouble for intercepting certaine monies' (1606, sig. 2A3r). In Massinger's play, however, each of the conspirators is given a more noble reason for their actions:

Parth[enius]: This for my Fathers death.

Domit[ia]: This for my *Paris*,

Julia: This for thy Incest

Domitilla: This for thy abuse of *Domitilla*.
(*Roman Actor*, sig. K4r)

---

[21]   See also the anonymous, *The Divine Right and Irresistibility of Kings and Supreme Magistrates* (1649, *passim*) and James VI and I's *True Lawe of Free Monarchies* (1603, especially sigs. C3v-C4r), where James argues that using singular biblical precedents for the deposition of a king is the same as arguing that murder and robbery can also be excused in all cases because these also have scriptural precedent.

[22]   In an otherwise comprehensive argument, Buchanan is notably reticent on the idea of the divine right of kings. He deals only with contract theories and the position of elected or hereditary monarchy, which give kings power from the people, not from God.

[23]   Howard (1985, p.125) also notes this.

It should be remembered that fear for their own lives is not entirely absent from the conspirators' motivation (*Roman Actor*, sigs. K2v-K3r), but significantly it is not emphasised here at the time of the assassination. In giving Domitian's crimes as reasons for the conspirators' actions, Howard argues, Massinger makes it clear that Domitian dies because of his crimes (1985, p.125). However, while the conspirators themselves draw attention to Domitian's tyranny as their reasons for participating in his assassination, the play emphasises that Domitian's fall is brought about not only by this, but by the offence he causes to the gods:

> Caesar: Let proud mortalitie but looke on *Caesar*
>   Compass'd of late with armies, in his eyes
>   Carrying both life, and death, and in his armes
>   Fadoming the earth; that would be stilde a God,
>   And is for that presumption cast beneath
>   The low condition of a common man,
>   Sincking with mine owne waight.
>   (*Roman Actor*, sig. K2v)

Domitian recognises he has overstepped the bounds of his position, acknowledging his 'presumption'. Having previously questioned who other than Caesar can judge Caesar (*Roman Actor*, sig. K1r), in this scene he comes to recognise that:

>   The offended Gods
> That now sit judges on me, from their envie
> Of my power and greatnesse here, conspire against me.
> (*Roman Actor*, sig. K2v)

Even whilst acknowledging that he has offended in his 'presumption' in being 'stilde a God', and that the gods are his judges, he is unable to contain his hubris in boasting here of the Gods' jealousy of his power.

Until the final Act, he has considered himself secure while Minerva is his patroness (*Roman Actor*, sig. I4v), but her desertion of him leaves him unprotected. Her reasons for this desertion are particularly significant:

> And me thought
> *Minerva* ravish'd hence whisper'd that she
> Was for my blasphemies disarm'd by *Jove*
> And could no more protect me. Yes twas so,
> His thunder does confirme it, against which   *thunder and*
> Howe're it spare the lawrell, this proud wreath   *lightning.*
> Is no assurance.
> (*Roman Actor*, sig. K1v)

Domitian here realises that he is only the 'weake feeble man' Domitia describes him to be (*Roman Actor*, sig. I3r), and his position as Caesar does not protect him from the anger of the gods. In light of this acceptance of his mortality, the Tribune's comment which follows Domitian's speech in which he claims that he would not 'lift an arme' against Domitian's '*sacred* head' (*Roman Actor*, sig. K1v, my emphasis) is ironic. The disarming of Minerva and the emphasis, both in Domitian's speech and through the stage directions, on thunder bring to mind Domitian's usurpation of Jove's weapon of thunder; his previous claim to be 'Guarded with our own thunder' against fate (*Roman Actor*, sig. G4r) is, here, shown to have been the empty bluster of a powerful but mortal man.

Whilst it is clearly his divine ambitions that are emphasised as the cause of his downfall, it remains that human agents bring about Domitian's death. The punishment of the conspirators anticipated at the end of the play denies the possibility of the legitimate killing of a monarch, even if he is a tyrant:

> 1 Trib[une]: What have you done.
>
> Parth[enius]: What *Rome* shall give us thanks for.
>
> Steph[anos]: Despatch'd a Monster.
>
> 1 Tribune: Yet he was our Prince
>   How ever wicked, a[n]d in you this murther
>   Which whosoe're succeeds him will revenge.
>   Nor will we that serv'd under his command
>   Consent that such a monster as thy selfe
>   (For in thy wickednesse, Augusta's title
>   Hath quite forsooke thee) thou that wert the ground
>   Of all these mischiefes, shall goe hence unpunished.
>   Lay hands on her. And drag her to sentence,
>   We will referre the hearing to the Senate
>   Who may at their best leisure censure you.
>   (*Roman Actor*, sigs. K4r-K4v)

In Stephanos's claim, there is something of the contract theorists' ideas of praise for those who remove tyrants. Buchanan, for example, argues that it is not only legitimate but praiseworthy to kill a tyrant, and describes such men as animals or monsters:

> If I were allowed to pass a law, I would order, as the Romans used to do in seeking expiation for monsters, that men like that [those who did not wish to live according to law for the good of the commonwealth] should be banished into desert lands or drowned in the sea far from the sight of land, lest even the contagion of their dead bodies infect living men; and that those who killed them would have rewards decreed to them, not only by the people as a whole but by individuals, as commonly happens in the case of those who have killed wolves or bears or have caught their cubs. (2004, p.89)

For Parthenius, his confident belief that Rome '*shall* give [them] thanks' (not 'should', for example), suggests that he anticipates no retribution for the act. The Tribunes, however, do not condone his action, and re-affirm the sovereign-subject positions of the assassinated Emperor and his killers: 'he was our Prince/ How ever wicked'. In the words of James VI & I, 'The wickednes therefore of the King can never make them, that are ordayned to be judged by him, to become his Judges' (1603, sig. D5v). Although the Tribune states that the hearing will be left to the senate, it is clear that it is not the senate but Domitian's successor as Emperor who will exact punishment. The inability of the Senate to act without the Emperor has already been illustrated at the beginning of the play in the abandoned trial of Paris, and here the Tribune's first comment that 'whosoe're succeeds [Domitian] will revenge' his murder emphasises the primary position of the Emperor. Thus the Emperor, however wicked, remains independently sovereign, set apart from and above the Senate.

The Roman Actor does not deny the divine right of kings, nor does it condone active resistance; instead it presents a ruler who oversteps the bounds of his prerogative, attempting to position himself as equal to, if not above, the gods. The Emperor's extra-legal prerogative, in fact, is not denied in this play; although, for example, his divorce of Lamia and Domitia is objectionable, his power to do so is not in question, and it is, conspicuously, not presented as a reason for his death. It is important to note that at the end of the play, it is not Domitian's illegal actions which are brought to the fore, but his cruelties:

> Take up his body. He in death hath payd
> For all his cruelties. Heere's the difference
> Good Kings are mourn'd for after life, but ill
> And such as govern'd onely by their will
> And not their reason. Unlamented fall
> No Goodmans teare shed at their Funerall.
> (*Roman Actor*, sig. K4v)

In placing an emphasis on reason here, Massinger also suggests a need for moderation in absolute power and this will be explored further in my discussion of *The Emperour of the East* below. Here, however, it is interesting to note in the Tribune's words an echo of a passage in James VI and I's *Basilikon Doron* in which he states the difference between a good king and a tyrant:

> For a good Kinge (after a happie and famous reigne) dyeth in peace, lamented by his subjectes, and admyred by his Neighbours... Where by the contrarie, a Tyrantes miserable and in-famous life, armeth in his owne subjectes to become his burreaux: And although that rebellion bee ever unlawful on their parte, yet is the worlde so wearied of him, that his fall is little meaned by the reste of his subjectes, and but smyled at by his neighboures. (1599, sigs. E3v-E4r)

Whilst it is possible that this is could be a commonplace saying (indeed, Bodin makes a similar argument),[24] it is not unreasonable to suggest a link between

---

[24]	Bodin makes this statement regarding the difference between kings and tyrants: 'the one is praised and honoured of all men whilest he liveth, and much missed after his death; whereas the other is defamed yet living, and most shamefully reviled both by word and writing when he is dead' (1606, p.213).

these passages. An echo of the former King's (absolutist) advice to his son for government in a play which deals with divine right and the dangers of resistance if a monarch is tyrannous, and is performed at the beginning of a new reign, allows the commercial theatre to speak to and of the new King, whilst paying tribute to the former ruler.

Decline from Divinity: *The Emperour of the East*

Whilst *The Roman Actor* presents the assassination of the Emperor, the play maintains the irresistibility of the monarch, demonstrating that it is his displeasing of the gods which really condemns Domitian. However, the desertion by Minerva and Domitian's submission to his passion in his desire for Domitia illustrate that Domitian is a mortal man, however powerful and divinely appointed. As the Caroline period progresses, this decline from divinity becomes increasingly apparent in stage monarchs. This section will discuss the ways in which the monarch comes to be seen more clearly as a fallible, mortal man rather than a divine figure of authority in *The Emperour of the East*. In this play, Massinger presents two monarchs: Theodosius (the Emperor) and his sister Pulcheria, who has ruled Constantinople during his minority. The juxtaposition of their methods of government dramatises a discussion on stage of the proper use of authority whilst maintaining the absolute power of the monarch; the reasons for Theodosius's fall from moderate absolutism to arbitrary rule suggest both his own fallibility and the importance of sensible counsel.

Theodosius has been educated in the arts of rule by his sister Pulcheria, who was appointed his protector with 'the disposure / Of his so many Kingdomes' (*The Emperour of the East*, sig. B1v) until he reached maturity.[25] It is clear that she has performed both duties very well, and is admired by her subjects at home and by foreign princes:

> Paulinus: Her soule is so immense,
>   And her strong faculties so apprehensive,
>   To search into the depth of deepe designes,
>   And of all natures, that the burthen which
>   To many men were insupportable,
>   To her is but a gentle exercise,
>   Made by the frequent use familiar to her.
>
> Cleon: With your good favour let me interrupt you.
>   Being as she is in every part so perfect,
>   Me thinkes that all kings of our Easterne world
>   Should become rivalls for her.

---

[25] In subsequent references, *The Emperour of the East* will be abbreviated to *Emperour*.

Paulinus: So they have,
    But to no purpose. She that knows her strength
    To rule, and governe monarchs, scornes to weare
    On her free necke the servile yoke of marriage.
    ...
    Shee's so impartiall when she sits upon
    The high tribunall, neither swayd with piety,
    Nor awd by feare beyond her equall scale,
    That 'tis not superstition to beleeve
    Astrea once more lives upon the earth,
    Pulcheriaes brest her temple.
    (*Emperour*, sig. B1v-B2r)

These references to the justice of Astraea, Pulcheria's refusal to marry, and references to her as a Phoenix and 'the moon' (*Emperour*, sigs. B1r, D2r) make clear allusion to Elizabeth I and situate the play in the growing trend of nostalgia for the chaste, just reign of Elizabeth in drama after her death.[26] The reference to a 'servile yoke' of marriage also serves to emphasise the sovereign independence of Elizabeth from the influence of foreign rulers. This nostalgia, which became manifest early in James's reign, took a variety of forms, from an image of chastity, to a politic prince maintaining an 'even keel in domestic and foreign affairs' to a 'Protestant Valkyrie' (Woolf, 1985, p.172). There is, in Pulcheria, a combination of these images. In his description of her, Paulinus establishes her skill in domestic rule, and her private lodgings are described as 'a chaste Nunnery' (*Emperour*, sig. B1v). Whilst she is not quite the warlike Protestant Queen defending her people from the Catholic threat, she is careful to maintain a distinction between religions, encouraging Athenais's conversion to her country's religion, and insisting on her baptism before Theodosius marries her (*Emperour*, sig. E4r). It is possible that contemporaries would have recognised in this a critical comment on Charles's marriage to Henrietta-Maria, a Catholic Princess; the marriage raised fears of Catholic influence in Charles's court, and with it developing ideas of absolutist prerogative rule which were associated with Catholicism. Athenais's growing insistence on the privileges of her position as empress, and Theodosius's increased arbitrariness after marriage support this reading.[27] Pulcheria's capabilities as governor are made clear in the ease with which she carries her responsibilities, emphasised in the comparison which suggests that many men would find the burden unsupportable which she, as a woman, bears with ease. It is important to note, however, that Pulcheria's good government, fairness and justice do not

---

[26]   Anne Barton argues similarly (1981, pp.717–19). Diana, goddess of the moon and of chastity, and the phoenix formed parts of Elizabeth's iconography and contributed to the distancing of the Queen from any human fallibility. See Barton (1981, *passim*).

[27]   Doris Adler argues similarly: 'With the hindsight of history, Theodosius and Athenais [...] seem dramatized types of Charles and Henrietta Maria, and the warnings to the young emperor and empress within the play seem very much the warnings that much of the nation would have their own king and queen heed' (1987, p.89).

preclude her from being an absolute monarch. It is clear that she alone manages her court and governs the empire.[28]

Despite the Elizabethan note, the problems at Pulcheria's court are noticeably Stuart. Those courtiers she condemns – the informer, the projector, the suburbs mignon and the master of the habit – embody some of the more controversial figures of both the Jacobean and Caroline Courts. However, her most scathing condemnation is reserved for the Projector:

> Projector, I treat first
> Of you and your disciples; you roare out,
> All is the Kings, his will above his lawes:
> And that fit tributes are too gentle yokes
> For his poore subiects; whispering in his eare,
> If he would have them feare, no man should dare
> To bring a sallad from his country garden,
> Without paying gubell; kill a hen,
> Without excise: and that if he desire
> To have his children, or his servants weare
> Their heads upon their shoulders, you affirme,
> In policy, tis fit the owner should
> Pay for 'em by the pole; or if the Prince want
> A present summe, he may command a city
> Impossibilities, and for non-performance
> Compell it to submit to any fine
> His Officers shall impose: is this the way
> To make our *E*mperor happy? Can the groanes
> Of his subjects yeeld him musick? Must his thresholds
> Be wash'd with widdowes and wrong'd orphans teares,
> Or his power grow contemptible?
> (*Emperour*, sig. C3v)

Projectors were particularly contentious figures in Caroline politics. That the projector should be associated with the advocation of the king's will as superior to the law is suggestive of the legal controversy over monopolies, which many common lawyers argued were an illegal way for Charles I to gain extra-parliamentary revenue.[29] Pulcheria's condemnation of this attitude suggests she rules in accordance with established law, as does her reference to the law when sentencing the wrong-doers to banishment from court (*Emperour*, sig. C4r). However, it is clear that this is a criticism of more than monopolies, and it is, in fact, a condemnation of arbitrary absolutism, extra-parliamentary finance and

---

[28]   This is not inconsistent with the reading of Pulcheria as an Elizabeth figure, as James VI and I respected Elizabeth for upholding the royal prerogative (Woolf, 1985, p.172).

[29]   Although monopolies had been made illegal by statute in 1624, Charles and his Attorney General had found ways around the legislation in order to raise more money for the King's coffers, 'in clear violation of the spirit of the law' (Orgel and Strong, 1973, p.64).

favouritism. The reference to the prince commanding a sum of money from cities ties this criticism closely to Charles's financial activities, referring to forced loans and the penalties imposed for those who did not or could not pay.[30] Describing such sums as 'impossibilities' here implies an unreasonableness in Charles's demand. The references to different ways of wresting taxes from the people ('gubell' and 'excise') too provide a comment upon Caroline fiscal activities.[31] Indeed, in using words such as 'poore', 'feare', 'groanes' and 'teares' Pulcheria casts these financial activities in a particularly negative light, and her question of whether this can make the Emperor happy encourages her audience (both on and off stage) to consider their effects. However, her final question, 'Must [...] his power grow contemptible?', addresses a monarch's sense of self-preservation, and provides a warning of the potential results of this behaviour.[32] Anne Barton wonders how such a tirade against Charles's activities passed the censorship of the Master of the Revels (1981, p.719), but as no comment from this process remains alongside the record of its licensing, it would seem that the play was not read, at least by the Master of the Revels, as constituting any severe criticism of the King.

Pulcheria's rejection of the activities which would oppress her people is representative of her benevolence which is emphasised throughout the play. She is respected for her justice both at home and abroad: Athenais is drawn to her court for help because of this, and she is always willing to hear the petitions of her subjects, instructing her servants to take 'especiall care too / That free accesse be granted unto all / Petitioners' (*Emperour*, sig. B2v). That Pulcheria's criticism is of those who maintain that 'All is the Kings, his will above his lawes' for their own benefit hints towards the idea of bad counsel which the play explores through the influence of Theodosius's courtiers.

---

[30]   See Richard Cust's *The Forced Loan and English Politics 1626–1628*.

[31]   Here, excise may refer to a general tax, not the more specific excise duty, which was not adopted in England until 1643. These were, however, exacted in Holland at Massinger's time of writing (*OED*, 'excise', 1, 2a). Although I have not been able to find an exact definition of 'gubell', there was a salt tax imposed in France before the revolution called a 'gabelle'. Sharpe notes that there was a project proposing to make salt from seawater, and the salt works at Newcastle on Tyne were supposed to bring £30,000 per year (1992, p.121). As this reference is made in the complaint against the projector, it may also be a comment on the monopoly for making saltpeter granted by James VI and I, and the proclamation confirming this issued by Charles I in 1627. Saltpeter was a controversial issue in the 1630s (Sanders, 1997, pp.461–2).

[32]   Although when it was published, *The Emperour of the East* included a Prologue at court, there is no evidence that this play was ever acted at court and no record of what Charles thought about the politics of the play (*JCS*, IV, pp.778–9). The Court Prologue, however, suggests that the play was not received particularly well in the theatre and appeals to the 'justice' of the King as 'supreme judge' to set the play above the envy of those who condemn it (*Emperour*, sig. A4v).

Philanax, Timantus, Chrysapius and Gratianus lament that Theodius has not yet taken over government from his sister. Chrysapius's reasons for this demonstrate his ambition:

> Wee that by
> The neerenesse of our service to his person,
> Should raise this man, or pull downe that, without
> Her licence hardly dare prefer a suit,
> Or if wee doe, 'tis cross'd.
> (*Emperour*, sig. D1v)

The powers he believes they should have are those which should be the province of the king, not his courtiers, suggesting an overstepping of appropriate bounds in Chrysapius's desires, and that this power and influence is denied to them at Pulcheria's just court suggests their impropriety. Philanax, pointing out the selfish concerns of Chrysapius's statement, claims that his interest is in raising the Emperor to his rightful position, not in elevating his own:

> You are troubled for
> Your proper ends, my aimes are high and honest.
> The wrong that's done to Majesty I repine at:
> I love the *E*mperor, and 'tis my ambition
> To have him know himselfe, and to that purpose
> Ile run the hazard of a check.
> (*Emperour*, sig. D1v)

This seems a little hollow following from Chrysapius's statement, and his mention of his 'ambition', whatever that may be, ties his desires to Chrysapius's. Philanax, of course, hopes that in knowing himself, Theodosius will also come to know what Philanax sees as the correct gifts and powers for his courtiers.

In their attempts to bring him to know 'himselfe' the courtiers argue that his current actions are not fit for a monarch:

> Timant[us]: You have not yet
>   Bene Master of one houre of your whole life,
>
> Chrys[apius]: Your will and faculties kept in more awe,
>   Then shee can doe her owne
>
> Philanax: And as a bondman
>   O let my zeale finde grace, and pardon from you,
>   That I descende so low, you are designed
>   To this or that imployment, suiting well
>   A private man I grant, but not a Prince,
>   To bee a perfit horseman, or to know
>   The words of the chace, or a faire man of armes,
>   Or to bee able to pierce to the depth,

> Or write a comment on th' obscurest Poets,
> I grant are ornaments, but your maine scope
> Should bee to governe men to guarde your owne,
> If not enlarge your empire.
> (*Emperour*, sig. D2v)

The activities for which they criticise him, and in which Pulcheria has made sure he has been educated, are those which were the marks of cultivated, reasonable manliness: mastery of horses and hunting were markers of mastery of the passions, and only when a man can be master of his own passions is he able to be ruler of others.[33] As James VI and I argued:

> As Hee can not bee thought worthie to rule & command others, that cannot rule and dantone his owne proper affections & unreasonable appetites; so can he not be thought worthy to governe a Christian people, knowing & fearing God, that in his own person and hart feareth not, and loveth not the Divine Majestie.
> (1599, sig. B2r)

Their suggestion that Pulcheria is more in control of Theodosius's will than she is of her own is not borne out by her actions in the play, and the lie suggests something of their pique at their lack of advancement. In their own ambitions and in pressing Theodosius to abandon these activities and do more to show his power – Timantus laments that the Emperor has staged 'No pompe, / Or glorious showes of royaltie, rendring it / Both lov'd and terrible' (*Emperour*, sig. D3r) – the play illustrates the bad influence that such ambitious courtiers can wield, and suggests that not only do they have a false idea of what is becoming of their own position (indicated in Chrysapius's wish to press suits), but also what is becoming of the Emperor's.

Theodosius's response, however, suggests the influence of Pulcheria's temperate government:

> will you not know
> The Lyon is a Lyon, though he show not
> His rending pawes? Or fill th'affrighted ayre
> With the thunder of this rorings? you bless'd Saints,
> How am I trenched on? Is that temperance
> So famous in your cited *Alexander*,
> Or Roman *Scipio* a crime in mee?
> Cannot I bee an Emperour, unlesse
> Your wives, and daughters bow to my proud lusts?
> And cause I ravish not their fairest buildings
> And fruitfull vineyards, or what is dearest,
> From such as are my vassals, must you conclude
> I doe not know the awfull power, and strength
> Of my prerogative?
> (*Emperour*, sigs. D3v-D4r)

---

[33] See Sharpe (2000, pp.99–100) for a discussion of the analogy between mastering one's will and horsemanship.

Absolute authority, Theodosius states, does not necessarily involve distressing his subjects merely to prove his power; rather, he places an emphasis on temperance, claiming heritage in earlier temperate and successful rulers.[34] There is, however, despite this condemnation of cruel and arbitrary acts, a much more worrying underlying absolutist claim here: should Theodosius wish to act in the way that he describes – ravishing wives, daughters, buildings and vineyards – it is within his prerogative as absolute monarch to do so.

In advocating benevolent rule, Theodosius stresses the good of the commonwealth over that of individual courtiers:

> am I close handed
> Because I scatter not among you that
> *I* must not call mine owne. Know you court leeches,
> A Prince is never so magnificent,
> As when hee's sparing to inrich a few
> With th'iniuries of many; could your hopes
> So grossely flatter you, as to beleeve
> *I* was born and traind up as an Emperour, only
> *In* my indulgence to give sanctuarie,
> *In* their unjust proceedings to the rapine
> And avarice of my groomes?
> (*Emperour*, sig. D4r)

Thus whilst it is clear that Theodosius is aware of his power and prerogative to take property from his subjects, he is also prepared to acknowledge the limits of what he can call his own property. This emphasis on the property rights of his subjects, like Pulcheria's criticism of extra taxes, strikes a contemporary chord with the arguments made against Charles's use of the prerogative taxation.[35] Emphasising in Theodosius's rebuke to the courtiers and through Pulcheria's actions that a ruler can be secure in the mere *knowledge* of an absolute prerogative, the play suggests that the royal prerogative need not be exercised unreasonably to be maintained. Pulcheria is no less absolute for her reasoned rule, and a 'Lyon is a Lyon, though he show not / His rending pawes' (*Emperour*, sig. D3v).

Despite his rejections of the courtiers' arguments, however, it is clear their comments have some impact, as Theodosius takes control over his empire almost immediately, saying to Pulcheria:

---

[34]   Scipio and Alexander (in his earlier years) were recognised for their temperance (*Plays and Poems*, V. p.220, note to II.i.136–7).

[35]   The rights of the king to levy extra-parliamentary taxes were under debate throughout the personal rule. That tyranny was associated with the illegal command of subjects' property is evident in Bodin's argument that there are three types of monarchy: lordly, kingly and tyrannical, where: 'The tyrannicall Monarchie, is where the prince contemning the lawes of nature and nations, imperiously abuseth the persons of his free borne subjects, and their goods as his owne' (1606, p.200).

Will you have mee
Your pupill ever? The downe on my chinne
Confirmes I am a man, a man of men,
The Emperour, that knowes his strength.
(*Emperour*, sig. E1r)

Whilst his repetition of man/men is an assertion of his maturity, and thus an indication that he no longer needs his sister to rule on his behalf, it also emphasises that he is indeed a *man*, not a god, despite Philanax's Biblical reference to the inscrutability of kings ('Wee had forgot 'tis found in holy writ, / That Kings hearts are inscrutable', *Emperour*, sig. D3v). This mortal fallibility soon becomes evident in his actions as Emperour, granting petitions arbitrarily so that he can 'send petitioners [away from him] with pleas'd lookes'. Indeed, when he attempts to excuse this folly he once again claims that he is a man, but this time, it is as an acknowledgement of his weaknesses, not a statement of his strength: 'I am a man, like other Monarchs, / I have defects and frayleties' (*Emperour*, sig. G4v). All monarchs, not only theatrical ones, are merely powerful men.

As in many plays of the Caroline period, the monarch's turn to arbitrary government and a rule of passion rather than reason, is closely related to his relationship with a woman, in this play, Athenais/Eudoxia.[36] Indeed it is Athenais who first suggests that Theodosius might be 'more than a man', stating 'sure there is divinity about him' and asking whether he expects her 'adoration' (*Emperour*, sig. E3r). Almost immediately before this, Theodosius has rejected the idea of his own divinity, noting God's sole power to make and unmake, to the approval of Pulcheria:

I applaud
This fit acknowledgement, since Princes then
Grow lesse than common men, when they contend
With him, by whom they are so.
(*Emperour*, sig. E2v)

This is an idea already familiar from the downfall of *The Roman Actor*'s Domitian. So, whilst the divinely appointed nature of monarchy is maintained throughout the play, Massinger goes on to raise questions over the divine nature of the kings themselves, emphasising that law and good counsel are needed to help mortal kings govern well.

Early in Theodosius's reign, it is not that Athenais exerts a deliberately corrupting influence over the Emperor, as the courtiers attempted; rather, she does not try to influence his behaviour at all, claiming she has 'no will, but what is

---

[36] See, for example, the influence of Honoria on Ladislaus in Massinger's *The Picture* (1629) and Alinda on Gonzago in Richard Brome's *The Queen and Concubine* (c.1635–6). This is a development from the association between passion and will in *The Roman Actor*, as Domitian asserted the power of his will over the laws before beginning his relationship with Domitia.

deriv'd from [his]' (*Emperour*, sig. F2). Pulcheria tries to convince Athenais to use her potential influence for good, to moderate Theodosius's behaviour:

> Pulcheria: Therefore, Madam,
>   Since 'tis your duty, as you are his wife,
>   To give him saving counsells, and in being
>   Almost his idoll, may command him to
>   Take any shape you please, with a powerfull hand,
>   To stop him in his precipice to ruine.
>   …
>
> Athenais: Do you think
>   Such arrogance, or usurpation, rather,
>   Of what is proper, and peculiar
>   To every private husband, and much more
>   To him an Emperor, can ranck with th'obedience
>   And duty of a wife? are we appointed
>   *In* our creation (let me reason with you)
>   To rule, or to obey? Or 'cause he loves me
>   With a kinde impotence, must I tyrannize
>   Over his weaknesse?
>   (*Emperour*, sigs. F3r-F3v)

In Theodosius's 'kinde impotence' there is an echo of Domitian's impotence concerning Domitia; submission to passion weakens an otherwise powerful ruler. Athenais's refusal to use her influence to help Theodosius govern reasonably is set alongside the frivolous and sycophantic courtiers' encouragement of his irrational actions, suggesting that unquestioning obedience is as harmful for the ruler and his country as giving bad advice. Indeed, Pulcheria argues that it is the duty of those capable of giving sound advice to do so. Although Athenais and the corrupt courtiers view Pulcheria's comments here as a means to regain control over the empire and Emperor through his wife, there is very little reason in Pulcheria's words or actions up to this point to doubt her stated motives. The political comment made here is complicated in this play by the mixing of domestic and political spheres. Wifely obedience is proper, and Athenais extends this in the well-known analogy between the domestic and political spheres to include unquestioning obedience to the Emperor. Ira Clark argues that the danger to the empire and Emperor caused by Athenais's submissiveness suggests that Massinger advocates strong women and their rights (1992, p.40), but Massinger already presents a more than able female monarch in this play; rather, what is at stake here is the importance of appropriate political counsel. In petitioning for and receiving Athenais as a slave through Theodosius's careless and arbitrary granting of petitions, Pulcheria teaches Theodosius, Athenais and the theatre audience that such political obedience is not always appropriate. There may also be, in this petition, a warning to courtiers regarding encouraging kings to act irrationally, as Theodosius's ambitious courtiers acknowledge the folly of encouraging his arbitrary gifts, worrying that Pulcheria's petition could have been to have them executed (*Emperour*, sig. G1r).

Although Theodosius accepts his sister's guidance after Athenais is restored to him, his passion for her continues to affect his reasonable judgement. He irrationally (and wrongly) assumes that when Paulinus sends to him an apple which he had earlier given to his wife, Paulinus sends it in scorn because he is weary of an affair with Athenais. In his anger, he orders Athenais's exile and sentences Paulinus to death. Although his subjects protest that Paulinus should be given the benefit of the due process of law, questioning the sentence whilst 'His cause [is] unheard', Theodosius sees this as a proper use of his absolute authority insisting, 'Is what I command, / To be disputed?' To the theatre audience, however, who know that Paulinus and Athenais are innocent of adultery, his action is, as the just and wise Pulcheria warns, mere 'rashnesse' (*Emperour*, sig. K2v); it is the wilful action of a powerful man.

When he believes the sentences have been carried out, Theodosius begins to doubt his actions:

> I play the foole, and am
> Unequall to my selfe, delinquents are
> To suffer, not the innocent. I have done
> Nothing, which will not hold waight in the scale
> Of my impartiall justice: neither feele
> The worme of conscience, upbraiding mee
> For one blacke deed of tyranny; whereof then
> Should I torment my selfe?
> (*Emperour*, sig. L2r)

The audience, however, know that his judgement was not impartial, and that Theodosius recognises this too is indicated, despite his denials, in his reference to his conscience and to tyranny. That his conscience does not allow him to be equal to '[him] selfe' suggests that he has now accepted as true the definition of his authority as entirely arbitrary that the ambitious courtiers propounded as 'knowing himself', and is unable to maintain this image. His assertions of his authority in the rest of this long speech (which is almost soliloquy, suggesting he wrangles with his own conscience and not with his subjects' judgements) serve to remind him of the power which was earlier claimed for him:

> shall I to whose power the law's a servant,
> That stand accomptable to none, for what
> My will calls an offence, being compell'd,
> And on such grounds to raise an Altar to
> My anger, though *I* grant 'tis cemented
> With a loose strumpets and adulterers gore,
> Repent the justice of my furie?
> (*Emperour*, sig. L2r)

Now it is not only the ambitious courtiers and projectors, but the Emperor who believes his will is above the law, and the possibility that it is this 'will' and not the law that decrees what should be considered an offence raises the spectre of a completely unrestrained arbitrary monarchy. The extent to which Theodosius has lost any moderation in reason is indicated in the deification of his anger, to which he claims he will raise an altar built with blood. The conflation of 'furie' (which has connotations of impetuosity and madness) and 'justice' is a disturbing indication of the potential excesses and injustice of such arbitrary rule.[37]

This assertion of monarchical power is, however, juxtaposed with an assertion of monarchical responsibility:

> Arc[adia]: As you are our Soveraigne, by the tyes of nature
> You are bound to bee a Father in your care
> To us poore Orphans.
> (*Emperour*, sig. L2r)

This is an echo of arguments of patriarchalism which asserted the responsibilities as well as the authorities for the king.[38] It is a philosophy to which Theodosius used to subscribe, arguing in Act 4, scene 1 that since God does not disdain to listen to kings' petitions, he is duty bound to offer his subjects as easy access to him (*Emperour*, sig. H3r). This previously acknowledged responsibility, and their kneeling to him, seems to remind Theodosius that he has not ruled in the best interests of his subjects, and he reflects upon his arbitrary acts:

> Wherefore pay you
> This adoration to a sinfull creature?
> I am flesh, and blood as you are, sensible
> Of heat, and cold, as much a slave unto
> The tyrannie of my passions, as the meanest
> Of my poore subjects the proud attributes
> (By oil'd tongu'd flatterie impos'd upon us)
> As sacred, glorious high, invincible,
> The deputies of heaven, and in that
> Omnipotent, with all false titles els
> Coind to abuse our frailetie, though compounded
> And by the breath of Sycophants appli'd
> Cure not the least fit of an ague in us.
> Wee may give poore men riches; confer honors
> On undeservers, raise, or ruine such

---

[37] *OED*, 'furie', 1, 2.

[38] James VI and I asserted that a king should behave 'as a loving Father, and carefull watchman, caring for [his subjects] more then for himselfe, knowing himselfe to be ordained for them, and they not for him; and therefore countable to that great God, who placed him as his lieutenant over them, upon the perill of his soule to procure that weale of both soules & bodies, as farre as in him lieth, of all them that are committed to his charge' (1603, sig. B4r).

> As are beneath us, and with this puff'd up,
> Ambition would perswade us to forget
> That wee are men.
> (*Emperour*, sig. L2v)

Most importantly here, Theodosius rejects the notion that an emperor is one of the 'deputies of heaven' along with other 'false titles', instead acknowledging his weaknesses as a mortal man. In describing himself as a 'sinfull creature', he recognises his own fallibility, and thus emphasises that he is a man, not a god.[39] Theodosius places emphasis on those things which may make a king feel more than mortal: power and, more significantly, the comments of those advisers who speak as if he *were* divine. As Buchanan argued, 'There is nothing which power equal to the gods dare not believe about itself when praised' (2004, p.95). This decline of and from divinity is accompanied by a recognition of the role played by passion, not reason, in the Emperor's arbitrary actions; indeed, passion is here directly associated with tyranny: in describing the 'tyrannie of [his] passions', Theodosius implies both that his passions have control over him, and that they cause him to act tyrannously. Again, the uselessness of flattery is brought to the fore in this play: those who obey unquestioningly, or refuse to offer good counsel cannot cure a sickness, either of wilfulness in the king himself, or an illness in the body politic. At the end of the play, Theodius, having discovered the truth (that Paulinus is a eunuch and could not have had an affair with Athenais), is reunited with his wife and released from the guilt of Paulinus's death by the revelation that Philanax did not carry out the execution. Thus it is the disobedience to arbitrary acts without due process of law which brings about a happy resolution to the play.

In contrast with *The Roman Actor* which emphasises the divine right of kings, even whilst questioning royal ambition, *The Emperour of the East* places increased emphasis on the impact of external influences on the monarch to moderate and guide his (or her) actions. In Theodosius, Massinger presents a movement away from a divine power and authority of a sovereign towards rule by a mortal and fallible man subject to passion. As Theodosius comes to recognise his weaknesses as a man, the need for good counsel and moderating reason is brought to the fore, and *The Emperour of the East* begins to hint at the possibility of established law being such a moderating influence over the monarch through the contrasting views Pulcheria and Theodosius give of the king's relation to the law.[40] This developing relationship between the monarch and the law, passion and reason in Caroline

---

[39]   One of Rutherford's arguments against the idea of a king's will being law in accordance with the notion that God's will is law, is that a king may will something unreasonable because he does not have the infinite wisdom and perfect will of God which mean that God can will only good (1644, pp.192–3).

[40]   The idea that laws were established as a form of reasoned moderation because kings are men, and thus subject to passions, is one of the arguments Buchanan gives for limiting monarchical authority through law (Buchanan, 2004, p.35). See also Rutherford (1644, p.184).

drama will be explored in more detail in Chapter 3; the final section of this chapter will examine the ways in which this shift in the foundation of monarchical authority from divinity to will is explored in *The Guardian*.

Subject to Will: Personal Authority in *The Guardian*

The decline from divinity of the theatrical rulers calls into question one of the legitimising foundations of royal authority. Although kings should rule according to reason, as suggested in *The Emperour of the East*, this is not always the case, and the intertwining discourses of will and prerogative in drama of the period, reflecting contemporary political debates as Charles continued his personal rule, begin to represent personal power as a point of authority for the king's rule. This section will examine the legitimacy of this position of authority as it is presented in *The Guardian*. In this play, as with the differing approaches to government of Pulcheria and Theodosius, Massinger uses a comparison of different rulers and governors to explore alternative methods of rule and foundations of authority.

The play opens with a discussion over the best way for the guardian of the title, Durazzo, to govern his ward. He has allowed Caldoro to be extravagant with his money, and the freedom to see whom and do what he pleases. His guardianship of Caldoro is benevolent, and as the play progresses it becomes clear that he does have his nephew's interests at heart, first offering him country pursuits to take his mind off his beloved, and then helping him to an engagement with Caliste. However, the Neapolitan gentlemen's warning that his 'too much indulgence' (*Guardian*, sig. G7v) will ruin his nephew, and Durazzo's own argument, indicate that this is a form of irrational arbitrary rule, despite his benevolence. His refusal to have his nephew master any means to support himself is clearly irresponsible, particularly as he encourages his thriftless spending: 'He wears rich clothes, I do so; he keeps horses, games, and wenches; / 'Tis not amiss, so it be done with decorum' (*Guardian*, sig. G8r). The reference to decorum does not necessarily imply that he expects his nephew to behave in an orderly or seemly way that pleases Neapolitan society – it is clear from the gentlemen's warnings that this is not the case – rather, he expects him to behave in accordance with his position and wealth.[41] What this entails, however, is not entirely clear, and a shadow of much less benevolent absolutism clouds Durazzo's joviality when he describes the pastimes he and Caldoro will enjoy in the country. He describes days of hunting, followed by evenings when he will:

> give [Caldoro] a Ticket,
> In which my name, *Durazzo*'s name subscrib'd,
> My Tenants Nutbrown daughters, wholsom Girls,
> At midnight shall contend to do thee service.
> I have bred them up to't; should their Fathers murmure,

---

[41] *OED*, 'decorum', 1a, b, 2b, 3.

> Their Leases are void; for that is the main point
> In my Indentures: And when we make our progress
> There is no entertainment perfect, if
> This last dish be not offer'd.
> (*Guardian*, sig. H5r)

Whilst, for the most part, the full description of the country pursuits does present the idealised life of country gentry (Clark, 1993, p.264), the liveliness and light-heartedness of the description and the emphasis on the positive aspects of the countryside (the girls are 'wholsom', for example) tend to obscure a more serious aspect of his plan: although some of the girls may go to his bed willingly, the threat of eviction if they refuse hangs over Durazzo's tenants. Indeed, he claims to have made this a condition of their tenancy! Despite this, as Philip Edwards argues, the 'amorality of the licentious old guardian is never rejected' in the play (1963, p.350). Nevertheless, the possibility of a monarch taking other men's wives and daughters arbitrarily is once again raised in Caroline drama, the monarchical analogy being confirmed in Durazzo's reference to their visits as royal progresses.[42]

Durazzo's benevolent governance of his nephew – and potentially tyrannical government of his estate – is juxtaposed with Iolante's strict guardianship of her daughter Caliste. Hearing that Caliste's 'fame and favours' have been the reason for a public quarrel between 'noted Libertines' (*Guardian*, sig. H5r), she threatens:

> Do not provoke me.
> If from this minute, thou ere stir abroad,
> Write Letter or receive one, or presume
> To look upon a man, though from a Window,
> I'll chain thee like a slave in some dark corner,
> Proscribe thy daily labor: Which omitted,
> Expect the usage of a Fury from me,
> Not an indulgent Mothers.
> (*Guardian*, sig. H6v)

The use of 'indulgent' draws a deliberate comparison with Durazzo's liberal governance, highlighting Iolante's severity. The extent of her demands – Caliste is not so much as to *look* at a man – and the harshness of her threatened punishments lead Mirtilla to claim that this is 'Flat tyranny, insupportable tyranny' (*Guardian*, sig. H6v), and ultimately leads to her daughter's rebellion and elopement with Caldoro (whom she thinks is Adorio). Indeed, the relationship between Iolante and her daughter is used in this play to explore possibilities of resistance to tyrannous monarchs. To Caliste's questioning 'She is my Mother, & how I should decline it?', Mirtilla responds:

---

[42]   In their discussions of Durazzo's description of his country pursuits, neither Clark nor Edwards acknowledge the uncomfortable coercive aspect of Durazzi's otherwise idealised description.

> 　　　　　　　I will not perswade you
> To disobedience: Yet my Confessor told me
> (And he you know is held a learned Clerk)
> When Parents do enjoyn unnatural things,
> Wise Children may evade 'em.
> (*Guardian*, sig. H7r)

This echoes the comment made in *The True Lawe of Free Monarchies*, that when kings act against God's laws, then subjects may disobey them, and raises the possibility of legitimate disobedience in running away from a monarch who issues such commands. The legitimacy of the argument, which Mirtilla attempts to confirm by citing her confessor as its source, is somewhat undermined by the appropriation of a moral and religious justification for refusal to obey sinful commands in order to follow their own desires and disobey Iolante's unreasonable, but not immoral edict.

That Iolante is representative of arbitrary absolutism in the play is confirmed through the now familiar theatrical equation of this kind of rule with complete surrender to desire. Despite her reputation for chastity, Iolante submits to a lustful desire for a French man, Laval, newly arrived at King Alphonso's court (he is actually her brother, whom she thinks is dead, in disguise):

> I am full of perplexed thoughts: Imperious Blood,
> Thou only art a tyrant; Judgement, Reason,
> To whatsoever thy Edicts proclaim,
> With vassal fear subscribe against themselves.
> (*Guardian*, sig. K6v)

The association of untempered passion with tyranny is made explicit here, as Iolante acknowledges that in her desire for Laval, her good judgement and reason have become subject to her passion. The unmanliness of such submission to passion and abandonment of reason, which has been suggested in the analyses of *The Roman Actor* and *The Emperour of the East* above, is emphasised here in the fact that a woman, the only female authority figure in this play, makes this statement.

Durazzo and Iolante's rights to absolute authority over their respective children is never questioned; their paternal/maternal position grants them a natural authority. It is, rather, their exercise of this authority which is brought under scrutiny. *The Guardian* does, however, also examine the foundation of legitimate kingly authority in its two figures of political authority, Alphonso and Severino. The play focuses particular attention on issues of law by presenting a forest kingdom of banditti with its own laws and sovereign in juxtaposition with the kingdom of Naples. This comparison allows a more detailed consideration of ideas of legitimate rule, personal power, law and prerogative, as Severino (King of the banditti), unlike Alphonso (King of Naples), has no theoretical right to rule. Whilst Butler and Adler have read Severino's forest kingdom as an ideal alternative to the corrupt Neapolitan kingdom (Butler, 1984, pp.256–7; Adler, 1987, p.103), and Rochester reads the play only as a 'self-consciously constructed greenworld comedy' in which the love plots are untangled in the woods in a manner reminiscent of *A Midsummer Night's Dream* (2010, p.68), I will argue that, in a greater demonstration of political engagement than these readings allow, Massinger's forest kingdom presents not an alternative to, but a critique of, absolute, arbitrary authority.

There is no direct assertion of the foundation of Alphonso's authority, but that he is 'anointed' as King suggests that he is given his authority by God; what is made explicit in the way that Alphonso describes his power, however, is that his position brings him certain responsibilities. When he apprehends Severino as King of the banditti at the end of the play, he states:

> Thy carriage in this unlawful course appears so noble,
> Especially in this last tryal, which
> I put upon you, that I wish the mercy
> You kneel in vain for, might fall gently on you.
> But when the holy Oyl was pour'd upon
> My head, and I anointed King, I swore
> Never to pardon murther; I could wink at
> Your robberies, though our Laws call 'em death;
> But to dispense with *Monteclaro's* blood
> Would ill become a King; in him I lost
> A worthy subject, and must take from you
> A strict accompt of't.
> (*Guardian*, sigs. N2r-v)

As Theodosius is brought to do, Alphonso recognises that in accepting the privileges of a king, he also must accept the duties to an authority higher than his own (to uphold heavenly law) which come with these prerogatives. A king's accountability to God is emphasised in Alphonso's earlier comment on being asked to pardon Severino for the supposed murder of Monteclaro that he '*dare* not pardon murther' (*Guardian*, sig. H8v, my emphasis). Nevertheless, it is also clear that Alphonso is not bound to act within the strict bounds of earthly law, and that he uses his prerogative power for pardons and punishment (he says that he would pardon the robberies 'though our Lawes call 'em death'). On more than one occasion, Alphonso pardons an offence in the hope that the perpetrator will behave better thereafter and deserve his forgiveness. He is not, though, an unduly lenient king, threatening that if they do not mend their ways they will 'deeply smart for't' (*Guardian*, sig. M1r). Importantly, whenever Alphonso acts outside or against the established law, it is to mitigate its harshness, not to further his own ends. This aligns him with the good king of James VI and I's *Basilikon Doron*, who will use justice with moderation (1599, sig. O3v). This use of prerogative is also the 'prerogative by way of dispensation of justice' that Rutherford allows as legitimate for the king (1644, p.194). Alphonso's obedience to heavenly laws, of course, does not diminish his absolutism.

Unlike Alphonso, whose anointment gives him legitimate authority, Severino has no external authority for his power, and imposes the rule of his will upon the forest band. Although he recognised his responsibility to make sure his followers are fed and clothed (*Guardian*, sig. M8r), there is no suggestion that this duty is imposed upon him by a higher authority, and this is to his credit. Since fleeing Naples and Alphonso's sentence for the supposed murder of his brother-in-law Monteclaro, Severino has become King of the banditti and given them laws by which to live:

3.   We lay our lives at your Highness feet.

4.   And will confess no King,
     Nor Laws, but what come from your mouth; and those
     We gladly will subscribe to.
     (*Guardian*, sig. I6r)

This statement clearly identifies Severino as the origin of law, and denies authority to any alternative source. If the royal word is the site of legal authority, then the king's will is law. It is also clear that this rule of will is maintained through demonstrations of personal power: Claudio states that Severino can command his subjects 'with a look' (*Guardian*, sig. I6r) and later the bandit King threatens not to leave any of his rebellious subjects alive when they refuse to give up their money to a just cause at the end of the play (*Guardian*, sig. N2r).

Severino's complete authority is confirmed when he invites Iolante to share his sovereignty in the forest, and the bandits present their loyalty to her:

From you our Swords take edge, our Hearts grow bold.
From you in Fee, their lives your Liegemen hold.
These Groves your Kingdom, and our Law your will;
Smile, and we spare; but if you frown, we kill.
(*Guardian*, sig. N4v)[43]

This, as has been the case with Domitian and Theodosius before, clearly identifies the sovereign's will with the law, but the phrasing of the statement 'our Law your will' allows two interpretations: first, that whatever the sovereign wills is law, but second, that the sovereign wills that there is law, or that law is obeyed. The feudal register of this passage connects the forest kingdom with the feudal structures of society imposed upon the Anglo-Saxons at the time of the Norman invasion, and this has significant implications for ideas of law. Common lawyers opposed to the extra-legal use of royal prerogative, such as Edward Coke, argued that there was a continuity in English common law from the Saxons (whose laws were made by consent of the people) through to the present, and for this reason, the king was not above the law, nor was he its origin.[44] However, others, including James VI and I,

---

[43]   The entertainment appears as 'II Song' at the end of the play in the 1655 edition. Edwards and Gibson insert it at the beginning of Act 5, scene 1.

[44]   See Burgess (1992, chapter 2) and Hill (1958, chapter 3). The ancient and customary nature of common law is discussed below in Chapter 3.

argued that after the Norman invasion William the Conqueror imposed his laws upon the (free) Saxons and thereafter his descendants ruled according to their own laws, not those made previously by the people:

> And although divers changes have bene in on-ther countries of the bloud Royall, and kingly house, the kingdome being rest by conquest from one to an other, as in our neighbour country in *England*, (which was never in ours,) yet the same ground of the Kings right over all the lande, and subjects thereof, remaineth alike in all other free Monarchies, as well as in this. For when the Bastard of *Normandie* came into *England*, & made himselfe King, was it not by force, and with a mighty army? Where he gave the law, & tooke none, changed the lawes, inverted the order of government ....
> And for conclusion of this poyn[t] that the king is over-lord over the whole landes, it is likewise daylie proved by the Lawe of our hoordes, ... want of Haires, and of Bastardies. (James VI and I, 1603, sigs. C8r-C8v)[45]

Such an understanding of conquest gives additional meaning to Severino's and Iolante's exchange:

> Iol[ante]: Would we might enjoy our own as Subjects.
>
> Sev[erino]:   What's got by the sword,
>   Is better than inheritance: All those Kingdoms
>   Subdu'd by *Alexander*, were by force extorted,
>   Though gilded ore with glorious stiles of conquest;
>   His victories but royal robberies,
>   And his true definition a Thief.
>   (*Guardian*, sig. M7r)

Iolante's reference is unclear, but perhaps indicates her desire to return home from the forest to enjoy their family wealth. Severino's response, that theft and conquest is better than inheritance, is understandable from a bandit. It is, however, less acceptable from a king in response to his subjects' property, raising the political stakes of this forest kingdom. Thus, whilst Norman conquest associations give added emphasis to Severino's absolutism, if they are read from a common law perspective, they allow for criticism of this absolutism in the loss of Saxon liberties.

Martin Butler and Doris Adler read Severino's kingdom as an ideal alternative to the corrupt Neapolitan kingdom (Butler, 1984, pp.256–7; Adler, 1987, p.103), placing the play in the dramatic tradition in which the exiled courtier and the values of the country present an honest, honourable contrast with the corrupt court. The substance of Severino's laws contributes to this impression by enforcing a kind of

---

[45] 'Hoordes', 'haires' and bastardies' are all aspects of the royal prerogative. A more general argument for the absolute power of kings through conquest can be found in writing throughout the period. See Sommerville (1999, pp.65–8). Bodin argues that a monarch who takes power through conquest can legitimately treat his subjects' person and property as his own property (1606, p.201). Rutherford specifically denies Maxwell's argument that conquest gives a ruler absolute power above the law (1644, pp.82–9).

social justice in preventing attacks upon the poor but allowing theft from the rich and greedy. Those who hoard grain or enclose commons, greedy usurers, 'builders of Iron Mills, that grub up Forests, With Timber Trees for shipping', dishonest shopkeepers and vintners are all fair targets for the outlaws (*Guardian*, sig. I6v); those who are not to be attacked include lawyers, scholars, soldiers, poor farmers, labourers and those who carry goods for others. However, Severino's laws place most emphasis on the protection of women:

> But above all, let none presume to offer
> Violence to women, for our King hath sworn,
> Who that way's a Delinquent; without mercy
> Hangs for't by Marshal law.
> (*Guardian*, sig. I7r)

The reference to martial law, even in the middle of these commands to uphold social justice, suggests the potentially arbitrary nature of Severino's power, and is reminiscent of the fears of Charles I's subjects in the late 1620s. The exclusion of lawyers from the list of those the banditti can rob because they 'may / To soon have a gripe at us' and are 'angry Hornets, / Not to be jested with' (*Guardian*, sig. I6v) suggests that it is only lawyers (with the common law) who provide a sustainable challenge to Severino's supremacy. However, the overtones of the Robin Hood legend evident in this strategy of robbing only the rich and greedy, emphasised by Alphonso's comments on the justice of Severino's distribution of his spoils and a reference to the outlaws as 'imitating / The courteous English Theeves' (*Guardian*, sig. M6r), suggests injustice in Neapolitan society against which Severino's band of men stands, and would support Butler and Adler's readings. These allusions to Robin Hood would not have been lost on the Caroline audience, particularly as the popularity of Robin Hood ballads and plays had increased in the preceding decades (Hill, 1997, p.71).

However, the presentation of Severino, his forest kingdom and his laws is more complicated than this court/country binary allows. I have already established that Alphonso is a just monarch, ruling according to heavenly laws, and exercising his prerogative only to ensure the equity of the law. Severino's laws must, then, have a different purpose. In this respect the forest setting of Severino's kingdom, along with the personal power that authorises his law, is significant; not only does the play comment on abstract notions of the right to rule and the foundation of legitimate authority, but through Severino's kingdom Massinger also comments extensively upon specific contemporary political issues.

Charles I's revival of the forest laws and extension of forest boundaries was very unpopular among his wealthier subjects as they saw this as an unscrupulous means of raising extra-parliamentary revenue through the royal prerogative. Forests became sites of noble resistance to monarchy, and Severino's law, which is in competition with Alphonso's, and his position as outlaw, suggest that the forests held an oppositional status. However, forests were also, George Keeton argues:

particularly subject to the will of the sovereign, and the laws which controlled
them were regarded as a special body of law, distinct from the Common Law
of the King's ordinary courts, and beyond the control of the ordinary justices of
Curia Regis. (1966, p.180)

There is, then, only prerogative law in the forest, identifying Charles more closely
with Severino than with Alphonso. The association of law and will in Severino's
kingdom discussed above also suggests an allusion to Charles's prerogative rule.
It should be remembered in this respect that Severino's laws are not customary
laws as those protecting common land were in Caroline England, but written
laws, imposed by the King, which are read, re-read and noted in table books by
Severino's forest subjects. In presenting these 'forest laws' as a means to protect
the poor by penalising the greedy, the play gives a positive light to Charles's
prerogative activities. Indeed, Kevin Sharpe notes that in many areas the forest
laws actually protected the peasant population from the threat of enclosure by
private individuals (1992, p.245), 'the grand Incloser of the Commons' and the
'Builders of Iron Mills, that grub up Forests, / With Timber Trees for shipping'
condemned by Severino's laws (*Guardian*, sig. I6v). This last reference also
emphasises the need to maintain forests to build ships to strengthen the navy,
an idea highlighted at the end of the play by Alphonso's story of his sons taken
captive by Turkish pirates. This story would have a deep resonance for the play's
Caroline audience because in 1631, not long before the play was licensed, there
was an assault by pirates on Baltimore in Cork during which 150 inhabitants were
captured. Severino's donation of all of the banditti's wealth to the disguised King
to ransom his sons and their companions from the pirates is a topical reference.[46]

There are, however, problems in reading Severino's kingdom as a positive
representation of personal rule, not in Severino's laws, but with his own actions.
Severino breaks his own laws. On venturing back to Naples to visit his wife,
Iolante, he finds her prepared to receive a lover. In rage he threatens to torture her
until she reveals her lover's identity, ties her to a chair and leaves her in the dark.
Iolante's comments draw attention to the fact that in his swift judgement, without
due process of law, Severino is not acting as a just ruler but rather as a passionate
man:

> Good sir, hold:
> For, my defence unheard, you wrong your justice,
> If you proceed to execution,
> And will too late repent it.
> (*Guardian*, sig. K7r)

---

[46]   The play was written too early for this to be understood in the context of Charles's
later contentious prerogative demands for ship money. Bodin argues that usually a king
does not have the right to levy extraordinary taxes outside those granted by agreement with
the people though parliament, but 'neverthlesse if the necessitie of the Commonweale be
such as cannot stay for the calling of a parliament, in that case the prince ought not to expect
the assemblie of the states, neither the consent of the people' (1606, p.97).

The association between passion and tyranny evident in the earlier plays is once again highlighted in the relationship between a man and the object of his (romantic) desire. Her warning echoes Philanax's concern in *The Emperour of the East* over the execution of Paulinus, 'his cause unheard' (*Emperour*, sig. K2v), but the emphasis here is placed on the effect such summary condemnation has on the image of the monarch's justice. Monarchs acting and judging rashly, the play warns, damage their own reputation for justice. Reluctantly, Severino hears her story but his sentence for her is unchanged. Iolante's maid, Calypso, returns and swaps places with her mistress so that Iolante can meet Laval (the gentleman she tried to seduce), believing that Severino will never really harm his wife. However, when Severino returns, thinking Calypso is Iolante, he stabs both her arms and slits her nose. This action breaks the most important of Severino's own laws: 'But above all, let none presume to offer / Violence to women' (*Guardian*, sig. I7r). Yet, Severino suffers no consequences for the action.

It is possible to read this law as a comment on sexual violence: the emphasis on chastity throughout the play would support this reading, and if this were the case, Severino commits no crime. However, there are no threats to female chastity in this play, except those posed by the women's passions themselves; rather the threats are of physical violence. Adorio threatens to torture Mirtilla (*Guardian*, sig. L7r), and when Claudio's appearance prevents Adorio's second threatened attack on Mirtilla it is not a sexual attack, despite his exclamation 'Forbear, libidinous Monsters', but a threat to 'rip [her] entrail' to recover a jewel he believes she has swallowed (*Guardian*, sig. M5v). Severino's violence, then, must be against his own law. Having complained of her injuries to Laval (Monteclaro), whose concern turns to the safety of his sister Iolante and her daughter, Calypso leaves the stage and does not return. Iolanthe and Severino are reconciled, and when Laval reveals his true identity as Monteclaro, Severino is accepted back into Neapolitan society under Alphonso's rule. The implication of this is that monarchs can break their own laws with impunity (the same is, of course, true of Iolante, who, breaking her own decrees of chastity, escapes punishment through a trick and is forgiven). This is an assertion with complex political implications for Charles's personal rule, particularly in respect of the debate surrounding the legal position of the royal prerogative, and the dubious legal manoeuvrings Charles and his advisers carried out.

Severino's violence to women jars awkwardly in a play which otherwise emphasises the need to uphold law both in Alphonso's refusal to pardon murder, and the re-iteration of Severino's laws. Finally, Severino must ask the pardon of the more moderate King for his offences against Alphonso's laws, and submit himself to Alphonso's sovereignty. Whilst this can be read as a suggestion that Charles may need to curb his absolutism to a more moderate level, the unresolved issue of Calypso's wounds leaves a worrying shadow over issues of sovereignty. It seems to emphasise that if a king does not choose to live by a rule of law – whoever's law this may be (God's, established law, his own edicts) – there is no redress for the injured subject.

* * *

Massinger's plays do not deny the ultimate sovereignty of the king. There is no suggestion that the people may legitimately revoke sovereignty or punish a tyrannous king, and the exercise of established law is entirely at the monarch's discretion; even Mirtilla's argument about disobedience advocates only running away, not revolution. What does change in the period covered by these plays, however, is the emphasised foundation for kingly authority. At the beginning of the Caroline period, the plays' grounds for royal absolutism are the theoretical claims of divine right kingship, but as the period progresses, authority comes increasingly to be seen as resting on the personal power of one wilful man. Because of this, emphasis is placed upon the need to moderate the behaviour of a powerful man subject to his passions, through the intervention of good counsel, reasoned argument and law. The intertwining of the abstract ideas of sovereignty and governance with specific aspects of Caroline political and legal policy, such as prerogative taxation, projectors and forest laws, suggests an increased public awareness of and debate over the employment of and foundation for royal authority. The decline from divinity provides an opportunity to question the ultimate legal authority of the monarch: a wilful man can be debated with, a demi-god cannot. The demonstrated need for a moderating force on the royal will allows the possibility of a legal authority independent from the monarch, and the advocation of the common law of England as such an authority, as presented on the Caroline stage, is the focus of the next chapter.

Chapter 3
Debating Legal Authorities:
Common Law and Prerogative

The movement in drama away from a divinely authorised monarch to a king who acts only according to his own will, discussed in the previous chapter, allows space to find a legitimate alternative to the monarch's legal authority. If a king's changeable will ought not to be the ultimate law, as Massinger's plays suggest, then a more stable alternative needs to be found. This chapter will develop this idea through readings of plays which contrast the untempered will of the monarch with the rationality of an independent law. Setting arbitrary absolutism against custom and established law, Richard Brome's *The Queenes Exchange* (c.1631–4), *The Antipodes* (1638) and *The Queen and Concubine* (c.1635–9) participate in contemporary arguments over the position of common law and prerogative using the ideas and vocabulary of Caroline legal debate, and suggest that the common law came to be seen as an alternative, legitimate legal authority to that of the king. Building on the ideas of love and lust which marked the arbitrary actions of rulers in the previous chapter, in each of the plays to be discussed here the state of the monarch-figure's marriage is an index of the stability of the country. However, as I will show, these plays go beyond advocating merely a marriage of law and prerogative, instead evoking images of monarchy governed by law. The first section of this chapter will summarise the legal contexts and arguments for and against the superiority of common law and prerogative, establishing the vocabulary and legal discourses with which these plays engage. In its concern with custom and reason, I will argue, *The Queenes Exchange* debates the contemporary arguments for the supremacy of the ancient constitution and the common law; *The Antipodes* contrasts the 'reason' of law with arbitrary action, and finally, *The Queen and Concubine* explores the destabilising consequences of favouring arbitrary action over established law and legal processes.

Discourses of Common Law

The common law of England is, according to Sir Edward Coke, equitable, excellent and ancient:

> [Y]et will I with a light touch set downe out of the consent of Storie some proofes of the Antiquitie, and ... somewhat of the equitie and excellencie of our Lawes; And that it doth appeare most plaine in successive authoritie in storie what I have positively affirmed out of record, That the grounds of our common laws at this day were beyond the memorie or register of any beginning, & the

same which the Norman conqueror then found within this realm of England. The laws that *Wil.* Conqueror sware to observe, were *bonae & approbatae antiquae regni leges*, that is, the lawes of this kingdome were in the beginning of the Conquerours raigne good, approved, and auncient. (1611, 2π4r–2π4v)

The existing system of common law, he argues, had been in place since time immemorial, emphatically before the Norman Conquest.[1] This ancient law formed the basis of the ancient constitution which maintained the liberties of the subject over the imposition of the will of a monarch.[2] As this form of law was ancient and without specific originator, the ancient constitution denied any possible claims that the law was imposed by a single monarchical figure, and therefore a contemporary king could not claim absolute prerogative and authority over the law as a descendant, literal or metaphorical, of the original lawgiver:

> Neither could any one man ever vaunt, that, like *Minos, Solon,* or *Lycurgus*, he was the first *Lawgiver* to our Nation: for neither did the King make his owne *prerogative*, nor the Judges make the *Rules* or *Maximes* of the lawe, nor the common subject prescribe and limitt the *liberties* which he enioyeth by the lawe …. Long experience, & many trialles of what was best for the common good, did make the Common lawe. (Davies, 1615, sig. *3r)[3]

Even those such as Francis Bacon who stated that there was a 'principal Law-giver of our nation' (1630, sig. A3r) claim that this was Edward I and so the institution of the law pre-dates the Norman Conquest, denying the possibility for a king to claim absolute monarchy through descent from the Conqueror.[4]

---

[1]   Conquest theories allowed absolute authority to the invading king to institute new, or deny any existing, laws. See Chapter 2.

[2]   The 'ancient constitution' is a term used by most political historians of the early Stuart period but very few of them attempt to describe what this is. J. G. A. Pocock summarises his arguments concerning the ancient constitution, thus:

> an 'immemorial' constitution, and … belief in it was built up in the following way. The relations of government and governed in England were assumed to be regulated by law; the law in force in England was assumed to be the common law; all common law was assumed to be custom, elaborated, summarized and enforced by statute; and all custom was assumed to be immemorial, in the sense that any declaration or even change of custom – uttered by a judge from his bench, recorded by a court in a precedent, or registered by king-in-parliament as a statute – presupposed a custom already ancient and not necessarily recorded at the time of writing. (1987, p.261)

In this chapter I will be discussing some of the claims made here in relation to the legal and political writings and the dramatic texts of the period.

[3]   Davies's 'Preface Dedicatory' was, significantly, reprinted in 1628.

[4]   Throughout the *Reports*, Coke acknowledges the role of Edward I in codifying the common law, but argues that the law was already ancient before the time of the conqueror and before Edward's codification.

In order for the common law to be seen as an independent, potentially competing, authority alongside the king's prerogative, however, its legitimacy as such first had to be established. The authority of the king, which had the legitimising sources of precedent both historically and biblically, could only be successfully matched by an alternative of significant historical authority.[5] This was in part the reasoning behind, and in part the conclusion taken from, the claims for common law's ancient and customary usage. The circularity of this argument reflects much of the contemporary thinking about the common law and the ancient constitution; custom feeds into law, and reason feeds into both custom and law and all three contribute to the nature of common law's legal authority, which is then compared in its fittingness as a form of government for England with the royal prerogative, an essentially personal, and potentially changeable and irrational 'law' as discussed in Chapter 2. This section will give an overview of the key terms of common law thought in the period, custom and reason, and their deployment in legal argument.

Custom

The common law was distinguished clearly from statute, civil and canon law by being *lex non scripta* – unwritten law. It was, in fact, a law based on customs which are of benefit to all in the community. Not all customs, however, could be treated as law:

> In respect of their forme, they are either generall throughout all the Realme, and so doe they constitute that part of the Common Law which is grounded upon the generall Custome of the Realme.
> Or else they are particular Customes to certaine places.
>
> (Doddridge, 1631, p.101)

In order to be considered law, a custom had to be effective throughout the whole country; local customs were, to an extent, exceptions to the law in the area in which they applied.[6] Even countrywide application was not in itself sufficient to merit custom being understood as law, however; the custom also had to have been in constant usage since time immemorial:

> [N]o custome is to bee allowed, but such custome as hath bin used by title of prescription, that is to say, from time out of minde. But divers opinions have beene of time out of mind, &c. and of title of prescription, which is all one in the Law. For some have said, that time of mind should bee said from time of limitation in a Writ of right, that is to say, from the time of King *Richard* the first after the Conquest, as is given by the statute of Westminster.... But they have

---

[5]   cf. Hill (1958, p.69).

[6]   In *A treatise of the principal grounds and maximes of the lawes of the kingdome*, William Noy argues in a similar vein to Doddridge, suggesting that customs in general use are maxims in the law (1642, p.19).

sayd that there is also another title of prescription that was at the Common law,
before any estatute of limitation of writs, &c. And that it was where a custome
or usage, or other thing hath beene used, for time whereof mind of man runneth
not to the contrary. And they have said that this is proved by the pleading... that
is as much to say, when such a matter is pleaded, that no man then alive hath
heard any proofe of the contrary, nor hath no knowledge to the contrary. (Coke,
1629, 113a–114a)

Coke's argument encompasses two notions of 'time immemorial', but it is the
latter – literally 'time out of mind' – which he most clearly emphasises to justify
the treatment of custom as law.[7]

Long usage also contributes to the superiority of the common law as a form of
government: 'such prescription, or any prescription used, if it be against reason, this
ought not, nor will not bee allowed before Judges, *Quia malus usus abolendus est*'
[because evil will be destroyed by experience/usage/custom] (Coke, 1629, 141a).
This statement is key to understanding the arguments and vocabularies of common
law: Coke's insistence on reason in customs will be examined in more detail
shortly; the importance of the notion that 'evil will be destroyed by experience'
emphasises the appropriateness of the common law for English government. A
custom which is not beneficial for the good of the people (commonwealth) will be
discontinued, and because of this:

> [T]his *Custumary lawe* is the most perfect, & most excellent, and without
> comparison the best, to make & preserve a commonwealth, for the *written lawes*
> which are made either by the edicts of Princes, or by Counselles of estate, are
> imposed uppon the subject before any Triall or Probation made, whether the
> same bee fitt & agreeable to the nature & disposition of the people, or whether
> they will breed any inconvenience or no. But a *Custome* doth never become a
> lawe to binde the people, untill it hath bin tried & approved time out of minde,
> during all which time there did thereby arise no *inconvenience*, for if it had
> beene found *inconvenient* at any time, it had beene used no longer, but had beene
> interrupted, & consequently it had lost the vertue & force of a lawe. (Davies,
> 1615, *2r)

This reason for preferring the common law over prerogative (that it has been
approved by long usage) also holds true as a reason for not introducing new laws,
or changing those already in place, unless, of course, they have been proved
contrary to reason, in which case, the custom loses its force as law:

> For any fundamentall point of the ancient Common lawes and customes of the
> Realme, it is a Maxime in policie, and a triall by experience, that the alteration
> of any of them is most daungerous; For that which hath been refined & perfected

---

7   Henry Finch also employed the 'time out of mind' formulation in his common law
argument: 'The Common law of England is a Law used time out of mind, or by prescription
throughout the Realme' (1627, p.77). For more information on both forms of 'time
immemorial' see Weston (1991, p.376) and Tubbs (1998, pp.365–9, especially p.367).

by all the wisest men in former succession of ages, and proved by continuall experience to be good and profitable for the common wealth, cannot without great hazzard and daunger be altered or changed. (Coke, 1635c, sig. B2v)

In his epistles to the reader of the books of *Reports* Coke often repeats that to change the common law is dangerous or will lead to inconvenience.[8] The idea is not specific to Coke, and can also be found in Bodin's *Six Bookes of a Common-weale*: 'to make the matter short, there is nothing more difficult to handle, nor more doubtful in event, nor more dangerous to mannage, than to bring in new decrees or lawes' (1606, p.470). The idea itself can be traced back to Aristotle, but it becomes particularly significant in Coke's attempts to assert the legitimate authority of the common law over the royal prerogative: the imposition of a new royal law, or, royal abrogation of established law is, according to this argument, a dangerous practice.[9]

The perfect nature of the common law for ruling England was asserted by James VI and I in *The Kings Maiesties Speach to the Lords and Common of this present Parliament at Whitehall on Wednesday the xxj of March, Anno Dom. 1609*:

> I am so farre from disallowing the Common Law, as I protest, that if it were in my hand to chuse a new Law for this kingdome, I would not onely preferre it before any other Nationall Law, but even before the very Judiciall Law of *Moyses*: and yet I speake no blasphemy in preferring it for conveniencie to this kingdome, and at this time, to the very Law of God: For God governed his selected people by these three Lawes, *Ceremoniall, Morall, and Judiciall*: The *Judiciall*, being onely fit for a certaine people, and a certaine time, which could not serve for the general of all other people and times. (1609, sigs. C2r-v)

In this speech James was attempting to defend himself from accusations that he intended to dispense with the common law of England and rule by Civil law, which allowed absolute rule by the monarch.[10] Earlier in this speech James does assert his

---

[8]   The idea appears in *Reports 3* (1635b, sig. D4r) and is emphasised and repeated at several points in *Reports 4* (1635c, 'To the reader' *passim*). See also John Davies's 'Preface Dedicatory':

> when our Parliaments have altered or changed any fundamentall pointes of the Common lawe, those alterations have beene found by experience to bee so inconvenient for the commonwealth, as that the common lawe hath in effect beene restored againe, in the same points, by other Actes of Parliament, in succeeding ages. (1615, *2r)

[9]   Burgess argues that there was almost universal agreement on the danger of changing or introducing new laws from Aristotle, Aquinas, Machiavelli and Bodin to Coke (1992, pp.23–4).

[10]   Absolutism became associated with the civil law, through the doctrine *quod principi placuit*: (Kelley, 1974, p.38): that which pleases the king (i.e. the king's will) is law. Francis Bacon and John Doddridge note some similarities between the civil law and the laws of England (Bacon, 1630, sigs. B2v-B3r; Doddridge, 1631, pp.158–9). The attitude of English

right to exercise the royal prerogative and claims that this is upheld, not limited, by the law (1609, sig. C1r).[11] It is clear, even from James's own writing, that he would not place the authority of the common law above his own judgement. Nevertheless the emphasis throughout James's text is placed on the status of the common law as the most suitable means to govern England.

Coke bases his argument for the ancient nature of common law on the arguments of Sir John Fortescue, Chief Justice of England under Henry VI, particularly Chapter XVII of his *De Laudibus Legum Angliae* (written between 1468 and 1471, first printed 1545–6):

> *The customs of England are very ancient, and have been used and accepted by five nations successively*
>
> The kingdom of England was first inhabited by Britons; then ruled by Romans, again by Britons, then possessed by Saxons, who changed its name from Britain to England. Then for a short time the kingdom was conquered by Danes, and again by Saxons, but finally by Normans, whose posterity hold the realm at the present time. And throughout the period of these nations and their kings, the realm has been continuously ruled by the same customs as it is now, customs which, if they had not been the best, some of those kings would have changed for the sake of justice or by the impulse of caprice, and totally abolished them, especially the Romans, who judged almost the whole of the rest of the world by their laws. Similarly, others of these aforesaid kings, who possessed the kingdom of England only by the sword, could, by that power, have destroyed its laws. Indeed, neither the civil laws of the Romans, so deeply rooted by the usage of so many ages, nor the laws of the Venetians, which are renowned above others for their antiquity – though their island was uninhabited, and Rome unbuilt at the time of the origin of the Britons – nor the laws of any Christian kingdom, are so rooted in antiquity. Hence there is no gainsaying nor legitimate doubt but that the customs of the English are not only good but the best. (1942, pp.39–41)

The long continuance of customary common law, then, confirmed its status as both legitimate legal authority and perfect for governing England. If the customary law was not the best method of government, various conquerors could and would have changed the law. Fortescue's original Latin when describing the reasons an invading king might change the laws reads: '*aliqui regum illorum iusticia racione vel affecione concitati eas mutassent*' [some of those kings would have changed

---

common lawyers, antiquaries and scholars towards the civil law is debated in a series of articles in *Past and Present* by Donald Kelley, and Christopher Brooks and Kevin Sharpe. See Kelley (1974); Brooks and Sharpe (1976) and Kelley (1976).

[11] In his 'Preface Dedicatory', Davies maintains both of these arguments – that the common law is the best law to rule this English nation, and that it upholds the king's prerogative – in his praise of the common law. However, he makes the point more strongly, stating that the common law 'is so framed and fitted to the nature & disposition of this people, as wee may properly say, it is *connaturall* to the *Nation*, so as it cannot possibly bee ruled by any other lawe' (1615, *2v).

them, moved by justice, *reason*, or caprice (my emphasis)]. Coke's translation, more accurate than Chrimes's, states that 'some of these Kings, mooved either with Justice, or with reason, or affection, would have changed them' (1636, sig. π3v).[12] Nevertheless, this acknowledgement of the possibility of a conqueror imposing his will as law did allow the prospect of absolute government after the Norman Conquest. This would have disrupted the ancient constitution which upheld the rights and liberties of the subject independently of the king, and entitled Charles, as a descendant of William, to absolute authority through conquest.[13] Importantly for the specific legal debates over ship money and non-parliamentary taxes of the period, this would also have given Charles absolute control over all land and property, and therefore the unquestionable right to impose prerogative taxation.[14] Coke, however, emphasised that the ancient laws continued throughout the reign of William the Conqueror and were restored by Henry I after William Rufus had attempted to impose his oppressive will on the people (1611, sigs. 2π4v-2π5r), thus neutralising the Conquest by absorbing it into the narrative of the ancient constitution. Davies, too, affirms that:

> the *Norman Conqueror* found the auncient lawes of England so honourable, & profitable, both for the Prince & people, as that he thought it not fitt to make any alteration in the fundamentall pointes or substance thereof: the change that was made was but in formulis iuris. (1615, sig. *3r)

John Hare, however, in *St Edwards Ghost: or Anti-Normanisme*, laments the changes made to the law and government at the Conquest and demands a return to the ancient laws and liberties enjoyed by the Saxons (1647, *passim*).[15]

---

[12] Coke acknowledges Fortescue as one of his authorities for maintaining the ancient establishment of the common law in the letter 'To the reader' of *Reports 6*. In his address 'to the learned reader' in the second book of *Reports*, Coke argues similarly to Fortescue that, 'If the ancient Lawes of this noble Island had not excelled all others, it could not be but some of the severall Conquerors, and Governors thereof [...] would (as every of them might) have altered or changed the same' (1635a, sig. π4v).

[13] cf. Hill (1958, p.63).

[14] Cromartie notes that Mary Tudor had successfully taken full advantage of her ability to impose extra-parliamentary taxation in the Book of Rates, but suggests that changes in the political climate (including the way in which the law was understood and described, along with an increased legalism amongst members of Parliament under James and Charles) meant that Charles was unable to exercise the same kind of power (2006, p.234).

[15] There is some debate over the extent to which it was argued that the conquest had made a significant difference to the systems of law and government in England. For a detailed discussion see Hill (1958, *passim*), Skinner (1965, *passim*) and Sommerville (1986, *passim*). Hill and Skinner give broader historiographical discussions of the Norman Conquest and its interpretation, whereas Sommerville focuses more closely on the early Stuart period.

The idea that the common law and ancient constitution had remained completely unchanged, as advocated by Fortescue followed by Coke, however, was not entirely satisfactory to some of Coke's contemporaries, such as John Selden and Henry Spelman, who argued that this is essentially non-historical, and does not allow for the developments in society. Selden questioned the argument for immutable customary law in his notes on Fortescue in the 1616 edition of *De Laudibus Legum Angliae*, instead arguing for an evolutionary development of common law, claiming, contrary to Fortescue, 'But questionlesse the *Saxons* made a mixture of the *British* customes with their own; the *Danes* with old *British*, the *Saxon* and their own; and the *Normans* the like' (1616, p.7). The comments Selden makes on this particular chapter of Fortescue's work are much longer than his commentary on any other chapter, suggesting the importance he places on this issue. His argument for the historical and evolutionary nature of law continues, responding to questions of the origin of common law:

> 'Tis their triviall demand, *When and how began your common laws*? Questionlesse its fittest answerd by affirming, when and in like kind as the laws of all other States, that is, *When there was first a State in that land, which the common law now governs*: then were naturall laws limited for the conveniencie of civill societie here, and those limitations have been from thence, increased, altered, interpreted, and brought to what now they are; although perhaps (saving the merely immutable part of nature) now, in regard of their first being, they are not otherwise then the ship, that by often mending had no piece of the first materialls, or as the house that's so often repaired, *ut nihil ex pristine materia superfit* [so that nothing is made of the original material], which yet (by the Civill law) is to be accounted the same still. (1616, p.19)

Although this need not entirely contradict the idea of law as customary, nor deny that the origin of law is immemorial, it does discredit the notion that common law has remained unchanged.[16] Selden's argument that the common law of England began at the same time as the laws that govern other nations also strikes against Fortescue's assertions, above, that the English laws are of greater antiquity than other laws, and for this reason are the best. Instead, Selden argues, the common law is the best law by which to govern England because it has evolved with the people and communities it governs: 'Those which best fit the state wherein they are, cleerly deserve the name of the best law' (1616, sig. C2v).

Reason

The legitimacy and superiority of the common law of England was not only based on its long usage, however; it was also considered to be a law constituted of reason, which derived in part from its customary nature, and in part from its basis in natural

---

[16]   In 'Of the Ancient Government of England', written in 1614, Henry Spelman also argues for a slow evolutionary process of legal development (1698, p.49).

law. Selden's commentary on Fortescue, aside from describing and emphasising the common law's fittingness to govern the nation, also draws attention to the idea that all law (at least all customary law) is based upon natural law.[17] The law of nature was thought to be the natural reason with which men governed themselves and was often equated with God's moral law. For Davies, common law's similarity to the natural law contributed to its authority and its perfection:

> Therefore as the *lawe of nature*, which the schoolmen call *Ius commune*, & which is also *Ius non scriptum*, being written onely in the hart of man, is better then all the written lawes in the worlde to make men honest & happy in this life, if they would observe the rules thereof: So the *custumary lawe* of England, which wee doe likewise call *Ius commune*, as comming neerest to the lawe of *Nature*, which is the roote and touchstone of all good lawes, & which is also *Ius non scriptum*, & written onely in the memory of man (for every *custome* though it tooke beginning beyond the memory of any living man, yet it is continued & preserved in the memory of men living) doth farre excell our *written* lawes. (1615, p.2)

However, natural law was also a law of reason. Natural law was the natural reason which every man possessed, and by which he should govern his own actions: 'The law of Nature is that soveraigne reason fixed in mans nature, which ministreth common principles of good and evill' (Finch, 1627, pp.3–4). The use of the word 'soveraigne' is significant: if reason should be sovereign in ruling a man's actions, it should also be sovereign over will in determining law. 'All men must agree,' Finch states, 'that lawes in deed repugnant to the law of reason, are aswell[sic] void, as those that crosse the law of nature' (1627, p.76).

Indeed, Finch asserts that the common law is 'nothing els but common reason'. It is not, however, merely the common reason, 'which everie one doth frame unto himselfe', he argues, 'but refined reason' (1627, p.75). Coke's *The first part of the Institutes of the Lawes of England* (hereafter, *Institutes I*) gives a more detailed explanation:

> And this is another strong argument in Law, *Nihil quod est contra rationem est licitum* [nothing which is against reason is lawful]. For the reason is the life of the Law, nay the common Law it selfe is nothing else but reason, which is to be understood of an artificiall perfection of reason, gotten by long study, observation, and experience, and not of every mans naturall reason, for, *Nemo nascitur artifex* [No one is born an expert]. This legall reason, *est summa ratio* [is the highest reason]. And therefore if all the reason that is dispersed into so many severall heads were united into one, yet could he not make such a law

---

17   The idea that all law derives from natural law is not specific to Selden (see, for example, Doddridge, 1631, pp.153, 158–9) nor new to the period, having its origins in the thinking of Thomas Aquinas (Burgess, 1992, p.33). Natural law, Aristotle believed, was also that which made men form political societies for government. For a detailed discussion of ideas of natural law, and its relationship with common law, see Sommerville (1999, pp.13–18).

as the Law of England is, because many succession of ages it hath beene fi[n]
ed and refined by an infinite number of grave and learned men, and by long
experience growne to such a perfection, for the government of this Realme,
as the old rule may be justly verified of it, *Neminem oportet esse sapientiorem
legibus*: No man (out of his owne private reason) ought to be wiser than the Law,
which is the perfection of reason. (1629, 97b)

Coke presents here dense and sophisticated arguments for the rationality of law.
The common law is the highest form of reason because it is not the wisdom of
one man in one time, but of many men through several ages, and their cumulative
wisdom must be greater than that of one man. Not only does Coke argue for the
rationality of common law here, but also for its superiority over a law imposed by
any one person. Included in his argument is the assertion that a man's personal,
natural, reason is not enough to be able to understand the complexities of law;
rather, it can only be understood through long study and experience, an 'artificial
reason' which only experienced lawyers and the judiciary possessed. They and
only they are capable of correctly interpreting and manipulating the law. If this
is the case, the king cannot hold authority over the law, either as law-giver or as
primary interpreter.[18]

In a variety of ways, then, the common law was viewed as a legitimate legal
authority, independent of the king. It has no single originating source (be that
indigenous king or conqueror), making it subject to the will of no single ruler;
instead it claims legitimate authority in its antiquity, its rationality or its perfect
fittingness to govern England. The common law had in its favour two different
assertions of its rationality: its derivation from the law of Nature, and its basis in
custom. Both of these arguments, by virtue of their emphasis on reason and testing,
favour common law over any rule imposed by a single lawgiver, and provide an
alternative, rational law in contrast with that imposed by the potentially capricious
will of the monarch.

In the sections which follow, I will examine the ways in which the understood
history and vocabularies of common law are employed, translated and debated
on the Caroline commercial stage. *The Queenes Exchange* engages with the
ancient constitution and the customary nature of common law; *The Antipodes*, by
illustrating the absurdity of irrational judgement, emphasises the need to temper
desire and act according to law, and *The Queen and Concubine* engages with the
rationality of law and the potential consequences of disregarding this in favour of
arbitrary absolutism. These plays, however, do not merely employ the vocabulary
of common law to present the ideas of contemporary legal argument, they also
present the potentially destabilising effect of competing legal authorities in the
common law and royal prerogative.

---

[18]   This assertion led to a direct confrontation between Coke and King James, common
law and the monarch. Although James had natural reason, Coke argued, he did not have the
'artificial reason' of the judiciary. James objected that this would mean that he was under
the law, and Coke quoted Bracton's argument that kings were under God and the Law
(Bracton, 1968–77, p.33). See Barnes (2004, pp.12–13) and Usher (1903, *passim*).

The Ancient Constitution: *The Queenes Exchange*

The Queenes Exchange centres on the marriage options of Bertha, Queen of the Saxons. The Saxon setting is unusual, and no source for the play has been identified, suggesting a deliberate association of the play with the idealised Saxon past employed by advocates of the common law.[19] In the course of the play, Bertha marries Anthynus, the son of one of her courtiers, believing he is the man to whom she is betrothed, King Osriik of Northumberland (the men are almost identical); the Queen's 'exchange' of the title is her exchange of one husband for another. More significant, however, are the legal authorities these possible husbands represent: Osriik embodies arbitrary absolute rule and Anthynus, rule by the customary common law. Bertha, in changing her husband, also changes the kind of legal authority she espouses.

At the beginning of the play, consistent with the Saxon setting, Queen Bertha has called a meeting of her Lords to ask their opinion on her proposed marriage to Osriik.[20] Bertha's first speech sets out clearly her claims to authority:

> Since it hath pleasd the highest Power to place me
> His substitute in Regal Soveraignty,
> Over this Kingdom, by the generall vote
> Of you my loyall Lords, and loving Subjects,
> Though grounded on my right of due Succession;
> Being immediate heir, and only child
> Of your late much deplored King my Father.
> I am in most reverend duty bound
> Unto that Power above me, and a wel-
> Befitting care towards you my faithfull people,
> To rule and govern so (at least so neere
> As by all possibility I may)
> That I may shun Heavens anger, and your grief.
> (*Queenes Exchange*, sig. B1r)

---

[19] Butler (1984, p.265) and Weston (1991, *passim*) note that the Saxons were the society to whom the Stuarts looked for customary rights and liberties, and it is indeed the Saxons to whom Coke (*Reports 8*, 'To the reader'), Hare (1647, *passim*, esp. 6) and Spelman (1698, *passim*), amongst others, refer their readers for the ancient nature of the law and the liberties of parliaments. Andrews states he has examined the chronicles of 'Hall, Holinshed, Fabyan etc' in vain for the source, but the names of the characters, however, can be found in Holinshed's chronicles referring to Saxons (1981, pp.79–80).

[20] Saxon kings ruled in association with a council of lords which later became the basis for rule by parliament. This provided a long, continuous (and pre-conquest) history for the notion of king-in-parliament, and added to claims that the king could not overrule parliament by virtue of their existing only after instigation by a previous king. See William Lambarde's *Archeion*, cited in Burgess (1992, p.62). This contrasts starkly with Robert Filmer's argument that 'all those liberties that are claimed in parliaments are the liberties of grace from the king, and not the liberties of nature to the people' (Filmer, 1680, sig. I5v).

As the opening speech, Bertha's focus on the foundations of her authority sets the scene for the ideas of legitimate authority to be contested throughout the play. This speech encompasses a variety of political theories on the nature and origin of royal power: she is the representative of God on earth, thus ruling by divine right, but she has also been elected through the Lords' vote and as such has the support of the council too. Her right to rule as the legitimate heir to the previous monarch is emphasised by her description of her father as 'late' and 'much deplored' (his death has been much lamented).[21] Her claims to authority encompass divine right and contract theories of government, and the deliberate conflation of these theories in the potential origins of Bertha's authority means she is undoubtedly sovereign in her kingdom: there is no position from which her authority can be questioned. What is at stake is the way in which she exercises her authority to govern. She is, at this point in the play, far from arbitrary absolutism; she acknowledges that her position comes with a duty, both to God and to her people, to rule justly.

Although most of the Lords express their approval of her marriage, Segebert does not. The reasons for his objection associate him closely with advocates of the common law:

> I beseech you my Lords,
> To weigh with your known wisdom the great danger
> This match may bring unto the Crown and Country.
> Tis true, the King *Osriik* as wel in person
> As in his dignity, may be thought fit
> To be endow'd with all you seem to yeild him.
> But what becomes of all the wholsome Laws,
> Customs, and all the nerves of Government
> Your no less prudent than Majestick Father
> With power & policy enricht this Land with;
> And made the Saxons happy, and your self
> A Queen of so great eminence.
> (*Queenes Exchange*, sigs. B1r-v)

Segebert's use of the discourse of custom of contemporary legal argument, and his reference to Saxons, connects the laws that he seeks to preserve with the ancient constitution. These laws are not only good for the wellbeing of the country – they are 'wholsome', suggesting health in the body politic – but they have also enriched it, and it is this legal wealth that gives Bertha her superiority over other monarchs. As part of the debate over the position of common law and prerogative, it is significant that here it is the customary law that maintains the Queen's position, not the Queen who gives power to the law, thus conforming to contemporary arguments that the royal prerogative was part of, or indeed granted by, the established law rather than the law being subject to the king's will. The 'great danger' Segebert fears for the country is that these laws will be lost and Bertha's happy, prospering and orderly realm will 'Be now subjected to a strangers foot; / And trod into disorder' (*Queenes Exchange*, sig. B1v) by subjection to Osriik's rule.

---

21 *OED*, 'deplored', 1.

Segebert does not want to deprive his Queen of the authority she currently wields or the privileges already ascribed to her; he wishes only to maintain the *status quo*:

> I know, and you, if you knew any thing,
> Might know the difference twixt the Northumbrian laws
> And ours: And sooner will their King pervert
> Your Priviledges and your Government,
> Then reduce his to yours.
> (*Queenes Exchange*, sig. B2r)

The audacity of this argument ('if you knew anything') suggests the extent of Segebert's concern for the maintenance of the common law. The government of the Saxons and indeed Bertha's privileges are, he argues, currently on the right course (that of moderate monarchical rule by common law), but this will be perverted in marriage to Osriik. The assertion that Osriik would not reduce his government to hers could suggest that he has greater power than Bertha which he will not diminish or bring under her control. However, 'reduce' had other meanings current in the seventeenth century including 'to lead or bring back from error on action, conduct, or belief, especially in matters of morality or religion' or 'to bring (a thing, institution, etc.) back to a former state'.[22] Segebert's concern is that Osriik will pervert the Saxon laws rather than turning his seemingly erroneous methods of government to those prudent and wholesome methods prevalent in Bertha's Saxon kingdom.[23]

The late King charged Segebert with the duty of protecting the law in Bertha's marriage. Concerned for his people, the King commanded:

> That rather then by marriage you should bring
> Your Subjects to such thraldome, and that if
> No Prince whose lawes coher'd with yours did seek you
> (As some there are, and nearer then the Northumbrian)
> That he would have you from some noble Stock
> To take a Subject in your owne Dominion.
> (*Queenes Exchange*, sig. B2r)

---

[22] *OED*, 'reduce', 8a, 9b. The first of these alternative, contemporary definitions also lends weight to the notion that the play might include some reference to the Catholic influence of the Queen at court.

[23] Marriage was, of course, an image used extensively by James VI and I to comment on the union of kingdoms under one monarch (Roberts Peters, 2004, pp.11–13). The contemporary concerns raised about the infraction of Scottish absolutism upon English law is a comparable argument to the one I am making here. Indeed, Matthew Steggle reads the play as a comment on the concerns of nationhood and Britishness related to the union of England and Scotland, arguing that the play 'does not offer practicable solutions to anxieties about the nature of the union between England and Scotland , but the play certainly articulates such anxieties'. As the union of Bertha's court with Osriik's does not actually happen, Steggle suggests that this is a separatist play (2004, pp.54–7, quotation at p.56). Steggle's reading is not incompatible with mine.

The customary laws of the ancient constitution safeguarded the liberties of the subject; that Osriik's government would bring the Saxons into 'thraldome' is the first clear indication of his absolutism. Segebert offers an alternative to this in suggesting marriage to one of her subjects, whose idea of law would necessarily coincide with her own. Segebert never suggests that he is the man she should marry and, despite the other Lords' pointed question, 'whom in your great wisdom / Would you allot the Queen?', he is cleared of any ambitious motive by his obvious concern for the law and the state, and in his condemnation of the other courtiers for their sycophantic acquiescence to Bertha's wishes 'though all / The Kingdom perish for't' (*Queenes Exchange*, sig. B1v). His care for the country is confirmed when he states that he does not grieve at his banishment (imposed for speaking out against the Queen's wishes) so much for himself as for what will become of his country (*Queenes Exchange*, sig. B4v).

The fear for the liberties of the people and the safety of the law Segebert invokes is intensified by the imagery Bertha chooses, in the same scene, to give her assent to the marriage to Osriik:

> A King sent forth a General to besiege
> A never conquered City. The siege was long,
> And no report came back unto the King;
> How well or ill his Expedition thriv'd;
> Until his doubtful thoughts had given lost,
> His hope oth' City, and his Army both
> When he being full of this despair, ariv'd
> Oth' suddam his brave General with Victory;
> Which made his thanks, as was his conquest double.
> (*Queenes Exchange*, sig. B2v)

There is nothing unusual about the analogy between a love won and a conquest but, in the context of Segebert's Saxon objections, the passage must have political resonance. If, as some absolutists claimed, the Norman Conquest introduced absolute kingship and disrupted the ancient constitution, Bertha's willing acquiescence to Osriik's conquest implies a submission to the will and whim of the conqueror and the abolition of the customary Saxon law. Her reference to a double conquest is a little ambiguous: whilst it is clear that in terms of the siege, 'double' refers to the greatness of the king's joy and victory, in Bertha's analogy the meaning is less clear, and to a politically alert audience could potentially link the conquest of Bertha's heart with the subordination of her laws and realm. The political and legal implications of the Queen's conquest analogy are confirmed in a sycophantic courtier's comment:

> I can but think what old Segebert said
> Concerning Laws, Customes and Priviledges,
> And how this match will change the Government.
> I fear, how e'er the Laws may go, our Customes will
> Be lost; for he [Northumbrian ambassador] me thinks out-flatters us already.
> (*Queenes Exchange*, sigs. B2v-B3r)

Although his second use of 'custom' quite clearly refers to court 'customs' of flattery, the emphasis is placed on the change in laws and customs and how this 'will change the Government'. Coming so soon after Bertha's conquest analogy and in the same scene as Segebert's objections to the marriage based on concern for law and liberty, this cannot but emphasise the play's engagement with contemporary legal argument.

The emphasis Segebert places on custom and law contrasts sharply with the terms he uses to criticise Bertha's marriage:

> All your wealth
> Your state, your laws, your subjects, and the hope
> Of flourishing future fortunes, which your Father
> By his continual care, and teadious study
> Gave as a Legacy unto this Kingdom:
> Must all be altered, or quite subverted,
> And all by a wilful gift unto a stranger.
> (*Queenes Exchange*, sig. B1v)

In describing Bertha's decision to marry Osriik as a 'wilful gift' Segebert undermines the Queen's prerogative, bringing it to the level of mere wilfulness, and raising the need for a moderating force. The royal prerogative has become mere will, not the reasoned government which, at least in Segebert's eyes, can be found in the legacy of customary law Bertha inherited. This legacy implies not only the long continuance of the law, but also a responsibility to preserve it to pass it on again at the Queen's death. Significantly, hope for the future for subjects, state and wealth are connected to the law, not to Bertha's will; indeed, indulging Bertha's will would overthrow or ruin (subvert) these hopes.

This questioning of the royal will causes the Queen to reassert her authority:

> Peace: stop his mouth. Unreaverend old man,
> How darst thou thus oppose thy Soveraignes will,
> So well approvd by all thy fellow Peers;
> Of which the meanest equals thee in judgement?
> (*Queenes Exchange*, sig. B1v)

Bertha tries to recover the authority of her 'Soveraignes will' from the imputations of whim both by reinforcing her authority in asking how he dares to oppose her, and by the approbation of the other Councillors. Segebert does not, however, accept the will of the Queen and the approval of his sycophantic peers as a sound method of judgement:

> Do you approve their judgements, Madam, which
> Are grounded on your will? I may not do't.
> Only I pray, that you may understand,
> (But not unto your loss) the difference
> Betwixt smooth flattery, and honest judgements.
> (*Queenes Exchange*, sig. B1v)

The repetition of the word 'will' in this interchange ('wilful gift', 'Soveraignes will', 'your will') emphasises that this action is on the whim of the Queen rather than a reasoned decision. The need for advisers' true judgement rather than the flattery of sycophants that Segebert highlights is not specific to drama of the Caroline period; here, however, the flattery of Bertha's courtiers not only encourages absolute, even arbitrary, rule but it is also explicitly connected with undermining the stability of her state, laws and subjects, and the 'hope / Of flourishing future fortunes' left as her legacy by her father.

Already, even before his appearance on stage, Osriik has tempted Bertha towards arbitrary rule. This can be seen most clearly in her banishment of Segebert for his advice; indeed, Anthynus later describes her as the 'Tyrannesse' who banished his father (*Queenes Exchange*, sig. D4v). Nevertheless, she does not yet rule with cruelty; she refuses to execute Segebert or confiscate his land because of his insolence, dismissing her courtiers' suggestions with 'Away, you'l be too cruel' (*Queenes Exchange*, sig. B2r). In Osriik himself, however, the traits of an arbitrary ruler can be found. He rules in conjunction with a court favourite, a stock figure of Jacobean and Caroline tragedy and a controversial figure in early Stuart politics. Reminiscent of Massinger's Severino, Osriik acts only according to his own will and his rule is clearly one of personal authority augmented with threats of severe punishment: 'And if my power be not a spell sufficient / To worke your secresie, I'l take your heads / To mine own custody' (*Queenes Exchange*, sig. E1v). This is not reasoned absolutism; rather it is the arbitrary threat of a wilful man, emphasising his power and ability to punish. There is no reason to believe he will not carry out his threats.

Osriik's complete surrender to will is illustrated in his uncontrollable passion for Mildred, Segebert's daughter. When Osriik first submits to his passion for Mildred, he describes it as an illness: 'I am not well, what kind of Changeling am I?' (*Queenes Exchange*, sig. C2r). His reference to being a 'Changeling' may refer to his sudden change of heart from Bertha to Mildred, but it could also refer to the danger to his friendship with his favourite Theodrick if he pursues Mildred as she has already been wooed by him.[24] In a dramatic parallel with Bertha's actions, Osriik, too, removes the courtier who obstructs his union with the desired partner, ordering Theodrick's house arrest. The King and his courtiers repeat throughout the following scenes at Osriik's court that the King is 'not well' or 'sick' (*Queenes Exchange*, sig. C2r, D2v), providing a stark contrast between the sickness caused by unrestrained will at Oriik's court and the 'wholsome Laws' (*Queenes Exchange*, sig. B1r) which Segebert claims for Bertha's kingdom. Indeed, Osriik's sickness does not only affect him, but those around him:

---

[24] That the desire that represents absolutism should also be concerned with taking what rightfully belongs to one of his subjects may also be a comment on the abuse of royal power and infraction of subjects' liberties in Charles's forced loans and prerogative taxation.

> Although I cannot properly call it
> A sickness: I am sure 'tis a disease
> Both to himself and all that come about him.
> I fear he's brain-crack'd, lunatick and Frantic, mad;
> And all the Doctors almost as mad as he,
> Because they cannot find the cause.
> (*Queenes Exchange*, sig. D2v)

All is not well in the Northumbrian body politic.

The possibility that Osriik's desire for Mildred has sent him mad also draws a comparison with Segebert's concern for the laws of Bertha's kingdom. Whilst he reprimands Bertha for acting wilfully, and her Lords for their sycophancy, they comment that he has lost his senses:

> [Bertha?]: Take hence the mad man.

> Colr.: We are sorry for you.

> Elk.: And wish the troublesome spirit were out of you
> That so distracts your reason.
> (*Queenes Exchange*, sig. B1v)[25]

It is clear, however, from his concern for his country and through comparison with Osriik's illness, that Segebert's reason is not distracted, although Osriik's, in his overwhelming desire, is. The claims for the reason of the common law are translated here into a madness of absolutism on the Caroline stage. This is a particularly key idea to Brome, and appears again in *The Queen and Concubine* and *The Antipodes* which will be discussed below. Osriik's courtiers explicitly associate this madness with his court favourites who, in having 'the rule here over [their] Ruler', have, they say, made the King mad (*Queenes Exchange*, sig. E4v). This is a subtle representation of the evil counsel argument, in which any unpopular or inappropriate actions taken by a king are the result of poor advice. It also associates the King's madness with the instruments of his absolute rule – his favourites. Here, however, it is not their poor counsel, but the King's own illegitimate desires which have brought about his 'illness'. Thus, the connection between madness and absolutism is confirmed in the audience's knowledge that Osriik's madness is really caused by his arbitrary will in his uncontrollable passion for Mildred. Although it seems, at least initially, that he wrestles with this passion, his arbitrary unconcern for his people is illustrated in his continued pursuit of Mildred even whilst acknowledging that his treatment of Theodrick is 'unjust' (*Queenes Exchange*, sig. D3v).

---

[25]   The 1657 edition of the text attributes the first of these lines to Segebert, but as he has just finished speaking, and the sentiment in it coincides with the other lords rather than Segebert it seems to have been misattributed. In her recent edition of the play for Richard Brome Online, Marion O'Connor attributes the line to Bertha (<http://www.hrionline.ac.uk/brome>, Modern Edition, 1.1.speech 16).

Despite Osriik's sickness, no harm comes to his country. However, in the linked sub-plot centred on Segebert's family, Brome illustrates the potential dangers for law and order in the total submission to will. As Segebert prepares to go into exile he asks his children for an expression of their gratitude. The echoes of *King Lear* in this scene are obvious, and contribute to the tragic atmosphere of Segebert's exile, invoking a potential political instability. They also suggest something of Bertha and Segebert's folly in wanting to hear their own praise, as well as preparing the audience for Offa's treachery, which endorses Segebert's warnings to the Queen about heeding flattery.[26] Mildred answers, like Cordelia and as becomes an obedient daughter, that she cannot speak his goodness to her; Offa replies with great flattery, and Anthynus reserves his praise, saying he will give his father no more and no less than his due respect because:

> I have observ'd, but specially at Court,
> Where flattery is too frequent, the great scorn
> You have ever cast upon it, and do fear
> To come within such danger of reproof.
> Knowing your reason may as well detest it
> In your own house, as in Kings Pallaces.
> (*Queenes Exchange*, sig. B4r)

Once again, Segebert is associated here with reason. This speech maintains the distance already established between Segebert's attitude and that of the other courtiers, but also creates an unmistakeable parallel between Segebert's home and the court.

Anthynus accompanies his father into exile, where they are attacked by Offa and the outlaws he has hired to kill them. Anthynus succeeds in fighting off the assailants, but Segebert is seriously injured:

> Seg[bert]: O I am weak.

> Anth[ynus]: Rest upon me, my strength, my all is yours.
>   *Aeneas* that true Trojan son, whose fame
>   For piety ever crowns his name

---

[26] For a more detailed examination of the *King Lear* resonances, see Shaw (1980, p.94); Andrews (1981, p.100) and Butler (1984, pp.266–7). Steggle notes that 'in recent years *King Lear* has increasingly come to be seen as an articulation of insecurities to do with national sovereignty and the division of the kingdoms', and argues that the echoes of Shakespeare's play here 'enters, in effect, into a form of intertextual dialogue with *King Lear*, addressing the same concerns about the borders of the nation but from a different perspective'. He also notes that the parade of Saxon kings who appear to Anthynus, reminiscent of *Macbeth*, are in this play actually 'guarantees of continuity with the past, not of changes in the future'. Whilst Steggle argues that this denotes a 'distinctly separatist agenda', it also suggests the continuity of the Saxon legacy of law and custom left by Bertha's father (2004, p.56).

Had not a will (although my means be poor)
Exceeding mine to answer nature more.
(*Queenes Exchange*, sig.C4v)

Anthynus's self-comparison with Aeneas not only draws attention to his care for his father, but also associates him with ancient Britain long before the Norman conquest, since in legend, Brutus, descendant of Aeneas, was thought to be the first King of the Britons.[27] More than this, though, the image of the burning of Troy is used again in the play in the representation of Osriik, as the comic figure Jeffrey claims that in celebration of the impending marriage of Osriik and Bertha, he is going 'To make the bravest bonfire that ever blaz'd since / *Troy*, or that which the Tyrant Emperor warm'd / His hands at' (*Queens Exchange*, sig. C3r). This statement implicitly, though comically, aligns Osriik with the tyrant Nero, who set Rome ablaze, and, somewhat forebodingly, connects the marriage of Bertha to Osriik with the fall of a strong, ancient nation.[28] The contrasting uses of the same classical story highlight the play's juxtaposition of destruction in the marriage of Bertha and Osriik with the potential for renewal embodied in the Aeneas-like Anthynus.

Offa attempts to murder his father and brother not only to clear his way to Anthynus's inheritance, but also to allow Offa to fulfil his uncontrolled and unnatural desire for his sister, Mildred, offering a sinister parallel with Osriik's desire for her. Although Offa's attempts are unsuccessful, this domestic disorder and disregard for law (moral, natural and positive) demonstrates the chaos which could potentially occur in the public political sphere if established law is supplanted by the rule of will only. Like Bertha's insistence on her will, and Osriik's pursuit of his, Offa's language and manner is threatening and arbitrary:

Thy cries shall be as fruitless as thy life
If thou offend'st me with 'em; hear but this
Impertinently peevish maid, and tremble
But to conceive a disobedient thought
Against my will.
(*Queenes Exchange*, sig. F2r)

Interrupted in his assault on Mildred by the arrival of Osriik claiming to be a Northumbrian gentleman wishing to see her, he assumes Osriik is Anthynus in disguise and summarily orders his death for the murder of their father. His servant Arnold prevents this claiming the action is 'too rash'. Whilst Offa tries to assert his authority, Arnold emphasises law and process over arbitrary action:

---

[27]   In Book 2 of *The Aeneid*, Virgil describes Aeneas carrying his father from the burning city of Troy.

[28]   Marion O'Connor notes that according to Suetonius, Nero dressed as a tragedian and recited verses about the fall of Troy whilst Rome burned (<http://www.hrionline.ac.uk/brome>, Modern edition, 2.2.speech 233), thus connecting Jeffrey's seemingly disconnected comments on Troy and Rome.

Off[a]: Are you
  Become my master, you old Ruffian?

Arn[old]: No
  Your Servant Sir, but subject to the Law;
  The Law that must determine this mans cause,
  Nor you, nor we, what ever he deserves.
  And till he shall be censur'd by that law
  We'l find a Prison for him.
  (*Queenes Exchange*, sig. F2v)

The emphatic repetition of 'law' suggests that Offa, like Arnold and despite being
his master, must subordinate his will to the law. Importantly, the law under which
Osriik is to be tried, and to which Offa's will is subject, is identified as the law of
Bertha's Saxon kingdom (*Queenes Exchange*, sig. F4v).

    Whilst Anthynus's loyalty to his father is rewarded at the end of the play with
marriage to Bertha, Offa is punished with madness, maintaining the association
of madness with submission to passion and arbitrary judgement. In this respect
it is particularly interesting to note that Offa's madness is closely associated with
attempts to corrupt justice:

    Offa: Whither do you hurry me?
      If I must answer't, give me yet some time,
      To make provision of befitting Presents,
      To supply the hard hands of my stern Judges,
      Into a tender feeling of my causes.
      I know what *Eacus* loves, what *Minos* likes,
      And what will make *Radamanthus* run.

    Anthynus: He is distracted.
      (*Queenes Exchange*, sig. G1r)

Minos, Rhadamanthys and Aecus were made judges of the souls of the dead in the
classical underworld because, when alive, they were renowned for their wisdom
and justice as lawgivers (March, 1998, p.258). Offa, in his distraction, believes his
judges will be these classical judges and asks time to prepare bribes for them; his
madness leads to an attempt to corrupt even the most fair of justices.[29] Significantly,
it is Anthynus, the subject whom the Queen will marry and therefore preserve the
Saxon's customary laws, who notes and comments on Offa's judicial distraction.
Untempered desire and madness are contrasted throughout this play with reason,
justice and customary law.

    Although no lasting damage is done to Osriik's kingdom through his pursuit of
will, it does cost him his possible marriage to Bertha. Anthynus, who looks almost
identical to Osriik, arrives in his kingdom and some of the courtiers take him to the

---

[29]   Rhadamanthys had such a reputation for justice that the people of the islands in the
southern Aegean voluntarily put themselves under his control (March, 1998, p.344).

palace thinking he is the King. Osriik takes this opportunity to leave the country unnoticed and pursue Mildred, leaving the kingdom in the hands of Ethelswick and Edelbert. However, the rest of his council dismiss these men, believing they are responsible for the King's madness, and they bring forward his wedding to Bertha, thinking this will cure him. Anthynus is then married to Bertha in Osriik's place in the literal exchange of the play's title. Butler argues that in dismissing these men, the council take rule 'into their own hands in the name of the national good' and that Osriik later 'applauds his subjects for having opposed him for his own good' (1984, p.266). Ira Clark gives a similar reading, stating that Osriik, 'who has been awakened to responsible monarchy, praises the allegiance and care of his country's lords, who counteracted his commands' (1992, p.162). However, the council did not know they were opposing the King; they were acting against his advisers, believed Anthynus was Osriik, and that they were bringing forward a marriage the King desired. Even when Anthynus lashes out at them, Theodwald claims that 'if your Majesty / Will tread our due allegiance into dust, / We are prepared to suffer' (*Queenes Exchange*, sig. F1r). As evidence for Osriik's submission to the common good, Butler quotes the following passage:

> Thy trespasse is thine honour…
> And I must thank your care my Lords, as it deserves,
> Your over-reaching care to give my Dignity
> As much as in you lay unto another.

However, Butler's editing, I believe, obscures the action of the play. Neither Butler nor Clark's readings takes account of the immediate context of these lines, which suggest a very different meaning:

> Theodr[ick]: O let me wash your feet Sir with my tears.
>
> Osr[iik]: Thy trespasse is thine honour my *Theodrick*
>   And I must thank your care my Lords, as it deserves,
>   Your over-reaching care to give my Dignity
>   As much as in you lay unto another.
>   And for your Letters counterfeit in my name
>   By which the Queen is mock'd into a marriage.
>
> Theod[wald]: That was your policy, your wit, my Lord.
>
> Eauf[ride]: A shame on't. Would I were hanged, that I
>   Might hear no more on't.
>   (*Queenes Exchange*, sig. G1r)

If the first line of Osriik's obvious praise is given where it is meant – to the erstwhile banished favourite – and the following lines directed towards Theodwald and Eaufride, it is clear that the King's tone is one of displeasure ('over-reaching', 'mock'd'), not applause, and his offer to thank their care 'as it deserves' becomes threatening. Theodwald's immediate attempt to shift responsibility to Eaufride is not the action of a courtier being praised. There is not, then, in Osriik, the promising change of heart in government that Butler allows him. Indeed, it is clear that little will change at Osriik's court: Theodrick will remain as Osriik's favourite (*Queenes Exchange*, sig. G1v), and despite his acknowledgement that he may be justly punished for pursuing his desires ('yet I must confesse, / In all that I am like to suffer, heaven is just' (*Queenes Exchange*, sig. F4r)), Osriik's will is upheld in that he is to marry Mildred. In the same way that the spectre of Severino's unpunished, arbitrary acts of violence haunt the end of *The Guardian*, nothing appears set to change in Osriik's kingdom.

For Bertha, however, the case is different. Through the literal exchange of future husbands, Bertha also exchanges one form of government for another. In happily accepting her marriage to Anthynus, and in her joyful pardon and acceptance of Segebert and Alberto (both had been banished for questioning their monarch's will, Alberto under Bertha's father) Bertha is seen to accept Segebert's values. She comments on her marriage:

> I take it as the providence of Heaven;
> And from the Son of that most injur'd Father,
> Whom now in my joys strength I could shed tears for.
> I yield you are my head, and I your handmaid.
> *(She sets him down, and kneels; he takes her up).*
> (*Queenes Exchange*, sig. G1r)

The image seen on stage is not merely one of monarchical acceptance of the law, but of her submission to it as she kneels to her husband. It is a presentation of the contemporary lawyers' arguments that the monarch should be subject to law. Monarchical will is brought under the control of the 'reason' of law, as Anthynus is the son of the representative of reason at Bertha's court. Bertha makes this submission happily; moreover, her reference to providence implies, radically, that such a submission is the will of God.

This reading of the scene is, however, potentially complicated by the ruler's gender. Because the monarch in question is female, the image is one of traditional wifely obedience, and this potentially undermines any radical implications of Bertha's kneeling to Anthynus, as the audience sees female wilfulness submitting to male reason. The relationship between women and wilfulness was commonly understood in the period and is spelled out in Massinger's *The Very Woman* (written 1634):

> Pedro: One reason for this would do well.

> Almira: My will
>   Shall now stand for a thousand; shall I lose
>   The priviledge of my sex, which is my Will
>   To yield a Reason like a man?
>   (*The Very Woman*, sig. O1v)

In kneeling to Anthynus, Bertha submits her female wilfulness to the control of masculine reason. However, in this conservative image is a suggestion that any monarch behaving wilfully is behaving in a less than masculine fashion. This connection between irrational womanly wilfulness and arbitrary absolutism is emphasised in Massinger's play in the lines following those quoted above:

> Or [shall] you
> Deny your Sister that which all true women
> Claim as their first prerogative, which Nature
> Gave to them for a law? and should I break it
> I were no more a woman.
> (*A Very Woman*, sigs. O1v-O2r)

This privilege to act wilfully, Almira asserts, is the only law that a woman need follow. A man, the passage suggests, should not act in the same way; reason is the law a man should follow. Her claim to be allowed, by nature, to act wilfully because she is a woman is couched in the language of prerogative and privilege, connecting her with absolutist claims for the unlimited exercise of the royal prerogative.[30] *The Queens Exchange*'s Jeffrey reminds the audience that Bertha's gender should not be relevant to her position as monarch. When he is told that the King's future bride is 'the bravest Woman', he states, 'Take heed o'that, woman did you say? Take heed, I / Give you warning. No man must know she is a woman / But the King himself. But a brave Queen she is they say' (*Queenes Exchange*, sig. C2v). This is, of course, a bawdy joke – no man other than the King should be so intimately acquainted with the Queen's body to *know* she is a woman – but, more than this, the play suggests that the Queen (or any monarch) should not show herself to be irrationally womanly. Claims of royal prerogative are set against a discourse of common law which claims that the common law is 'nothing else but reason'.[31] Bertha's kneeling to Anthynus is much more than an enforcement of gender roles and stereotypes: it emphasises the rational nature of customary law and suggests that will and prerogative should be subject to this kind of reason.

It is, however, made clear in Anthynus's physical raising of the Queen that rule by the established customs and law of the kingdom will not diminish her status, but rather will maintain her position, if not raise her higher. It is perhaps significant in this respect that Anthynus and Osriik look almost identical: there is, to the uninformed observer, no apparent difference in Bertha's position in marrying one or the other man, adopting one or the other position regarding law; her status

---

[30] *The Very Woman* was performed by the King's Men at the Blackfriars theatre. As *The Queenes Exchange* was also a King's Men play it is possible that both plays were performed at Blackfriars, and along with Brome's *The Queen and Concubine*, suggest a sustained engagement with ideas of reason, masculinity and wilful behaviour in the audiences for which the King's Men performed at that theatre.

[31] Coke (1629, 97b); Finch (1627, p.75). See also Davies (1615, p.4); Doddridge (1631, p.194) and Noy (1642, sig. B1r).

looks the same. The dramatic motif of mistaken identity allows the adoption of the common law as the best method of government without suggesting a decrease in the monarch's powerful image. That Bertha and Osriik's pardons are necessary for all those who acted against their will, or without their authority, in order to bring about a satisfactory resolution to the play, also emphasises that the Queen remains sovereign in her country, despite her acceptance of custom and law. There is not a radical change in the ways Bertha governs; the marriage of the Queen to her subject (and her country's law) maintains the ancient constitution of the Saxon kingdom.

Inverting Law and Authority: *The Antipodes*

Whilst *The Queenes Exchange* pays sustained attention to contemporary arguments for the superiority of common law in the ancient constitution, and suggests the union, if not a complete submission, of the monarch to the law, Brome's *The Antipodes* deals more obliquely, but no less critically, with the notions of conquest, custom, reason and madness in relation to legal authority explored in that play. The play presents a young man, Peregrine, who has been taken to London by his family to see Doctor Hughball because his overwhelming desire to travel has made him mad. Hughball and Letoy stage a play in which the doctor pretends to take Peregrine to Anti-London, where all things are supposedly opposite to London in order to cure him. However, the 'fantasy of travel is in the end a means of reinterpreting one's own place and space' (Sanders, 1999b, p.142), and Anti-London provides a means to explore issues connected with contemporary London. Through the theatrical device of the play-within-the-play the notions of custom, reason and law already established are explored simultaneously in familial and political, domestic and foreign spheres, with the on-stage audience being at once part of and commentators on this exploration.

Although Joyless attributes his son's madness to reading too many travel narratives and an intemperate desire to travel, it is not only this which has sent Peregrine mad; it is because his desire to travel has been frustrated by his father's seemingly arbitrary decision not to let him go:

> When he grew up towards twenty,
> His minde was all on fire to be abroad;
> Nothing but travaile was all his aime;
> … His mother and
> My selfe oppos'd him still in all, and strongly
> Against his will, still held him in; and wonne
> Him into marriage; hoping that would call
> In his extravagant thoughts, but all prevail'd not,
> Nor stayd him (though at home) from travailing
> So farre beyond himselfe, that now too late,
> I wish he had gone abroad to meet his fate.
> (*Antipodes*, sig. B3r)

This attempt to cure Peregrine of his sickness through marriage recalls the Northumbrian advisers' attempts to cure Osriik in bringing forward his marriage to Bertha. In this case, though, the marriage does not facilitate an unwitting but satisfactory end in marrying the monarch to the law; rather, it brings about madness in Peregrine's wife, Martha:

> Joy[less]: He takes no joy in her; and she no comfort
>   *In* him: for though they have bin three yeeres wed,
>   They are yet ignorant of the marriage bed.
>
> Doct[or]: I shall finde her the madder of the two then.
>
> Joy.:   *In*deed she's full of passion, which she utters
>   By the effects, as diversly, as severall
>   Objects reflect upon her wandering fancy. (*Antipodes*, sig. B3v)

The arbitrary will of the father encourages madness in the son, and in turn the madness of the husband provokes madness in the wife. Analogically, as in Osriik's Northumbria, the sickness at the head of the body politic also affects – or infects – the body of the subjects.

The Joyless family are brought to the house of Letoy, a gentleman for whom 'Stage-playes, and Masques, are nightly … pastimes' (*Antipodes*, sig. C2r) to witness an elaborate play-within-the-play engineered by Letoy and the Doctor, performed by Letoy's own troop of actors. Letoy's fondness for plays leads Hughball to assert, 'O y'are the Lord of fancy'. Whilst this may be an indication of his skill in inventing the play ('Your fancy and my cure shall be cry'd up / Miraculous') (*Antipodes*, sig. D2r), 'fancy' also connects him with Martha's 'wandering fancy', and with madness, arbitrariness and caprice.[32] Letoy's response, 'I'm not ambitious of that title Sir, / No, the Letoy's are of Antiquity, / Ages before the fancyes were begot' (*Antipodes*, sig. D2r) can then be read as a denial of arbitrariness, claiming that his long lineage precludes any possibility of irrationality, and as asserting his high social status through his genealogy, as tracing his family name back to the Norman Conquest would legitimise his privileged status as part of an ancient family in the contemporary socio-political order.[33] That he has actively sought out his claim to this status is clear from an earlier conversation with Blaze over Letoy's 'Armes and Pedegree':

---

[32] *OED*, 'fancy', 4a, 5a, 6, 7.

[33] When glossing these lines, Anthony Parr notes that in *The Compleat Gentleman* Henry Peacham explains that 'the ancients of our Nobility for the greater part, acknowledge themselves to bee descended out of *Normandy*, and to have come in with the Conquerour, many retaining their *French* names' (1622, p.142) (Brome, 1995, p. 233, note to I.ii.7–9). Letoy's desire to trace his ancestry may also be an appeal to the interests of the gentry in the audience, as Lisa Hopkins notes that 'the study of genealogy, along with that of heraldry, was one of the great crazes of the Jacobean and Caroline periods' (1994, p.56).

Let.: But has he gone to the root, has he deriv'd me,
      Ex origine, ab antiquo? Has he fetched me
      Farre enough *Blaze*?

Bla.: Full foure descents beyond
      The conquest my good Lord, and findes that one
      Of your French ancestry came in with the conqueror.

Let.: *Jefrey Letoy*, twas he, from whom the English
      Letoy's have our descent; and here have tooke
      Such footing, that we'll never out while France
      Is France, and England England,
      And the Sea passable to transport a fashion. (*Antipodes*, sig. C1r-v)

Whilst his concern for his heraldry is trivialised by the emphasis on his family importing fashion from France, particularly as Letoy himself dresses 'more like a pedlar, / Then like a Lord' (*Antipodes*, sig. C1v), this may be a comment on the importation of French fashions at the Caroline court because of the Queen's influence. There is, potentially, an underlying concern here that France may not be as separate from England in fashion or governance as 'France / Is France, and England England' ought to suggest. Moreover, Letoy's Norman ancestry alerts us to a possible arbitrariness in his nature and authority – illustrated by his eccentricities of dress and habit – when read in light of conquest theories of government, which could undermine his claims to reason (in lack of 'fancy') through his inherited position.

It is in this context of madness, conquest and antiquity that the play-within-the-play is produced. In order to cure Peregrine's travel madness, Hughball pretends to have taken him to the Antipodes where:

> The people through the whole world of *Antipodes*,
> In outward feature, language, and religion,
> Resemble those to whom they are supposite.
> ...
>   but in their manners,
> Their carriage, and condition of life
> Extreamly contrary.
> (*Antipodes*, sig. C4r)

During Peregrine's travels in Anti-London, he and the on-stage audience are told of, and witness, many of these contrary practices, most of which concern issues of law, authority and governance: sergeants running away from a gentleman who wants to be arrested, wives ruling their husbands, servants governing their masters/mistresses and children instructing their parents. The interjections of Peregrine's observing family, particularly Diana, commenting on the differences between anti-London and its English counterpart serve, in part, to highlight the points of similarity as well as the differences (Butler, 1984, p.215).

The first thing Hughball tells Peregrine about the Antipodes is that although in London 'the Magistrates / Governe the people: there the people rule / The Magistrates' (*Antipodes*, sig. C4r), suggesting that the focus of this play-within-the-play will be issues of governance. In a domestic version of such issues, Peregrine witnesses a conversation between the gentleman, his wife and her serving-woman, in which the Lady, endorsing Antipodean practices, instructs her husband that he must sleep with the merchant's wife:

La[dy]: You know your charge, obey it.
…

Wom[an]: What is his charge? or whom must he obey?
    Good madam with your wilde authority;
    You are his wife, tis true, and therein may
    According to our law, rule, and controwle him.
    But you must know withall, I am your servant,
    And bound by the same law to governe you,
    And be a stay to you in declining age,
    To curbe and qualifie your head-strong will,
    Which otherwise would ruine you…

La[dy]: Insooth she speaks but reason.
    (*Antipodes*, sig. E3v)

Despite the Lady's assertion that her instruction is unproblematically clear, the servant's response suggests otherwise. Associating the Lady's legitimate authority with her 'head-strong will' implies an arbitrariness in her commands which undermines this authority by making it 'wilde', thus leaving her husband in doubt of exactly what he is supposed to do. As '*The Antipodes* presents an anti-London which is at once an inverted image of London and an accurate representation of it' (Steggle, 2004, p.111), the play here contains a warning about the consequences of Charles's arbitrary authority and manipulation of law (for example, in projectors and the award of monopolies, which are also shown to be Antipodean practices).[34] If law and its representatives are inconsistent or arbitrary, the play suggests here, subjects will be left with no clear law to follow. Moreover, this wilfulness not only leads to confusion but to the potential 'ruine' of the ruler. To prevent this, the law places the Lady under the influence of her servant, who is bound to 'curbe and qualifie' her wilfulness. If this is Anti-London, then London has no check on the ruler's authority and the audience is left to question, given the already suggested outcomes of arbitrary action, whether this really should be the case. That the

---

[34] Particular projects were excluded from the condemnation of the 1624 Statute; monopolies held by corporations, and for limited periods, inventions were legal (Butler, 1987, p.30). In including monopolies and projectors in his vision of anti-London, Brome perhaps illustrates 'the unfitness and ridiculousness of these Projects against the Law' that Bulstrode Whitelocke noted in the projectors of James Shirley's 1634 masque, *The Triumph of Peace* (quoted in Orgel and Strong, 1973, I, p.65).

mistress's 'head-strong will' is contrasted with her servant's 'reason' suggests a tempering influence over Charles in the common law itself, but there is also the possibility that the servants who should be called to stabilise the King's 'wilde authority' are members of Parliament, servants of the King in being his subjects and representatives of the law in proposing and debating statutes. Indeed, in the Caroline period, a high proportion of Members of Parliament were trained in the law, making this identification stronger.[35]

During his visit to the Antipodes, Peregrine does not merely watch the action, he participates in it. Finding his way into Letoy's actors' tiring house, Peregrine attacks the stage properties and proclaims himself King by conquest:

> on the suddaine, with thrice knightly force,
> And thrice, thrice, puissant arme he snatcheth downe
> The sword and shield that *I* playd *Bevis* with,
> Rusheth amongst the foresaid properties,
> Kils Monster, after Monster; takes the Puppets
> Prisoners, knocks downe the Cyclops, tumbles all
> Our jigambobs and trinckets to the wall.
> Spying at last the Crowne and royall Robes
> *I*th upper wardrobe, next to which by chance,
> The divells visors hung, and their flame painted
> Skin coates; those he remov'd with greater fury,
> And having cut the infernall ugly faces,
> All into mamocks) with a reverend hand,
> He takes the imperiall diadem and crownes
> Himselfe King of the *Antipodes*, and beleeves
> He has justly gaind the Kingdome by his conquest.
> (*Antipodes*, sigs. G1v-G2r)

Despite the doctor's previous explanation that the Antipodes is not full of monsters and exotic creatures, but of people with contrary customs and manners, Peregrine's '*Mandevile* madnesse' (*Antipodes*, sig. I4v) leads him to believe that he does really see a Cyclops, and his desire to take possession of the 'imperiall diadem' emphasises his desire to explore and conquer foreign lands prefigured in his talk of Drake, 'Candish' [Cavendish], Hawkins and Frobisher (*Antipodes*, sig. C3r). Julie Sanders reads Peregrine's conquest of the tiring room as a rite of passage in freeing himself from his father's influence: 'The infantilising prohibitions of his family are swept away in the assertive role he assumes as a romance hero in his attack on the stage properties of the actors' tiring house' (1999b, p.146). However, in light of the concern the play-within-the-play shows with law and authority, it is significant that Peregrine claims kingship through conquest, and in his madness, thinks this is just. Letoy's comment on this, 'Let him injoy his fancy' (*Antipodes*,

---

[35] Interestingly, Cromartie notes that Coke believed that even parliamentary statutes should be held as secondary authorities to the common law interpreted by judges (2006, p.215).

sig. G2r), further undermines the idea of right to absolute rule through conquest which the ridiculousness of taking a country through conquering an army of stage properties already calls into question.

Nevertheless, in what his rights and conquest suggest to be an inverted echo of *The Queenes Exchange*, Peregrine sets about 'to governe / With purpose to reduce the manners / Of this country to his owne' (*Antipodes*, sig. G2r) through imposing his absolute authority on the people of the Antipodes. His knighting of a judge who presides over a trial where only the judge is satisfied by the verdict, exclaiming 'Most admirable Justice' (*Antipodes*, sig. G4v) suggests that this is not the bringing back of unreasonable government to one of reason and custom which would have been promised if Bertha had reduced Osriik's government to hers. Whilst 'mak[ing] discovery of passages / Among the people' (*Antipodes*, sig. H1v), in disguise, Peregrine begins to come to his senses. Watching the arrest of a gentleman because a woman assaulted him, Peregrine intervenes:

> Per. Call you this justice?
>
> Doct. In th' *Antipodes*.
>
> Per. Here's much to be reform'd. (*Antipodes*, sig. H3r)

Peregrine's acknowledgement that this is not justice marks a step in his recovery from madness. He frees the gentleman, and begins to order that the lady is taken to prison, until the Doctor reminds him, 'At first shew mercy' (*Antipodes*, sig. H3r). Hughball's double role as King Peregrine's chief Officer in the play-within-the-play, and as physician for Peregrine's madness, places him in a position to educate the King in a more temperate method of government and the husband in a more temperate way of living, suggesting a cure for madness in the King and the country.

On recognising how much there is to be 'reform'd' in the Antipodes, Peregrine considers sending for advice: 'What if *I* crav'd a Counsell from New *England* / The old will spare me none' (*Antipodes*, sig. I1v). There may be here a direct reference to the absence of a parliament from real London (Butler, 1984, p.218). Old England either cannot spare a 'Counsell' for Peregrine because Charles is currently ruling without a parliament, or because were one to be called it would be needed there. Doctor Hughball's response, '*Is* this man mad?' (*Antipodes*, sig. I1v), suggests that his wish to call a parliament is a step towards his recovery from arbitrary madness. His movement away from madness and immediate imposition of his absolute power by Conquest is indicated when Peregrine ruefully claims ''Twill aske long time and study to reduce / Their manners to our government' (*Antipodes*, sig. H4r) on seeing a man-scold on a ducking stool. Unlike the earlier suggestion that reducing their manners to his own may involve the imposition of his own madness on the country, here he not only refers to the extent of the contrary behaviour in the country, but calls to mind the long study which Coke claims in *Institutes I* is necessary for a true familiarity with the common law (Coke,

1629, 97b). This change will not be a rapid imposition of the will of an arbitrary monarch by conquest, but a careful introduction of reason into the activities of the Antipodes.

The final straw for the new King of the Antipodes, and the indication of Peregrine's return to rationality, comes when he fully understands the arbitrary nature of justice and law in his kingdom:

> Doe you provide whips, brands; and ordaine death,
> For men that suffer under fire, or shipwracke,
> The losse of all their honest gotten wealth:
> And finde reliefe for Cheaters, Bawdes, and Thieves?
> I'll hang ye all.
> (*Antipodes*, sig. I3r)

The Antipodeans' response is given in terms of custom and law:

> Let not our ignorance suffer in your wrath,
> Before we understand your highnesse Lawes,
> We went by custome, and the warrant, which
> We had in your late Predecessor's raigne;
> But let us know your pleasure, you shall finde
> The State and Common-wealth in all obedient,
> To alter Custome, Law, Religion, all,
> To be conformable to your commands.
> (*Antipodes*, sig. I3r)

This vocabulary for debating legal positions is now familiar, but here the terms are used unexpectedly. In an inversion of the assertion of the supremacy of customary law presented in *The Queenes Exchange* and contemporary legal tracts, here the ridiculousness of the Antipodean's customs and their willingness to conform to Peregrine's commands invites the audience to accept the imposition of monarchical law. That Byplay claims Peregrine's predecessor had allowed the customs also jars with notions of customary common law existing independently of the monarch.[36] It may be that this too is the Antipodean reverse of how things are in London; however, what is significant about Peregrine's attempt to change the laws in the Antipodes is that his laws, in contrast with those of the Antipodeans, will be laws of *reason*, not arbitrary judgements. His outburst against the irrational customs of the Antipodes marks his return to reason from madness.

At the end of his journey through the Antipodes, Peregrine is introduced to the Antipodean Princess, played by the (still mad) Martha, who has been bequeathed to him by the late sovereign. Although he momentarily 'falls backe againe to *Mandevile* madness', concerned over marrying the Princess in case she is a

---

[36] Parr's gloss to this line suggests that this is a 'clear allusion to the reign of James I, when the court was a place of licence and excess and was perceived to set a bad example to the country' (Brome, 1995, p. 300, note to IV.iv.373–4).

Gadlibrien, Byplay advises him, 'For the safety of your Kingdome, you must do it' (*Antipodes*, sig. I4v). Whilst this advice could suggest that dynastic marriage to the legitimate heir of the kingdom would make his claim to the throne less questionable, or that marriage and the production of heirs was necessary to maintain political stability, in the domestic and political analogy in which Peregrine's kingly madness affects his subject/wife, his (re)marriage to Martha will also cure her of her madness, returning his (English) household to correct order. Peregrine states that he cannot marry the Princess because he already has a wife at home, and 'A Crowne secures not an unlawfull marriage' (*Antipodes*, sig. I4r). Significantly, Peregrine's new embrace of reasoned law brings him to recognise the limits to his kingly power. Although Hughball removes this problem by claiming that Martha is dead and her spirit now 'animates this Princesse' (*Antipodes*, sig. I4r), Peregrine's objection positions the king, by his own admission, as undoubtedly subject to law. Lawful, productive marriage is not, then, the solution to the problem of law and prerogative in this play as it was in *The Queenes Exchange*; rather, it is symbolic of a well-ordered household (political or domestic) where all concerned hold their proper place: subject to reason and law.

In stark contrast with Peregrine's regal concern that his marriage to the Princess must be lawful, outside the Antipodean play, in 'Kingly humour' (*Antipodes*, sig. K1r), Letoy (whose powerful social position by virtue of the Norman conquest has now been undermined) attempts to seduce Joyless's wife, Diana. In a similar way to Massinger's Domitian, he claims power as his authority: 'trust to me, my power, and your owne, / To make all good with [Joyless]' (*Antipodes*, sig. L1r). Indeed, Joyless's suspicions of Letoy lead him to worry that 'Lords actions all are lawfull.' However, his questions which immediately follow, 'And how? And how?' (*Antipodes*, sig. K2r), undermine the implied truth of this statement. Letoy is, indeed, challenged in his attempt by Diana herself, and the terms of their argument are telling. Letoy offers Diana first wealth, which she refuses, and then pleasures 'comparative with those / Which *Jupiter* got the Demy-gods with', to which she responds:

> My Lord, you may
> Glose o'er and gild the vice, which you call pleasure,
> With god-like attributes; when it is, at best
> A sensuality, so farre below
> Dishonourable, that it is meere beastly;
> Which reason ought to abhorre.
> (*Antipodes*, sig. K4r)

On the surface, Diana, who shares her name with the Roman goddess of chastity, exposes the mythical justification that Letoy gives as being merely stories of Jupiter's lust. However, in relation to the argument the play-within-the-play has made regarding legal marriage as beyond the power of a monarch to change, Diana's rebuff suggests that such actions – those which are contrary to law and deprive subjects of their legal rights – cannot be justified or gilded over by comparison with the divine. In his right *reason*, she argues, Letoy should recognise these actions as 'beastly' rather than sanctified by divine precedent. Neither conquest, nor divine right, then, allows the king to take action contrary to the law.

When assertions of power fail, Letoy threatens to tell Joyless that Diana has been unfaithful anyway, and hand her over to his anger, but Diana remains steadfast in her refusal. *The Antipodes* is diverted from this potentially tragic path by the revelation that once again Letoy is 'playing', and Joyless has been in the audience to her witness his wife's resistance. Letoy pretends to seduce Diana to test her loyalty to her husband, and determine if she is obedient enough to be acknowledged as his own daughter, whom he had given away, believing that her mother had been unfaithful. Indeed, Letoy claims he would have punished Diana severely had she given in to his advances. Diana is, then, placed in an impossible position: obedience to the lord *or* to her husband might have brought about her downfall. (Indeed, in Shirley's *The Traytor* such a test of obedience leads to the tragic death of Amidea at her brother Sciarrha's hands when she pretends to agree to sleep with the Duke in order to buy his pardon.) The subject cannot know how best to act in relation to arbitrary or divided authority, so she follows her own moral judgement. In the context of *The Antipodes*'s concern with reason, law and good governance, the repeated assertions of hearers of his story that Letoy is mad (*Antipodes*, sigs. L1v-L2r) can be read as a critical comment upon arbitrary patriarchal or monarchical 'tests' of subjects' obedience. In not trusting their wives, both Joyless and Letoy could have lost sole rule of their domestic kingdoms (suggested by the comic presence of Mrs Blaze, whom it is clear Letoy did indeed seduce to cure Blaze's fear of cuckolding). Thus, *The Antipodes* uses its multiple levels of theatrical action to juxtapose modes of authority: that the courtly world outside the now-reasoned Antipodes is still mad within the play suggests that the world outside Brome's play is also 'mad', yet it could, the play suggests, be brought to reason through a renewed trust between King and subjects, created by mutual adherence to one, reasoned legal authority – the common law.

Destabilising Legal Authority: *The Queen and Concubine*

Although *The Antipodes* glances towards the potential for confusion over law and legal actions when authority is not rational, and advocates a return to reasoned government subject to law, this play, like *The Queenes Exchange*, does not explore the consequences of irrational, arbitrary rule in any detail. It is with these consequences that *The Queen and Concubine* is concerned. In this play, Brome takes the 'madness' of absolutism in a different direction. It is no longer set clearly against the law in terms of conquest and custom; rather, it is set against an embodiment of law as the common good in Queen Eulalia. The play, Butler asserts, 'recalls those Elizabethan dilemma dramas in which the spectator (usually the queen) was faced with a choice between two deities or dignitaries who represented alternative attitudes to government or courses of action' (1984, p.35). Like Brome's own Bertha, King Gonzago must choose between modes of government in his choice of spouse: either his wife of 20 years, Eulalia (law, due process and the commonweal), or his new mistress, Alinda (the madness of absolute sovereignty). From the beginning of the play, King Gonzago has conflated law and will; his rule is already personal and powerful. What Gonzago must choose is the way in which he exercises that power; what is at stake is the health of the country (literal and metaphorical) and the stability of law and authority.

It is clear almost from the beginning of the play that Gonzago is prone to act irrationally and arbitrarily. His strangely and rapidly conceived jealousy of his wife's commendations of Sforza, a general in his army who has given the King good military service, and his consequent change of heart towards Petruccio, a banished courtier, leads Horatio to comment on Petruccio's return to court that: 'It must be so, this is one of his un-to-be-examin'd hastie Humours, one of his starts: these and a devillish gift He has in Venerie, are all his faults' (*Queen and Concubine*, sig. B4r). Although Horatio makes light of these as Gonzago's only faults, as the play progresses it becomes clear that it is these faults in the King which bring about a crisis in government and potential chaos in the country. This mention of his 'devillish gift in Venerie' in relation to his rapidly changing humours paves the way for his pursuit of the young, beautiful Alinda (Sforza's daughter) and the divorce and banishment of his wife Eulalia whom he falsely accuses of adultery with Sforza.

To Lodovico's questioning of the King's 'dotage' on Alinda, Horatio replies: 'Come, think upon Law and Regal Authoritie. The king's Power Warrants his Acts' (*Queen and Concubine*, sig. C6v). For King Gonzago and Horatio, the king's will is law, enforceable by his power. Although he makes a show of ruling in accordance with legal procedures (Eulalia, for example, is tried for adultery in a court, albeit a corrupt one) and governs in conjunction with a parliament, it is clear that Gonzago exercises an absolute authority. Unlike *The Queenes Exchange*'s Bertha, of whom we can initially think more generously in calling her Lords as council, Gonzago calls his parliament to approve his divorce and remarriage only for the sake of appearance:

> King: Now to this Censure, for due Orders sake.
>   And for which end this Parliament was call'd;
>   Your Voyces are requir'd: do ye all approve it?
>
> Omnes: We do.
>
> Lodovico: We must.
>
> King: What say you, Lodovico?
>
> Lodovico: We do; Heaven knows against my heart.
> (*Queen and Concubine*, sigs. C4r-C4v)

Gonzago's assertion that parliament was called for 'due Orders sake' suggests something of his own aversion to sharing any judicial power; moreover, it also serves to highlight Gonzago's undermining of order even whilst he claims to uphold it. This is an early indication that arbitrary royal action undermines the stability of legal authority, an idea which becomes increasingly evident later in the play. That Lodovico feels compelled to condemn Eulalia, however reluctantly, is clear from his 'we must' set against the easy 'we do' of the other courtiers. One of the reasons he must condemn her is that she has been found guilty of adultery in a court of law, albeit through perjured witnesses and falsified evidence engineered by Alinda and her sycophant courtier, Flavello. Throughout the scenes at court, legal processes are manipulated and undermined by the exercise of self-seeking power. To emphasise this, the audience are given two representations of Eulalia's trial: first, Flavello describes it to Alinda, along with the ways in which he had 'work[ed] the witnesses' (*Queen and Concubine*, sig. C2v) to falsify their testimony; second, immediately following this, we watch the trial and the uncrowning of the Queen in dumb show, emphasising that in this trial justice is only *seen* to be done; what is said or, indeed, true is irrelevant.

For Gonzago's Parliament, too, what is true means very little. Whatever the lords may think, it is clear from the King's speech regarding his new Queen, Alinda, that Lodovico has no safe choice other than to give his assent:

> I your King
> Am Subject to this all-deserving Lady,
> And do require you not alone to hear
> What I can say, but without all denial
> That you approve, confirm what I will say.
> ...
> I hope none rates our will or his own life
> So meanly, as to give least contradiction.
> (*Queen and Concubine*, sig. C5r)

The Parliament must be seen to approve of the King's marriage to Alinda, and of her coronation. Gonzago's vocabulary is commanding ('I... do require you'), and his threat of execution for dissent is apparent. The emphasis throughout the parliament scene is on obedience to, and ratification of, Gonzago's kingly will. There is, however, a strange contradiction in his claims to be both able to command their obedience and yet be subject to Alinda himself. This signals his complete submission to will and with this, the play suggests, comes a reduction of kingly authority. Reminiscent of the impotence of Massinger's Domitian and Theodosius regarding their wives, Alinda herself describes Gonzago's 'raging dotage' on her as 'the weakness of the King' (*Queen and Concubine*, sig. C2r).

More than Gonzago's dotage on her, Alinda herself comes to represent the excesses of arbitrary monarchy. It is Alinda who explicitly asserts the independence of royal power, telling her father in response to his objection to her relationship with the King that 'Soveraignty you know, admits no Parentage' (*Queen and Concubine*, sig. B8r). In a physical manifestation of the metaphorical poisoning of good kings through the bad counsel of ambitious courtiers, Alinda's own ambition is accelerated by Flavello's administration of 'Pills that puff'd her up / To an high longing, till she saw the hopes / She had to grow by' (*Queen and Concubine*, sig. B6v). Indeed, her ambition grows to such an extent that she attempts to bring about the realisation of her claims for independent sovereignty by asking Gonzago to have her father killed. In a sinister iteration of Horatio's claims for royal power – 'the Kings Power Warrants his Acts' (*Queen and Concubine*, sig. C6v) – Alinda states, in her madness, that 'she thought, that being now a Queen, / She might by her Prerogative take Heads, / Whose and as many as she listed' (*Queen and Concubine*, sig. H4v). Her arbitrary cruelty is continued when she persuades the King to banish his son, and sends assassins to attempt Eulalia's life in her exile in order to secure her own position. Indeed, her demands become increasingly cruel and arbitrary, provoking even Horatio, the courtier who loves and hates just as the King does (*Queen and Concubine*, sig. B5v) to state, 'She's mad beyond all cure' (*Queen and Concubine*, sig. H1r) and the King to observe:

> What wild Affections do in women raign!
> But this is a Passion past all President.
> O 'tis meer Madness, mix'd with Divellish cunning,
> To hurl me upon more and endless mischiefes.
> (*Queen and Concubine*, sig. H1v)

This combines the theatrical presentation of wilfulness as being womanly with the now established presentation of arbitrary absolutism as madness. Alinda's madness is beyond even any precedent the arbitrary Gonzago has seen, and his reference to 'Divellish cunning' takes such action as far away from divine right as possible. Moreover, her madness is potentially infectious:

> ... The Queen. The Queen, the Queen's distracted,
> And I am like to be, and you, and any man
> That loves the King, unless some Conjurer
> Be found to lay the Devil: I mean *Sforza*.
> (*Queen and Concubine*, sig. H4r)

Whilst Horatio revises his statement to clarify that by 'devil' he means the imagined ghost of Sforza, his first statement suggests widespread madness in the State if Alinda's madness continues. Horatio's claim that this is particularly problematic for men who love the King also gestures towards problems that good subjects might face in obedience if a king is unjust, or authority becomes divided.

In contrast with Alinda's dangerous, 'mad', unreasonable exercise of prerogative power, Eulalia is presented as an idealised image of restraint:

> you know too well the King,
> How apt his Nature is to fell oppression.
> The burden of whose crueltie long since,
> If by the virtuous Clemencie of his Wife
> It had not been alay'd and mitigated,
> Had been a general subversion.
> And now that Peerless Princesse being depos'd,
> Whose vertue made her famous, and us happy;

> And he re-married to this shame of women,
> Whose vileness breeds her envie and our mischief,
> What can we look for but destruction?
> (*Queen and Concubine*, sig. C7v)

The description of Eulalia's clemency mitigating Gonzago's cruelty is reminiscent of the arguments discussed in Chapter 2 for the need for law to moderate the passionate acts of a fallible, human king. A link is also made here between Eulalia and established law in the use of the word 'Clemencie', which has been used once before in the play to describe the laws of Sicily which 'are so well rebated / With Clemencie, and mercie' that they prevent Eulalia's execution for alleged adultery (*Queen and Concubine*, sig. C4r). Eulalia's clemency has not only prevented Gonzago's cruelty, but also averted a 'general subversion', the word associated in *The Queenes Exchange* with the replacement of established customary law with the rule of an absolute monarch (*Queenes Exchange*, sig. B1v). Here, Eulalia's compassion, as well as her maintenance of due order emphasised throughout the play, has prevented chaos and potential rebellion against the King, something later threatened in the soldiers' rebellion over the supposed death of Sforza, ordered on the King's command, without justification of law or legal process. In sharp contrast with Eulalia's maintenance of order, Lodovico claims that Alinda will prove to be the 'destruction' of the state. Lodovico hints that the only way to prevent this subversion and destruction is through Alinda's death, and Horatio assents to this, saying, 'You and the Common Good have won me' (*Queen and Concubine*, sig. C8r). That even the ridiculously loyal Horatio agrees to this suggests an urgent need to curtail arbitrary prerogative rule for the good of the King, the government and the country.

Whilst Alinda potentially spreads illness in the body politic in her focus on her own desires, Eulalia is associated with the health of the body politic and the common good. (Indeed, that Lodovico is one of her strongest advocates and convinces Horatio to act against Alinda allows a conflation of Eulalia and the 'Common Good' that wins Horatio to Lodovico's opinion.) The province of Palermo, which 'Kings have customarily laid out / For their Queens Dowry' and where lawyers and doctors were never previously needed, has been struck by 'foul Infection, Pain and Sorrow' (*Queen and Concubine*, sigs. E2v, E2r) since the King banished Eulalia. Although Pedro suggests that this is a punishment for them as the people of her province in lieu of the king's execution of Eulalia, the Queen herself provides an alternative: 'Might you not judge as well, it was th' injustice and the wrongs the innocent Queen hath suffer'd, that has brought sense of her injuries upon her Province?' (*Queen and Concubine*, sig. E3v). With the gift of healing that a genius gave her to help sustain her, Eulalia sets about curing the illnesses of her people, because, as Lodovico claims, 'perfect health I think dwells only where / Good Eulalia remains'. Andrea's repeated complaint 'I am out of joynt… Out a joynt, out a joynt, I am all out a joynt' (*Queen and Concubine*, sigs. E4r-v) is representative of the state of the country when the king acts beyond the law and neglects the common good to pursue his own will.

It is not only in terms of the health and sickness of the body politic, though, that Eulalia is presented in opposition to the court. As she and her followers are exiled, Horatio rifles through Andrea's belongings, accusing him of taking 'Plate and Jewels'. Andrea's response chimes with Caroline concerns over prerogative taxation: 'you will not take my own proper goods from me, will ye?' (*Queen and Concubine*, sig. D1v). It is not only that Gonzago follows his own desires in his abandonment of Eulalia in favour of Alinda, but that this move further towards arbitrary absolutism raises fears in his subjects that he will take more than his due. Eulalia, however, actively refuses to take the money and goods of her countrymen more than she should take in payment for her healing and teaching services. Indeed, in teaching the daughters of Palermo skills in needlework, she increases their chances to make money rather than taking it from them. The comparison between the Sicilian court and the activities in Palermo is made explicit in this interchange:

> Poggio: Madam, the Court in all the Braverie
> It boasts and borrows, cannot so rejoyce
> In the bright shining Beauty of their Queen,
> As we in your enjoying in this plainness.
> Their Bells, and Bonfires, Tilts and Tournaments,
> Their feasts and Banquets, Musicks and costly shews
> (How ere unpaid for) shall not outpass our loves.
>
> Eulalia: Be you as confident, I will not wrong
> A man among you: therefore pray reserve
> What is your own, and warrant your own safety.
> (*Queen and Concubine*, sigs. F6r-v)

Whilst the court celebrates using what is not clearly its own ('borrows', 'unpaid for'), Eulalia assures the countrymen that with her they should keep what is theirs. Her reference to their safety is, for her, a reference to the King's proclamation that no one should help the Queen in her exile. However, in the context of prerogative loans and taxation, Andrea's reference to the 'King and Queen's Takers' (*Queen and Concubine*, sig. D1v) and this assertion of royal exploitation of others' monies, it is possible to read her speech as having a more radical meaning: I will not wrong you by trying to take what is not mine; therefore, keep the goods and money which rightly belong to you and no harm will come to you through me. Thus, the virtuous and popular Eulalia is presented in opposition to the unpopular and extra-legal practices of the Caroline court.[37]

As Martin Butler and Catherine Shaw point out, the country and the court are deliberately juxtaposed in this play. Shaw argues that the movement from court

---

[37] Such arguments, along with the arbitrary imprisonment of Sforza which I will discuss later in the chapter, may reflect back on the Petition of Right, which sought to define a limit to the bounds of Charles's prerogative actions in law, and which continued to resonate throughout the period. See Chapter 1. L. J. Reeve notes that the Petition was often cited in John Hampden's case in the Exchequer Chamber in 1637 and 1638 regarding his obligation to pay ship money (1986, p.261).

to country is restorative: 'The action moves from the court world dominated by fortune and the desire for material growth and social advancement to a green world dominated by nature and the desire for spiritual growth and moral advancement' (1980, pp.102, 100). This is true, to an extent, but does not really take account of the political actions which take place in the country as well as at court. Butler reads the play's movement from court to country as a 'shift to more popular forms of government' and the play's final country festival as representing a nostalgia for an 'Elizabethan idea of an organic community in which the members participate fully' (1984, pp.40, 39). The play does, I think, consider such ideas of a more participatory governance in its representation of Palermo's local officials, its comic 'Sages' (self-appointed judges) and 'pettie Parliament' (*Queen and Concubine*, sigs. I3r, I2v), but ultimately rejects them in favour of a monarch who will rule according to law and legal processes and in favour of the common good. Indeed, that Eulalia overturns all of the decisions made by the 'pettie Parliament' suggests that we are not to see their decisions or authority as particularly desirable. I argue that the shift to multiple authorities in Palermo signifies the potential instability in the country caused by the King's rejection of law and legal processes, by offering parallel actions and events in and away from the court.

The 'pettie Parliament' of Palermo provides both a contrast to and a comic echo of Gonzago's pretended parliament to banish Eulalia and recognise Alinda as Queen:

> Do not I understand the purpose of our meeting
> Here in our pettie Parliament, if I may so call it?
> Is it no[t] for a Reformation, to pull down
> The Queens mercy, and set up our Justice?
> For the prevention of a superabundance of Treason
> Dayly practiced against her?
> (*Queen and Concubine*, sig. I2v)

Palermo's parliament is 'pettie' in being a less important (that is less official) version of Gonzago's parliament, constituted by men of lesser rank, and in being largely ineffective as its decisions are all overturned by the Queen in a restoration of order that is juxtaposed with Gonzago's destruction of it in forcing his parliament to assent to the banishment of Eulalia and accept Alinda.[38] It seems from this speech that their concerns are far from trivial in their care for the safety of the Queen, but the expressed purpose of their meeting – to pull down the Queen's mercy and set up their own justice – is a baldly stated version of what Gonzago achieved with his parliament in banishing the Queen and her 'clemencie' and instituting his and Alinda's arbitrary judgement.[39] In a similar way, the 'pettie Parliament' wish to impose summary execution, without trial or processes of law, upon those who attempt Eulalia's life. In arguing the need to introduce summary justice to prevent treason, the 'pettie Parliament' also echoes one of the reasons given for Charles I's

---

[38]   *OED*, 'petty' *adj.* and *n.*, 1a, 1b, 2a.
[39]   *OED*, 'petty' *adj.* and *n.*, 2b.

resort to arbitrary imprisonment without showing cause, an idea presented in this play in the imprisonment of Sforza who is told only that he is imprisoned because ''Tis the Kings pleasure' (*Queen and Concubine*, sig. D2r). This, of course, is reminiscent of the royal argument, discussed in Chapter 1, that the knights of the Five Knights' Case were imprisoned *per speciale mandatum domini regis* ('by his majesty's special command'). The possibility for abuse of this practice is evident in Petruccio's concern that Sforza's life may be forfeit to the King's fury rather than his law (*Queen and Concubine*, sig. D3r). Eulalia makes clear to the rustics, however, that the institution of summary execution would make them no better, and certainly no less guilty, than her attackers: 'you transgresse / As much his Laws in spilling of their blood, / As they had done in mine' (*Queen and Concubine*, sig. F8v). Her concern is always with the maintenance of law and order. Her obedience to the King's arbitrary will as law, even to her own detriment, suggests, somewhat conservatively, that even tyrannous monarchs should be obeyed to maintain order in the commonwealth.

Despite her arguments to the contrary, the rustics name Eulalia as Queen, establishing in her a legal authority separate from that of the King:

> Alphonso: Your selves are Traytors
>   In succouring 'gainst the Law, a dissolute woman
>   Whom I command you, in the Kings high name
>   To yield into my hands:
>
> Lollio, Poggio, Andrea: You shall be hang'd first.
>
> Alphonso: By whose Authority?
>
> Lollio: By the said womans Sir.
>   She is our Queen and her Authority is in our hands.
>   (*Queen and Concubine*, sig. I3v)

Despite the King's decree that Eulalia should not be aided and that she is no longer Queen, she has become, to the rustics of Palermo, the figurehead of an independent legal authority, and this authority is held in higher regard than the King's. Eulalia herself refuses this title of Queen (*Queen and Concubine*, sigs. G3v-G4r), emphasising that it is Gonzago, not Eulalia, who is responsible for the rustics' institution of a separate legal authority through his misuse of law, and his embrace (literal and figurative) of arbitrary absolutism in Alinda.[40] Indeed, Eulalia's obedience maintains order by refusing to legitimise two separate 'laws', and it is this orderliness and her associated virtue (set against Alinda's mad ambition and disorder) which finally bring Gonzago to realise his error in divorcing the rightful Queen.

In his divorce from Eulalia and his marriage to Alinda, Gonzago moves away from the forms and procedures of established law. The imprisonment and death

---

[40]   I have taken the image of embracing arbitrary rule in Alinda from Butler (1984, p.36).

of Sforza are commanded at the King's (and Alinda's) whim, not through any legal channels, and the various attempts on Eulalia's life engineered by Alinda and Flavello provide clear examples of the disrespect for law and order at Gonzago's court. As the play progresses, this divorce of royal authority and law destabilises both law and authority. The King himself comes under threat as the soldiers, revolting against Petruccio for the death of Sforza, come to the palace:

> in the late Execution
> Of Death-doom'd *Sforza*, which the Souldier
> (Not looking on [the King's] justice, but the Feud
> That was betwixt *Petruccio* and him)
> Resents as if it were *Petruccio's* Act,
> Not yours, that cut him off.
> (*Queen and Concubine*, sig. H2v)

The soldiers believe Petruccio's life should be forfeit for the murder of Sforza, despite his royal warrant. However, when he claims (truthfully) that he disobeyed the King's order, the soldiers accuse him of lying and maintain their claim to his blood, but simultaneously offer him to the King's punishment for disobedience:

> We dare to kill the Hangman of our General,
> And think it fits our Office best: though you
> Have Law enough to wave our care and pain,
> And hang him up your self: for he affirms
> That he let *Sforza* live 'gainst your command;
> And that's the lie we treat of.
> (*Queen and Concubine*, sig. H3v)

The claims of the King, law and justice have been separated and thus undermined to such an extent that there is no possibility of justice for Petruccio whether he did or did not carry out the King's command. Although the soldiers do not believe his claims of innocence, his admission of disobedience gives the King 'Law enough', that is, sufficient evidence whatever the truth of the matter, to punish him for his action. The confusion that accompanies the soldiers' demands is indicative of the potential chaos of a State without due legal process. The only way to defuse the situation is for Sforza to return, unharmed, to the King's favour. This can be achieved in the play because Petruccio has deceived Gonzago in reporting Sforza's death; significantly, this method of restoring order requires the reversal of all of the King's arbitrary judgements on Sforza.

The difficulty of Petruccio's position and scene of confusion caused by arbitrary action is echoed in the concerns of the country rustics that in rescuing Eulalia from those Alinda sent to kill her they have fallen foul of an edict ordering that no one is to aid the former Queen in her banishment:

> Poggio: How? what have we done? In relieving her from killing, we are all become Traytors.

Lollio: That's an idle fear: we knew her not,
       Which now we do, we may again reliver her
       Into their hands, for them to kill her yet:
       And then there's no harm done.

Poggio: So let us give them their swords again; and when they have done their
work, to make all sure, we'll hang them for their pains, and so keep the Law in
our own hands while we have it.

Curate: *O homines insani.* (*Queen and Concubine*, sigs. E6r-E6v)

The ridiculousness of this situation masks its more serious undertones. This is one
of several similar incidents in the play, all of which suggest that the uncertainty
caused by arbitrary actions leaves subjects in doubt over what is and is not legal.
That the rustics can logically claim that if they hand the Queen over to her killers
'then there's no harm done', though couched in comedy, is a shocking realisation of
the chaos that the will of Gonzago and Alinda can bring about, and it is significant
here that the Curate's response to the rustics' decisions is to call them 'mad men'.
The need to take law into their own hands in order to keep on the right side of
it allows the possibility that subjects will disregard established law if kings set
them such an example. The comedy of the situation, which remains comedy only
because Eulalia's insistence on the due process of law prevents a lynching, hides
the chaos which would result from the countrymen's arbitrary 'legal' decisions.
The 'destruction' (*Queen and Concubine*, sig. C7v) Lodovico feared for the court
when Eulalia was banished is only kept in check in Palermo by her presence.

At the end of the play, brought to recognise the absolute cruelty and madness
of his new bride, Gonzago rejects Alinda and reinstates Eulalia as his Queen.
Unlike the happy resolution of *The Queenes Exchange* brought about by the
marriage of the monarch and the common law, and the restoration of reason in the
reunion of Peregrine and Martha, the reacceptance of Eulalia as Queen, and thus
the remarriage of royal authority and due legal process for the common good, is
not sufficient in *The Queen and Concubine* to bring about a satisfactory resolution.
Alinda is quite literally brought to her senses and recognises her folly, begging
pardon from her father, the King, the Queen and the Prince before asking to be
allowed to retire to a convent 'To spend this life in Tears for [her] amiss' (*Queen
and Concubine*, sig. K1r). Importantly, Gonzago, too, having recognised his own
errors, is to leave the political arena and retire to a monastery, leaving the kingdom
to the Prince's government:

King: So haste we to *Nicosia*, where (my Son)
       In lieu of former wrongs, Ile yield thee up my Crown and Kingdom.
       Your vertuous mother (whom may you for ever
       Honour for her pietie) with these true
       Statesmen, will enable you to govern well.

Horatio: Who makes a doubt of that?
       (*Queen and Concubine*, sig. K1r)

A play that had seemed conservative in advocating obedience to even a tyrannous king shifts here to a much more radical position. Arbitrary rule must not only be recognised as inappropriate, and even dangerous to the stability of the state, it must be entirely removed from the political sphere. That Gonzago emphasises to his son that ruling in conjunction with his mother will enable him 'to govern well' highlights the importance of law, order and maintenance of the common good for good governance, and implies that his government with Alinda, and without Eulalia, has been far from this. Horatio's comment here on the future good government of Sicily is consistent with his characteristic agreement with the King; throughout the play he has, in a ridiculous caricature of the sycophantic courtiers of Bertha's court, done the King 'that service, just to love / Or hate as the King does' (*Queen and Concubine*, sig. B5v). Nevertheless, this statement reinforces Gonzago's acknowledgement of the need for rule by established law and due order, suggested in his praise of Eulalia's piety. However, Horatio's rhetorical question also invites the audience to pass judgement on the legal politics which have been presented to them in the course of the play. There is very little basis for disagreement.

* * *

The movement towards the subjection of monarchical authority to law in these plays is set alongside the disintegration of reason into madness, which is representative of, and brought on by, the unrestrained exercise of prerogative powers. Attempts to manipulate the law are shown to be acts of madness, literally in Offa and Alinda, fictionally in the Antipodes, but also metaphorically, as such actions destabilise the State, threatening both the monarch and the commonwealth. This association of intemperate monarchical will with madness in the theatre coincides with an increased emphasis in the contemporary politico-legal arena upon the reason of the law, both inherent in law itself and in the cumulative wisdom of the lawyers, set against the potentially arbitrary judgements of absolute monarchy. Whilst the dramatic confines of the theatre, and the generic boundaries of tragi-comedy and comedy, allow the exploration of the destabilising effects of absolutism without real consequences, the political arena does not. The only means to maintain a stable, just government and a prosperous commonwealth, these plays suggest, is to subordinate royal authority to the power of independent, established law.

Chapter 4
Decentralising Legal Authority:
From the Centre to the Provinces

Positions of legal authority in the localities fell to men from a variety of social strata, from the local petty constable (often a man of humble background) to the Justices of Peace (often local landowners or gentry) to the Lords Lieutenant (usually titled men).[1] Such figures were responsible for the enforcement of central law and policy in their area, and were officially the representatives of central authority in delivering justice. The responsibilities of local authority figures were wide-ranging, and will be summarised, along with the structures and hierarchies of authority that led from the centre to the provinces, in the first section of this chapter. Justices of Peace:

> be called Justices (of the peace) because they be Judges of Record; and withal to put them in minde (by their name) that they are to doe justice (which is, to yeeld to every man in his owne by even portions, and according to the Lawes, Customes, and Statutes of this Realme,) without respect of person.
>   They are named also Commissioners (of the peace) because they have their authority by the Kings Commission. (Dalton, 1635, p.7)

Appointed by the king through the Privy Council, justices were the main representatives of central authority in the localities, and, I will argue in a reading of Brome's *The Weeding of Covent Garden* (1632), on the Caroline stage. However, figures of local authority were also involved much more in the negotiation and mediation of central law, than in its direct enforcement; Justices of Peace and, particularly, constables walked a precarious line between following their instructions from higher authorities and maintaining peace and their place in local society. As Keith Wrightson argues:

> The order of the village community could survive occasional drunkenness, erratic church attendance, profane language, neglect of the licensing and

---

[1]   Indeed, Keith Wrightson suggests that petty constables, at least, were often poor men pressed to take the position because villagers were notoriously reluctant to accept the responsibility (1980, p.26). For a detailed discussion of the selection, responsibilities and activities of village constables, see Joan Kent (1986). Thomas Cogswell (1998) provides a discussion of the position and activities of the Earl of Huntingdon, Lord Lieutenant of Leicestershire. For a more general discussion of the power and position of Lords Lieutenant, and their relationship with local sheriffs and justices, see Stater (1994, especially the introduction and chapters 1 and 2).

apprenticeship laws. It was more likely to be disturbed by the enforcement of the host of penal laws which might excite new conflicts and drain, in fines, its resources. What really mattered was the maintenance of specific, local, personal relationships, not conformity to impersonal law. (1980, p.25)

The division of central legislation and local government into two separate concepts of order that this implies suggests a negotiation of law enforcement in the localities which took into account not only the relationship of the 'offender' to the law, but also of the official to the law and to the community. Such complexities of local authority will be explored here with regard to Ben Jonson's *A Tale of a Tub* (1633). Finally, I will argue that increased attempts to centralise legal authority in the provinces, in parallel with Charles I's exercise of prerogative rule at the centre, emphasised the divisions between concepts of central and local legal governance, and brought about, Brome's *A Joviall Crew* (1641) suggests, a fragmentation of law, government and society.

From the Centre to the Provinces

Aside from the Lords Lieutenant whose main responsibility was military (although they occasionally, as a figure of high local standing, attempted to resolve disputes amongst their neighbours), the Justice of the Peace was the most prominent figure of permanent judicial authority in many regions in the Caroline period.[2] Justices were appointed by the Privy Council, served indefinitely and could only be removed from office at the king's will. They reported their activities to the Judges of Assize, who in turn reported to the Privy Council on the justices. However, this system of monitoring was not all one way; the local justices, Kevin Sharpe notes, were also encouraged to report back to the Council on the activities of the judges whilst in their area (1992, p.435). The hierarchy of justice figures was not for monitoring purposes only, however; it also acted as a chain of communication: the king gave his address in Star Chamber to the Assize Judges, who then passed on new (or emphasised) issues of policy to the local justices on their circuit.

The Justices of Peace in each county met every three months for the quarter sessions, the main forum for local justice.[3] Some justices, however, chose to meet more often in 'petty sessions' in order to deal with pressing county business, or to reduce the workload for the quarter sessions. These petty sessions were initially set

---

[2]   Victor Stater suggests that the responsibilities of the Lords Lieutenant increased throughout the early Stuart period, and that this was a reflection of the *ad hoc* nature of early Stuart government (1994, p.26). J. A. Sharpe notes that 'arbitration through friends, respected members of the community, the local clergyman, or even through the intercession of justices of the peace, must have kept many disputes and differences from entering the courts' (1980, p.112).

[3]   Much of this paragraph is based upon Sharpe (1992, p.430–38). See also A. J. Fletcher (1986, *passim*).

up on an informal basis but the Book of Orders (*Orders and Directions*) of January 1631, which sought to increase officials' co-operation and impose a greater order upon local governance, ordered the institution of regular monthly petty sessions:

> Orders 1.
> That the Justices of Peace of every Shire within the Realme doe divide themselves, and allot amongst themselves what Justices of the peace, and what Hundreds [a division of land in the county] shall attend monethly at some certain places of the Shire. And at this day and place, the High Constables, petty Constables, and Churchwardens, and Overseers for the poore of those Hundreds, shall attend the said Justices. And there inquirie shall be made, and Information taken by the Justices, how every of these Officers in their severall places have done their duties in Execution of the Lawes mentioned in the Commission annexed, and what persons have offended against any of the said Lawes. (Charles I, 1630, sigs. E4r-E4v)

Those officers who had neglected their duties were to be punished, and note taken of this, along with any fines levied and how these had been spent. Details were then to be sent quarterly in a written report to the High Sheriff of the County, for him to report back to the Privy Council. The extent to which this order was carried out varied from county to county.

Despite the importance of their position in law enforcement, local governance and county welfare, Justices of the Peace received no formal training. However, there were some 'handbooks' for justices, which laid out their responsibilities and the statutes for their enforcement. William Lambarde's *Eirenarcha* (first published in 1581) and Michael Dalton's *The Countrey Justice* (first published 1618) presented the statutes pertinent to their office, and justices' jurisdiction with respect to felony, larceny, theft and the raising of hue and cry. Apart from their expected judicial responsibilities, however, *The Countrey Justice* showed that justices were also responsible for determining paternity, poor relief and road maintenance. The popularity of such manuals is attested by the fact that by 1620, *Eirenarcha* had reached its twelfth edition (Sharpe, 1992, p.431n.217), and *The Countrey Justice* was reprinted for the fifth time in 1635. The anonymous *The Complete Justice A Compendium of the particulars incident to Justices of the Peace, either in Sessions or out of Sessions* (1637), containing not only information from the statutes, resolutions of judges and approved authorities, but also references to the relevant passages of Dalton's and Lambarde's works, suggests the authority these volumes carried.

Primarily, Dalton stated, the justices were commissioned by the king to keep his peace:

> The conservation of this peace (and therein the care of the Justice of Peace) consisteth in three things, *viz.*
> 1. In preventing the breach of the Peace, (wisely foreseeing and repressing the beginnings thereof) by taking surety for the keeping of it, or for the good behaviour of the offenders, as the case shall require.

　　　2. In pacifying such as are in breaking of the peace[...]
　　　3. In punishing (according to Law) such as have broken the peace.
But of the three, the first, the preventing Justice, is most worthy to be commended
to the care of the Justices of Peace. (1635, p.10)

Before stating the Justices' responsibilities, however, Dalton also notes that:

> Justice may be perverted in many wayes, (if [the justices] shall not arme
> themselves with the feare of God, the love of Truth and Justice, and with the
> authority and knowledge of the Lawes and Statutes of this Realme). (1635, p.7)

These are, he says: fear of 'the power or countenance of another'; attempts to
favour friends or family; hatred of one party or another; expectation of a gift, fee
or reward; 'Perturbation of minde; as anger, or such like passion'; ignorance of
knowing what should be done; 'presumption' (when a justice acts on their own
will without law or warrant); 'Delay; which in effect is a denying of justice' and
'precipitation' (rash actions without due examination) (1635 p.7).

　　Justices of Peace, however, were not the only law enforcement officials.
Amongst their responsibilities was that of appointing High Constables (two in
each Hundred), who were assisted by Petty Constables. Of the local officials,
the High and Petty Constables were most integrated into the society they served,
and were mostly yeomanry/farmers and ordinary men like husbandmen or
shopkeepers respectively. They were more engaged in the everyday life of their
local community, and as such faced a more complex negotiation between their
responsibilities and life in their community than the justices, and indeed are the
primary focus of Wrightson's essay, 'Two Concepts of Order', quoted above. They
were responsible for effecting hue and cry (rousing the local people to search for
criminals), collecting taxes / loans, making presentments to the assembled justices
at petty and quarter sessions and escorting those who were summoned to appear
before the sessions. In this way, it was they, not the justices, who were directly
responsible for reporting their friends, family and neighbours' misdemeanours.
Unlike justices, they were not protected by a high social status, nor were they
appointed by the Privy Council. Constables usually held their position only
for 12 months, after which they had to go back to their everyday lives in the
same community, facing any repercussions from their neighbours, without what
little protection their post had previously offered.[4] That they had to live in the
community, and thus with the consequences of their actions, must have held
substantial influence over the decisions made by all local officials, but this does not
necessarily imply widespread corruption (although figures such as the constables
and clerks of Brome's *The Northern Lasse* and Thomas Nabbes's *Covent Garden*
suggest a perceived undercurrent of dishonesty amongst local lawmen). The

---

　　[4]　For a detailed discussion of position of constables, see Wrightson (1980); Sharpe
(1980) and Kent (1986). The same problems arose for ship money sheriffs (Lake, 1981,
p.57).

increased demands upon constables brought about by the Book of Orders and ship money collection in the 1630s exacerbated the constables' problems, making recruitment to the post more difficult. Justices were forced to appoint men from a broader base of lower status men and new families (Sharpe, 1992, p.439), and these men would inevitably carry less natural authority than those of locally established families or men of higher status.

The collection of the forced loan (1626) and ship money (during the 1630s) not only tested the constables and those above them in the chain of local governance, but also highlighted the tensions between the priorities of local and central authorities.[5] Charles's attempts to raise these extra-parliamentary monies were met with some resistance, in part because of their dubious legality (extra parliamentary taxation was technically illegal) – there were those who refused to collect or pay their allotted amount for this reason – and in part because those commissioned to collect the money chose to do what was best for the financial well-being of their local community.[6] Ship money sheriffs with responsibility only for the collection of such funds were appointed in the localities, and although this 'constituted a decision to bypass the usual hierarchies of county government' (Lake, 1981, p.59), it did not sidestep the clash of local and national interests present in local officials. Nevertheless, some managed to assert the rights and concerns of their community with regard to ship money assessments, whilst also appearing loyal to the King and Privy Council.[7] The Privy Council, too, exploited the dual loyalties (and personal concerns) of the ship money sheriffs, who were financially responsible for any shortfall in the collection in their year of office:

> [T]hey were not only playing on his sense of obligation to the King's service
> (and his fear of the practical consequences of any failure on his part) but were
> also exploiting his sense of obligation towards his own county. Left with no
> choice but to administer the writ the sheriff could be relied on to minimize its

---

[5] For a detailed discussion of the introduction, enforcement and implications of the Forced Loan, see Richard Cust's *The Forced Loan and English Politics 1626–1628* (1987, *passim*). For more detail on ship money, see Sharpe (1992, 567–98); Peter Lake's discussion of Cheshire ship money provides a close focus upon the different methods of the individuals involved in its collection, and of their communication with the Privy Council (1981, *passim*). In contrast to the more usual negative discussions of ship money, Richard Cust notes that the levy was, initially, a considerable financial success (2005, p.191), and that 'it might have been possible to contain the opposition caused by ship money had it not been for Hampden's case', since the concerns over the extent of prerogative power involved here 'did not become really widespread until after the publicity given to the arguments at Hampden's trial' (2005, p.193).

[6] Lords Lieutenant who displeased the King over the forced loan temporarily lost their position (Stater, 1994, p.17), and Fletcher states that some country justices were also dismissed for opposition to ship money (1986, p.10). Sharpe, however, argues that there is little evidence to support this statement (1992, p.436).

[7] See Peter Lake's discussion of the sheriffs involved in the collection of ship money in Cheshire (1981, *passim*, especially pp.45–50).

effects in the local context. After all he had to live there after his year in office.
(Lake, 1981, p.57)

The localism that could be detrimental to central authority's will here was turned
to its advantage.

The disadvantage of bypassing the usual county hierarchy in such a way,
however, was that it allowed the direct questioning of the royal prerogative in the
authority given by the King to the sheriffs. Unlike the Justices of Peace, who were
given authority by the King to uphold and provide justice within common and
statute law, ship money sheriffs acted only with the authority of royal prerogative,
making them 'a direct link … through which the unalloyed power of the King's
prerogative was to be brought to the locality' (Lake, 1981, p.59).[8] The extent of
the King's prerogative was, in this case, not a matter for debate amongst lawyers,
Parliament and the King in the way that passing the Petition of Right had been,
but a matter that affected all subjects in the localities directly and financially.
Their reaction to the sheriffs' authority could then be seen as a reaction to the
prerogative, and, thus, Peter Lake argues, 'it was not possible to react against
ship money without also raising a whole series of questions about the nature and
limits of the King's authority' (1981, p.61). If people were unco-operative with
the sheriff, they were disobedient to the King. In attempting to bypass the chain
of local authority in the provinces, ship money and its sheriffs created a fissure in
the presentation of royal authority by subjecting it to the mediation of individuals'
capabilities and influence.

The enforcement of law and royal policy, then, depended upon the influence,
charisma and efficiency of the local authority figure(s), and upon the co-operation of
the local people. Although Caroline local officials were not always representatives
of the prerogative (as in the case of the ship money sheriffs) they were always
representatives of the king's judicial authority. The next section will discuss this
representation of central authority in *The Weeding of Covent Garden*.

Central Authority: *The Weeding of Covent Garden*

Brome's *The Weeding of Covent Garden* presents several figures of authority: the
local Justice (Cockbrayne), two fathers (Crosswill and Rooksbill) and the Captain
of a band of youths called the Philoblathici (Driblow). The parallel positions these
men hold might suggest a proliferation of authorities in the play; indeed, Butler has
argued that 'Brome's Covent Garden is full of law of all varieties, but order and
authority there is none' (1984, p.157). In what follows I will argue that, whilst the
play does present a variety of potential authorities, ultimately, the legal authority

---

    [8]   By contrast with the sheriffs, Richard Cust and Peter Lake argue in their discussion
of the ideals and ideologies espoused by Sir Richard Grosvenor (Chief Justice of the Peace
in Cheshire), that the institutions of local government were seen primarily as representatives
of parliamentary authority in the localities (1981, p.45).

in this play resides in the single figure of the Justice of the Peace, suggesting a single, unified focus of legitimate legal authority.

Cockbrayne is a particularly proactive local official, who takes his responsibilities very seriously, reminding himself of his duties regarding bawdy houses and prostitutes ('I guess what she is, what ere I have said. O Justice look to thine office' (*The Weeding of Covent-Garden*, sig. B5r)), and actively seeking out wrong doers to punish in order to rid Covent Garden of its 'weeds', suggesting a concern that the newly built houses are filled by appropriate people.[9] Cockbrayne compliments Rooksbill, a developer of Covent Garden, on the state of the building, saying 'All, all as't should be!'. Rooksbill's response, 'If all were as well tenanted and inhabited by worthy persons', leads the Justice to a lengthy discussion of the progress of all new developments:

> Cockbrayne: Phew; that will follow. What new Plantation was ever peopled with the better sort at first; nay commonly the lewdest blades, and naughty-packs are either necessitated to 'hem, or else do prove the most forward venturers ... And do not weeds creep up first in all Gardens? and why not then in this? ... And for the weeds in it, let me alone for the weeding of them out. And so as my Reverend Ancestor *Justice Adam Overdoe*, was wont to say, *In Heavens name and the Kings*, and for the good of the Common-wealth I will go about it.

> Rooksbill: I would a few more of the Worshipful here-abouts (whether they be in Commission or not) were as well minded that way as you are Sir; we should then have all sweet and clean, and that quickly too. (*Weeding*, sigs. B1v-B2r)

Rooksbill's desire for more local participation in maintaining order chimes with the ideas of unofficial, local, participatory governance that Steve Hindle describes in early modern parish authorities (2000, pp.204–23). However, such participation seems to be lacking in Brome's Covent Garden, and does not, then raise an alternative or further form of authority from the designated officials as it might have done in *The Love-sick Court* or *The Queen and Concubine*. Here, Cockbrayne's declaration that he acts in heaven's name, and the king's and for the good of the common wealth justifies his actions through all possible authorities from the highest seat of justice (heaven), through the king to the people, and his earlier decision to actively seek out criminals suggests something of the demands of central authority in the Book of Orders for an increased efficiency in its local officials. In this statement, he also claims heritage in Jonson's Jacobean justice, Adam Overdo (*Bartholomew Fayre*) and like Overdo, his officiousness will do him little good. This heritage also hints towards the way Cockbrayne intends to weed Covent Garden: in disguise. His comparison between the development of Covent Garden and colonial expansion ('new Plantation') is significant as a comment upon the expansion of London into greenfield areas on its outskirts. At

---

[9] Hereafter *The Weeding of Covent Garden* will be abbreviated in references to *Weeding*.

the time, there were royal proclamations against further building around London, except for on existing foundations (Sanders, 1999a, p.51), and the Earl of Bedford had to petition the King in order to build at Covent Garden.[10] However, if central authority was against any further expansion of London, this does not fully explain the colonial analogy. The explanation lies, I suggest, in the intended market for the houses, to which Rooksbill hints in his wish for 'worthy persons' and Cockbrayne refers in his compliments on the building: 'I Marry Sir! This is something like! These appear like Buildings! Here's Architecture exprest indeed! It is a most sightly scituation, and fit for Gentry and Nobility' (*Weeding*, sig. B1r). Martin Butler states that '[t]he square was designed deliberately as an area of fashionable housing' and 'Covent Garden … was the newest and most prominent example of the gentry's foothold in London' (1984, p.147). The country gentry, then, are 'colonising' London. Charles sought to deal with this – and the potential problems of local government it brought – with the proclamation of 1632, 'Commaunding the gentry to keep their Residence at the Mansions in the Country, and forbidding them to make their Habitations in *London* and places adjoining'.[11] *The Weeding of Covent Garden*'s Will Crosswill, however, has contrary ideas: 'He has had an aime these dozen years to live in town here but never was fully bent on't until the Proclamation of restraint spurr'd him up' (*Weeding*, sig. C2r). He has, however, found a way to circumvent the proclamation; he has 'sold all [his] land to live upon [his] money in Town here, out of danger of the Statute' (*Weeding*, sig. F5v). His deliberate crossing of the proclamation is representative of Crosswill's intentionally contradictory attitude.

Crosswill sees his authority as the ability to act utterly arbitrarily and embodies the extreme of untempered will. The dramatic convention, and patriarchal political theory, which equates fathers with kings suggests that he should be seen as a representation of the king's authority.[12] Julie Sanders makes this point particularly succinctly, arguing that in *The Weeding of Covent Garden* and other such plays: 'the space of the family is used as a means for exploring the wider problems of the monarch-father's relationship with his children-subjects in the body politic or wider commonweath' (1999a, p.68). Crosswill arrives in Covent Garden as a potential tenant for Rooksbill's properties, and when he first appears, he is

---

[10]   Matthew Steggle notes that until the Earl of Bedford commissioned its redevelopment for housing in 1631, Covent Garden had been a greenfield area (2004, p.47). Julia Merritt discusses the layout of the Covent Garden development, suggesting it was designed to exclude the undesirable poor 'by eliminating the types of areas in which the poor traditionally congregated' (2005, pp.196–9, quotation at p.197). For early seventeenth-century testimony regarding the movement of undesirables to colonies before more respectable gentlemen, see Miller (1990, p.357).

[11]   Butler argues that Charles I's commanding the gentry back to their country estates sought in part to reinstate the gentry's order-keeping through hospitality, whilst maintaining better communication between Whitehall and the provinces during the personal rule (1992b, pp.181–2).

[12]   For a discussion of patriarchalism, see Chapter 2.

complaining of his children's behaviour. Although they behave in ways that 'other fathers would rejoice at' (*Weeding*, sig. B2v), it is not enough that they speak of obedience 'Or that [they] are obedient. But I will be obeyed in my own way' (*Weeding*, sig. B2r). For his daughter, this is choosing her own husband:

> But she has a humour, forsooth, since we put your son by her, to make me a match-broker, her marriage-Maker; when I tell you friend, there has been so many untoward matches of Parents making, that I had sworn she shall make her own choice, though it be of one I hate. Make me her match-maker! Must I obey her, or she me, ha? (*Weeding*, sig. B3v)

Katherine's refusal to make her own choice is a response to Crosswill and Cockbrayne's sudden and irrational decision to call off her marriage with Cockbrayne's son, Anthony. Crosswill believes his fatherly authority gives him the power to do whatever he pleases and exercises this power at every opportunity, and in this way embodies the fears of arbitrary action by the King raised by the imposition of Charles's personal rule. Often Crosswill's arbitrary decisions are merely a test of his children's obedience, yet this backfires, as Crosswill's arbitrariness raises in his children a spirit of opposition and deviousness that would not necessarily have arisen if he did not attempt to thwart their plans at every turn. Mihil states:

> thou know'st 'tis his custome to crosse me, and the rest of his children in all we do, to try and urge his obedience; 'tis an odde way: therefore to help my self I seem to covet the things that I hate, and he pulls them from me; and make shew of loathing the things I covet, and he hurles them doubly at me, as now in this money. (*Weeding*, sigs. C6r-C6v)

After a long soliloquy on his own actions and his children's response, Crosswill himself acknowledges his fault in creating their behaviour, saying '*I* could beat my selfe for getting such children' (*Weeding*, sig. F7v). (A comic parallel for this can be found in the play's Captain Driblow, leader of the Philoblathici, who actively encourages disorder in his followers, suggesting that too much insistence on authority is as bad for the commonwealth as too little.)[13] In the same way as Mihil tricks money from his father, Katherine pretends to want to leave Rooksbill's house to trick her father, who had decided to leave, into staying. This deliberately contrary behaviour in his children and his own repentance for creating it serve as a warning to Charles about the dangers of imposing arbitrary rule. Wilfulness in the ruler provokes wilfulness in the subjects.

More significant than his daughter's behaviour in this respect are the 'disobediences' of his sons: Gabriel has changed from 'imitating a soldier' (*Weeding*, sig. E2r) to behaving like a Puritan, and Mihil has, Crosswill believes, become a student of law at the Inns of Court. Puritans and lawyers were both groups

---

[13] cf. Butler (1984, p.156).

with whom Charles I wrangled on occasion, the former objecting to the potential Catholicising of the English church, and the latter for Charles's prerogative infringements upon common and statute law. Gabriel admits at the end of the play, when Dorcas's honour is restored though marriage with Nicholas, that he was merely acting the Puritan to displease his father in return for being sent away earlier (a decision which unintentionally allowed Nicholas to seduce and leave Dorcas). His choice of words here, however, is significant, as he 'acknowledg[es] [his] formal habit was more of *stubbornnesse* then true devotion' (*Weeding*, sig. G7v, my emphasis). This suggests a certain contrariness in all Caroline Puritans, emphasised by Katherine and Lucie's earlier interchange:

> Kat: … *I* think verily he does it but to crosse my father, for sending him out of the way when the mischief was done.
>
> Luc: *I* will not then beleeve 'tis Religion in any of the gang of 'em, but mere wilful affectation. (*Weeding*, sig. E3r)

Gabriel's 'affectation' however, not only displeased his father, but gave him a religious vocabulary which suggests heavenly retribution for Nicholas, but also allows personal violence:

> It had been good to have humbled him, though into the knowledge of his Transgression. And of himself for his soules good, either by course of Law, or else in case of necessity, where the Law promiseth no releese, by your own right hand you might have smote him, smote him with great force, yea, smote him unto the earth, until he had prayed that the evil might be taken from him. (*Weeding*, sig. E8r)

The comic repetition of 'smote' both emphasises Gabriel's anger with Nicholas and ridicules the zealous fervour of seventeenth-century puritans. It should be noted, though, that this violence becomes an option only 'where the Law promiseth no releese'. Submission to appropriate authority is still important to Gabriel. In fact neither 'smiting' nor law catches up with Nicholas who is, instead, upon hearing her story and recognising his part in it, persuaded by his friends to marry Dorcas without official intervention. This circumvention of authority by the Philoblathici perhaps gestures towards the community negotiation of law I suggested in the opening to this chapter.

Mihil's ostensible study of the law also infuriates his father. Although Crosswill himself placed Mihil as a student in London, his disappointment to find his son studying law rather than reading romances plays on the knowledge that the Inns of Court were as much a 'college' for young gentlemen who wished to enjoy London society and advance themselves at court as places to study the law. Mihil's demonstration of his legal knowledge, put on as a show to his father using borrowed books and gowns, and other pretend students (the shoemaker and tailor to whom he owes money), leads Crosswill himself to admit as much:

> Did I leave thee here to learn fashion and manners, that thou mightst carry thy self like a Gentleman, and dost thou wast thy brains in learning a language that I understand not a word of? ha! I had been as good have brought thee up amongst the wild Irish. (*Weeding*, sig. C4v)

The reference to the Irish perhaps continues the colonisation analogy, but more significant is Crosswill's objection to Mihil's legal learning: he does not understand it. I do not wish to argue that Brome is suggesting Charles I is ignorant of the law, but that this may suggest a (deliberate?) misunderstanding of the law on the King's part. The terms that Crosswill uses to prevent Mihil continuing his study too are significant: 'Away with books. Away with Law. Away with madnesse. *I*, God blesse thee, and make thee his servant, and defend thee from Law, *I* say' (*Weeding*, sig. C4r), and again later, an interchange between Crosswill and Mihil confirms this association of studying law and madness:

> Mi: They are Gentlemen of my standing, Sir, that have a little over-studied themselves, and are somewhat –
>
> Cros: Mad; are they not? And so will you be shortly, if you follow these courses. Mooting do they call it? you shall moote nor mute here no longer. (*Weeding*, sig. C5r)

This is, of course, an inversion of the law/reason, madness/arbitrary rule equations evident in Caroline drama I discussed in Chapter 3. The explanation for this may lie in Crosswill's deliberately contrary nature, and thus it might be expected that he should reverse the convention. His prayer that Mihil be defended from law could be taken as a slight upon crooked lawyers and legal practices, but in terms of Crosswill as a representative of Charles I, his wish that heaven may defend him and his sons from law evokes the divine right of kings in protection of royal prerogative (Crosswill's arbitrary authority) against the claims of law.[14] As this is *Crosswill's* prayer though, it can be understood as a perverse wish.

Mihil's apparent studiousness, however, is a cover for his real 'occupation' in town as a member of the Philoblathici, the 'brothers of the blade and battoon' led by Captain Driblow (a further figure of authority), who swear to protect each other and their companions, be disrespectful to all but their brotherhood unless they can gain from them ('let no man take wall of you, but such as you suppose will either beat you or lend you money'), and to undermine the law:

> That you be ever at deadly defiance with all such people, as Protections are directed to in Parliament, and that you watch all occasions to prevent or rescue Gentlemen from the gripes of the Law brissons. That you may thereby endear your selfe into noble society, and drink the juice of the Varlets labours for your officious intrusions. (*Weeding*, sig. D3v)

---

[14] Mihil's exposition of 'remitter' to his pretend students is taken from Coke's *Institutes*, fol.347b-348a, and is close to direct quotation. The choice to quote from Coke is also significant in this presentation of the clash between law and kingly authority, as Coke was one of the main proponents of rule by common law against prerogative (see Chapter 3).

Protections were warrants for safe conduct or immunity from arrest usually issued by the king to those in his service. That the protections here are offered by Parliament suggests an intention to undermine *all* forms of authority.[15] In this respect, it is interesting that Nicholas draws a comparison between his Philoblathici brothers and Gabriel's puritan brothers:

> But we are brethren, sir, and as factsous [*sic*] as you, though we differ in the Grounds, for you, sir, defie Orders, and so do we, you of the Church, we of the Civil Magistrate; many of us speak i'th'nose, as you do; you out of humility of spirit, we by the wantonnesse of the flesh; now in devotion we go beyond you, for you will not kneel to a ghostly father, and we do to a carnal Mystresse. (*Weeding*, sig. F4v)

This comparison of Mihil, Nicholas and Gabriel's positions suggests that puritans, like the Philoblathici, deliberately set out to flout authority.

That the brothers of the blade can so easily 'convert' Gabriel from his Puritan ways to drunkenness may, like the revelation of his pretence, also be a comment on the sincerity of Puritans. His transformation from Puritan to Militia Captain threatening to 'do Martial Justice on you all' (*Weeding*, sig. G4v) is not too far in violence from his previous desire to 'smite' his enemies, but presents him as more acceptable to his father (and thus Caroline central authorities) but also as an embodiment of several contentious issues of the period. His complaint that his 'troops' are ill-trained and equipped (*Weeding*, sigs. G4v-G5r) was a real problem for the Caroline militia, and his threats of martial law reflect fears of its imposition in towns with military garrisons which had been argued against in the Petition of Right.[16] This opens the question as to what forms of behaviour are acceptable to both the Caroline populace and the King. Gabriel's threat to enforce such law changes the threat to order he embodies from one of disobedience to Church authority to a threat to local authority, as commissions of martial law undermined the authority of Justices of the Peace.[17]

Cockbrayne's attempts to 'tread out the spark of impiety, whilest it is yet a spark and not a flame; and break the egge of a mischief, whilest it is yet an egge and not a Cockatrice' (*Weeding*, sig. B2r), and thus weed Covent Garden, involve infiltrating the Philoblathici. His attempts result in his first being soundly beaten by the brothers, then left to pay their inn bill with Clotpoll, and then being beaten by two prostitutes, Bettie and Francisca (Frank). His determined statement, 'I will not yet desist; but suffer private affliction with a Romane resolution for the

---

[15]   Matthew Steggle argues, alternatively, that the reference to the parliamentary protections is a topical reference relating to the revival of the play in 1641, as parliamentary protections were a contentious issue at that point (2001, paragraph 20).

[16]   Cogswell's discussion of Huntingdon's efforts in training and equipping the local militia is particularly informative regarding these problems (1998, *passim*). See Lockyer (1999, p.272) and Chapter 1 for concerns over the imposition of martial law raised in the Petition of Right.

[17]   See Russell (1979, p.359) and Lockyer (1999, p.272).

publicke welfare' (*Weeding*, sig. D6r) is admirable and suggests a genuine concern for the common good. However, his letter to Crosswill explaining his absence suggests ulterior motives:

> He is upon the point of discovery in a most excellent project for the weeding of this Garden? What Garden? What project? A project he says here for the good of the Republike, Repudding... He is ambitious to be call'd into authority by notice taken of some special service he is able to do the state aforehand. (*Weeding*, sig. F7r)

Crosswill's easy dismissal of any concern for the common good ('Republicke, Repudding') is unsurprising given his cross-will and arbitrary nature, and perhaps suggests a lack of concern for this in Charles's arbitrary government. Cockbrayne's motives here, too, are less than altruistic in wishing to advance his own position in weeding Covent Garden. In seeking to advance himself through his enforcement of the law rather than in acting for the common good despite his earlier claims that he would do so, Cockbrayne can be seen to represent Charles I's dubious use of law for his own gain.[18]

Cockbrayne's scheme advances him very little. His infiltration of the Philoblathici and storming of the tavern result in confusion as he finds respectable community members amongst the carousers who agree to stand as surety for each other and their relatives in the Philoblathici. Cockbrayne finds that he cannot arrest Crosswill and his children, or Rooksbill and his, and discovers that another of the Philoblathici is his own son: 'Why *I* know not whom to commit now', he says (*Weeding*, sig. G8v). In this confusion, Brome nods towards the ties of friendship and community which Wrightson (1980) argues complicated the activities of local officials. However, this confusion merely facilitates a satisfactory resolution to the play; it is not the dominating issue. Rather, the proper exercise of authority and obedience is brought to the fore. The parallel positions of Cockbrayne, Crosswill, Rooksbill and Driblow, along with Gabriel's puritan authorities, have led critics to argue that the proliferation of authority figures in this play suggests a complete lack of authority in Covent Garden. Matthew Steggle has associated this lack of authority closely with the play's setting, as Covent Garden had strong puritan links, and it did not become a parish in its own right until 14 years after the play was written and therefore did not have its own local authority figures (2004, pp.47–8). Butler argues that there is a more general confusion over legitimate legal authority:

> Brome simply [sets] these various sorts of authority at war with one another, the point being that no one figure can claim any more 'authority' than the next, since the actions of each arise from a narrow personal (and often contradictory) idea of what constitutes law. (1984, pp.154–5)

However, I would argue that despite their parallel positions as authority figures, Cockbrayne, Crosswill, Rooksbill and Driblow are not really competing authorities

---

[18]   Butler argues similarly (1984, p.153).

(unlike, for example, *The Queen and Concubine*'s King Gonzago and the unwilling Eulalia). Indeed, a satisfactory resolution to this play is ultimately brought about through the intervention of, and submission to, the appropriate officials:

> Vintner: There's no escaping forth. And Gentlemen, It will but breed more scandal on my house, and the whole plantation here, if now you make rebellious uproar. Yield your weapons, and welcome Justice but like subjects new, and peace will follow.
>
> ...
>
> Mihil: They shall yield up their weapons. So do you.
>
> Capt: Yes yes 'tis best.
>
> Clot: Shall we, sir, shall we?
>
> Mih: Yes sir, you shall.
> 　　(*Weeding*, sig. G6v)

Mihil's insistence that the Philoblathici give up their swords to the local authority figure, and Crosswill and Rooksbill's legitimate desire to bail their relatives rather than stand unofficially in the way of their arrest, imply deference to the constable and Justice Cockbrayne. Although there are other authority figures in the play, they do not hold higher power than Cockbrayne, and they know this. Even Captain Driblow, who potentially fights against Cockbrayne's authority, acknowledges this in his interchange with Clotpoll before the Justice's arrival:

> Clot: If our sight offend you,
> 　　Know we are men that dare forbear the place.
>
> Capt: I son, let's go, our stay is dangerous.
> 　　They look like Peace-maintainers, we'll fall off.
> 　　(*Weeding*, sig. G6v)

The harmonious ending to the play is brought about by acknowledgement of the legitimate authority of the Justice, and Covent Garden is eventually weeded when those who have not been submitting to the relevant authorities do so. That Cockbrayne chooses not to enact his powers of arrest suggests the necessary mediation of strict laws to bring about a satisfactory resolution. Nevertheless, this does not cause a dilemma for Cockbrayne; the authority to enforce or mitigate the law is his alone. There is no divided authority in this play.

Divided Loyalties: *A Tale of a Tub*

Although *The Weeding of Covent Garden* nods towards the conflicting loyalties experienced by local officials, its primary concern is with the appropriate imposition of, and obedience to, authority. As a representative of kingly judicial power, Justice Cockbrayne ultimately holds the highest authority in the locality of Covent Garden. Matthew Steggle's comment that Covent Garden had to rely on the services of officials shared with neighbouring areas (2004, p.48) may go some way to explaining this lack of personal conflict, although Cockbrayne's ties of friendship and family are not entirely irrelevant to the resolution of the play. Instead, I would like to argue that there is little conflict in Covent Garden because there is only one legitimate authority figure here (however dubious his motives and activities may be); there is no hierarchy. The conflict for figures of local authority comes with the need to reconcile the demands of higher authorities with those of the community.

Throughout the personal rule, Charles I sought to impose a greater sense of order upon what central government saw as the often haphazard enforcement of law in the provinces. Thus he issued the Book of Orders (*Orders and Directions*) in 1631:

> Whereas divers good Lawes and Statutes, most necessary for these times, have ... been with great wisedome, pietie, and policie, made and enacted in Parliament ... And whereas we are informed that the defect of the execution of the said good and politique Lawes and Constitutions in that behalfe made, proceedeth espicially from the neglect of duetie in some of Our Justices of the Peace and other Officers, Magistrates, and Ministers of the Peace, within the severall Counties, Cities and townes. (Charles I, 1630, sigs. B3r-B4r)

Accordingly, the Book of Orders attempted to institute regular meetings of Justices of Peace within each county to monitor the activities of all local officials and punish those who were lax in law enforcement (*Orders and Directions*, sigs. E4v-F3r). This attempt to impose central control over the localities was met with differing levels of enthusiasm; 'the Book of Orders ... failed not so much because it was openly resisted as because it was not properly enforced' (Fletcher, 1986, p.57). The criticism of officials in *Orders and Directions* assumes an easy choice between the neglect of duty and enforcement of law, failing to take account of local circumstances:

> [T]he Book presupposed a common pattern of priorities, a national agenda for magisterial effort. Justices of Peace, however, believed they knew their own counties, the needs of their countrymen and the most glaring deficiencies of their subordinates better than anyone in London. (Fletcher, 1986, p.57)

The local law enforcers acted in what they saw as the best interests of their county, and, as with the collection of the forced loan and ship money, problems arose when this conflicted with central government's policies and directions. For example, the forced acceptance of apprentices ordered in 1618 and 1627, and restated in *Orders and Directions*, proved difficult in the 1630s; '[t]he matter had been allowed to lapse for so long that in some areas it was not easy all of a sudden to find enough suitable masters for large numbers of boys and girls' (Fletcher, 1986, p.216).

The disruption caused by attempts to enforce apprenticeship would cause greater disorder than the unemployed youth.

Justices' flexibility regarding the opening and licensing of alehouses too paid attention to the sustained peace of the area rather than the strict enforcement of central legislation. On one hand, justices had to acknowledge the interests of local suppliers and brewers, the wishes of their clerks who received fees for awarding licenses, and the demands of local inhabitants for a place to drink and socialise (Fletcher, 1986, p.247); on the other, was the tightening of alehouse regulation determined by central government (to whom the justice was ultimately, if haphazardly, answerable). This particular balance of interests can be seen in Thomas Nabbes's Justice, Sir Generous Worthy, in *Covent Garden*, as he arrives at an alehouse:

> Sir Gen.: Ha! My sonne here; and Mr *Ierker*!
>   I came i'th' person of authoritie,
>   Invited by your noise. But put that off,
>   Out of my love borne to the generall good,
>   I doe advise you to be temperate:
>   That the faire hope conceiv'd of growing virtues
>   Might not be lost.
>   (*Covent Garden*, sig. H1v)

Sir Generous sees no need to be heavy handed with his judicial authority in this case, but nevertheless, the mention of it suggests a warning to those present that they are in breech of regulations. His reasoning, 'Out of my love borne to the generall good', could relate to the previous phrase (he has put off his authority because of his love for the general good), or to that following (out of concern for their good, he advises temperance). Either way, his concern for the local community overrides the strict enforcement of law. It is also worth pausing here to discuss the drinkers' response:

> Ierk[er]: Sir, we are Gentlemen; and by that priviledge
>   Though we submit to politique Government
>   In publique things may be our owne law-makers
>   In morall life. If we offend the law
>   The law may punish us; which onely strives
>   To take away excess, not the necessity
>   Or use of what's indifferent, and is made
>   Or good or bad by'ts use.
>   (*Covent Garden*, sig. H1v)

Jerker takes the interference as an affront to his gentlemanly honour and privilege to regulate his own moral behaviour. Perhaps, then, Nabbes suggests that alcohol consumption should not be a matter for law, particularly amongst gentlemen. Butler places emphasis on the drinkers' gentlemanly status, suggesting that the play presents gentlemen as being capable of governing themselves, especially in their personal lives, arguing that in 'Nabbes's Covent Garden, an independently minded gentry indignantly criticise the rigours of a repressive authority' (1984, p.151). Whilst this is true, to an extent, it does not take account of Sir Generous's mediation of these stricter laws, and indeed, the fact that Sir Generous is also a gentleman. His decision not to press his authority at the alehouse is not specifically related to the drinkers' gentlemanly status, or to the fact that one of them is his son, but rather for the 'generall good'. It is important to note that Jerker does not claim a 'privilege' for gentlemen above the law in its appropriate jurisdiction ('If we offend the law / The law may punish us'). This does, of course, raise questions as to what the law should regulate and who should make these decisions, which are not resolved in the play. The scene ends with Sir Generous buying wine from the vintner, admonishing him to 'keepe good orders' (*Covent Garden*, sig. H3r), and inviting all of the gentlemen to his house for dinner in a demonstration of ideal gentlemanly hospitality, a significant part of the establishment and maintenance of good order.[19] This complex set of relations between centre and locality, officer and local community forms the background, and even, I would argue, the subject, of Jonson's *A Tale of a Tub*.[20]

The setting of *A Tale of a Tub* is Valentine's Day in Finsbury Hundred. The Marian or Elizabethan period setting of the play suggests a deliberate nostalgia, but the problems of law and order presented are, as Julie Sanders suggests, those of a 1630s Caroline community (1997, p.456).[21] The action of the play takes place in Finsbury and other specifically named places which are not quite in London, but not quite far enough away to be essentially provincial. Sanders argues that Finsbury Hundred is in an 'uncomfortable proximity to London', and this contributes to the undercurrent of political tension in the play (1997, p.459).[22] Whilst I do not wish to disagree with her argument, I believe the play's geography – being not quite inside London, and not quite outside it – also emphasises the 'in between' central and provincial status of local law officers which I have already established, and encourages such a reading of the play's High Constable Toby Turf.

Turf has arranged the marriage of his daughter Audrey to John Clay, through the traditional Valentine's Day marriage lottery during which Turf and his wife

---

[19] See also Heywood and Brome's *Late Lancashire Witches* (1634) where the hospitality of the local gentleman is the only stable factor in the disorder caused by the witches, and Shirley's *Lady of Pleasure* in which the balance between privilege and hospitality suggested in Nabbes's scene between the alehouse gallants and Sir Generous is given a more direct contrast in the positions of Bornwell, who used to be renowned for his hospitality in the country, and his wife who now claims privilege in the city.

[20] Lorna Hutson has also recently commented on the play's exploration of the relationship between local officials and central authority in this play (2010, pp.226–7).

[21] For a discussion of the potential explanations of the pre-Stuart setting, see Butler (1990, pp.5, 26), (1992b, pp.180, 183–4).

[22] Sanders associates this with the radicalism of Essex in the period discussed by Keith Wrightson in 'Two Concepts of Order', and the autonomous stance near-London communities adopted on political issues (1997, p.459).

were married 30 years before. The choice of husband seems to have involved the whole community as 'All the wise o'th' hundred' (all local officials: the petty constable, headborough and thirdborough) are met at Turf's house 'to conclude in Counsell, / A Husband, or a Make for Mrs Awdrey' (*Tale of a Tub*, sigs. J3r-v).[23] Thus the spirit of community and neighbourliness of the hundred under Turf's authority is illustrated by the festive gathering of Audrey's wedding. However, the wedding is consistently delayed, and the festivities postponed, whilst Turf goes about the business required of him by his position. Leah Marcus argues that Audrey's marriage to Pol-Martin at the end of the play presents the triumph of festival (evident in the Valentine's Day ritual) which local officials and dignitaries seek to suppress through imposition of various forms of law, suggesting that what is at stake in the play is festival versus law, making the play a celebration of Charles I's reissue of the Book of Sports in 1633 (1986, pp.133, 107). However, the interferences with the wedding are not planned, ultimately, to prevent the festivities taking place, but to allow a change of groom. The wedding is, rather, the demonstration of a peaceful neighbourliness which is disturbed by the intervention of authorities from outside the community for their own gain. What disturbs the peace of this village is, as Butler argues, the 'interference of the external world of law into the communal peace of the hundred' (1990, p.21).

The first demand on Turf is created by a dispute between Hannibal (Ball) Puppy (Turf's man) and Basket Hilts (Squire Tub's Governor) who has come, sent by Squire Tub, to disrupt the festivities. Turf intervenes, asserting the origin of his authority:

> Turf: I charge you in the Queenes name, keepe the peace.
>
> Hilts: Tell me o' no Queene, or *Keysar*: I must have
>   A legge, or a hanch of him, ere I goe.
>
> Medlay: But zir,
>   You must obey the Queenes high Officers.
>
> Hilts: Why must I, Good-man *Must*?
>
> Medlay: You must, an' you wull.
>   (*Tub*, sig. K4v)

The necessity of obedience to local officials and the authorities they represent is thus asserted as the first plot to delay the wedding begins. There is an equation of the queen's power with the constable's, and there is no immediate conflict in these authorities. Hilts's reference to 'Keysar' here, however, draws attention to an almost incidental tale of a Roman constable that Scriben, Medlay and Turf later discuss:

---

[23]   *A Tale of a Tub* will be abbreviated to *Tub* in subsequent references.

Scriben:	I can tell you

A thousand, of great *Pompei, Caesar, Trajan,*
All the high Constables there.

Turf:	That was their place:

There were no more.

Scriben:	*Dictator*, and high Constable

Were both the same.

Medlay:	High constable was more, tho'!

He laid *Dick*: *Tator* by the heeles.

Pan:	*Dick*: *Tator*!

H' was one o' the Waights o' the Citie. I ha' read o' hun.
(*Tub*, sig. M4v)

On the surface, this comic interchange highlights the rustic simplicity of the provincial officials Medlay and To-Pan, who believe Dick Tator was a real person. However, Scriben and Turf's comments have a more serious political undertone. In suggesting that the constable and the dictator were the same in ancient Rome, Scriben elevates the lowly constable to the status of imperial power, leading Sanders to infer an oblique criticism of Charles's government:

> [W]as it so far a leap of the imagination to consider that in 1633 there was a real person who used the title of Caesar in order to aggrandize his position rhetorically, and that very possibly his attempt to rule without Parliament came close to constituting a form of dictatorship? (1997, p.459)

However, Scriben's constable does not merely assume imperial status in their conversation, but goes beyond it, placing 'Dick Tator' in the stocks (laying Dick Taytor 'by the heels'). In the provincial Hundreds, the High Constable is the highest local authority; kingly dictation will receive little favour. It is perhaps worth noting at this point that Turf is also capable of discoursing 'of the great Charty' (Magna Charta) to his subordinates (*Tub*, sig. I4v). Thus divisions begin to appear in the implied unity of local and central authority that was suggested in Turf's command to keep the peace in the 'Queenes name'. That the discussion about Dick Tator comes shortly after Turf's claim that he will 'triumph over this Justice, as becomes a Constable' (that is, foil Justice Preamble's plans to marry Audrey) suggests that these divisions affect all levels of the local authority judicial hierarchy.

Turf does eventually manage to impose order on the near-brawling Puppy and Hilts, pledging his own authority as promise of punishment for the offender (Puppy): 'For him, / On my authority, he shall lie by the heeles'. Puppy appeals to Turf's clerk (Clench) to intercede so that he will not have to miss the wedding, but Turf is adamant that 'If he lye not by the heeles, / Ile lie there for 'hun' implying an absolute determination to see justice done (*Tub*, sig. K4v). The demands of justice and the wedding festivities can both be met as Hilts drops his charge, and Turf insists that Puppy will make amends. As soon as this potential obstacle to the festivities is overcome though, Hilts presents a further problem for Turf, charging him to raise hue and cry to find robbers who, he falsely claims, attacked him and his captain, Captain Thumbs (in fact this is a ruse to delay the wedding so that Squire Tub can steal Audrey away, and Thumbs is really Chanon Hugh in disguise). Turf is immediately torn between community life epitomised in the wedding plans and doing his duty:

> Turf: As Fortune mend me, now, or any office
> Of a thousand pound, if I know what to zay,
> Would I were dead, or vaire hang'd up at *Tiburne*
> If I doe know what course to take, or how
> To turne my selfe, just at this time too, now,
> My Daughter is to be married: Ile but goe
> To *Pancridge* Church, hard by, and returne instantly,
> And all my Neighbour-hood shall goe about it.
>
> Hilts: Tut, *Pancridge* me no *Pancridge*, if you let it
> Slip, you will answer it, and your Cap be of wooll;
> Therefore take heed, you'll feele the smart else, Constable.
> (*Tub*, sigs. L1r-L1v)

Hilts's assertion that the constable will have to answer if the hue and cry is not raised immediately is no empty threat; village constables were often held responsible for the value of stolen items, or indeed for the ship money they were commissioned to collect on behalf of the sheriff. Turf himself acknowledges this: 'shud we leave the zearch / I am in danger, to reburse as much / As he was rob'd on; I and pay his hurts' (*Tub*, sig. M1v).

In an example of the ways in which local government hierarchy was supposed to function (in accordance with the Book of Orders) Turf is later brought before Justice Preamble to answer both dropping the hue and cry and hiding Clay, who is accused of the robbery. However, this hearing illustrates how open the system is to corruption, as Preamble uses it to extort money from Turf. Preamble's choice of language at this meeting contributes to the interplay of law, order and community in the play:

> Pre: I cannot choose but grieve a Soldiers losse:
> And I am sory too for your neglect,
> Being my neighbour; this is all I object.
>
> Hug[h]: This is not all; I can alledge far more
>   …
>   Let not neighbour-hood
> Make him secure, or stand on priviledge.
> (*Tub*, sig. N3r)

Preamble's seeming concern that his neighbour should be so remiss plays on Turf's own understanding of his position in society, but is, in fact, merely a cover for Preamble's plot against Turf to keep him away from the church and his daughter. He uses the same feigned rhetoric of neighbourliness during his engineered 'arrest' of Squire Tub (*Tub*, sig. L4r). Preamble's obsequious response to Captain Thums's (Chanon Hugh) concern, 'Sir, I dare use no partiality' (*Tub*, sig. N3r), contrasts starkly with Turf's sincere determination justifying his arrest of his intended son-in-law: 'I will doe mine office, / An' he were my owne begotten a thousand times' (*Tub*, sig. L2r). Preamble again uses this language of community to pretend a favour to Turf, asking Captain Thums, 'then Ile pray you, 'cause he is my neighbour, / To take a hundred pound, and give him day' (*Tub*, sig. N4r). As an abuse of the discourse of neighbourliness which maintained peace in the provinces, this could be seen as representative of the Crown's (mis)use of the local and national loyalties of its officers to make central policy seem less incompatible with the wishes of the community.[24] That Preamble intends to take this money himself is further evidence of the exploitation of provincial officers for the personal gain of higher authorities.

Preamble's plans to disrupt Audrey's wedding to Squire Tub involve the introduction of a third layer of authority into the province. He arranges for his Clerk, Miles Metaphor, to dress as a pursuivant to arrest Tub:

> Pre: Ha you acquaintance with him [a pursuivant]
> To borrow his coat an houre?
>
> Hugh: Or but his badge,
> 'Twill serve: A little thing he weares on his brest.
>
> Pre: His coat, I say, is of more authority:
> Borrow his coat for an houre. I doe love
> To doe all things compleately, Chanon *Hugh*;
> Borrow his coat, *Miles Metaphor*, or nothing.
> (*Tub*, sig. K2r)

Butler suggests that, throughout, the play dwells on the way authority lies in the signs of office rather than the person of the office holder, arguing that this presents a failure of local authority (1990, p.23). However, here it is the agent of central authority who needs to command respect through his dress. The badge of their office means less, according to Justice Preamble, than the clothes central officials wear which demonstrate their higher status. Turf, on the other hand, seems to be highly respected in the community, at least by his inferiors ('A right good man!' (*Tub*, sig. K4r)), and his clothing is not mentioned. If this does suggest a failure of authority in the provinces, then, it lies, more subversively, with the central

---

[24] cf. Lake (1981, p.57).

authorities not the local. Metaphor's pursuivant adds a higher authority to which the Justice must defer:

> Pre: It is a warrant,
>   In speciall from the Councell, and commands
>   Your personall appearance. Sir, your weapon
>   I must require: And then deliver you
>   A Prisoner to this officer, Squire *Tub*.
>   (*Tub*, sig. L4r)

Personally making Tub's arrest 'I' the Queenes Majesties name, and all the Councels' (*Tub*, sig. L4r), the pursuivant provides a direct link between Whitehall and the province, and as Butler argues, presents the direct incursion of the 'arm of princely government' into the locality (1992b, p.181). Once again the interference of authority and imposition of law from outside the Hundred causes delay to Audrey's wedding, and she is snatched away by Justice Preamble.

    Although Preamble's claims of neighbourhood and community are bogus, the other local officials attempt more carefully to balance upholding the law with causing as little disruption to the community as possible. During the officers' search for criminals, Medlay voices concerns: 'Masters, take heed, let's not vind too many: /One's enough to stay the Hang-mans stomack' (*Tub*, sig. M1r). The occasional prosecution is enough to show central authority their willingness to enforce law without being over-officious. Turf himself genuinely struggles to negotiate the demands of the community (Audrey's wedding) and the demands of his position:

> Turf: Were never honest Varmers thus perplext.
>   …
>
> Turf: Hath Justice *Bramble* got my daughter *Awdrey*?
>   A little while, shall he enjoy her, zure.
>   But O the *Huy* and *Cry*! That hinders me:
>   I must pursue that, or neglect my journey:
>   Ile ene leave all: and with the patient Asse,
>   The over-laden Asse, throw off my burden,
>   And cast mine office …
>   … Ile no more High Constables.
>   (*Tub*, sig. M2v)

On discovering Preamble's plot, Turf can no longer negotiate his divided loyalties, and chooses to abandon his post to salvage the wedding. His plaintive comment about 'honest Varmers' reminds the audience that High Constables were not professional officials; rather, they were local yeoman farmers, who took on the post in addition to their usual occupation. Whilst his references to the overburdened ass indicate the pressure Turf is under, to the theatre audience who know that the robbery is a ruse, the repetition of 'asse' also hints that the High Constable's superiors are using their legal authority 'to make and ass out of him'. Turf's problem of pursuing Hue and Cry or preventing Preamble's seduction of Audrey is not resolved, but dissolved: Squire Tub tells Turf that the robbery was a trick concocted by Preamble to seize Audrey. Although Tub's explanation is not quite the truth (Clay's guilt was his plot) it does allow Turf to resume his post, 'I take my office back: and my authority/ ... Neighbours, I am / High Constable againe' (*Tub*, sig. M3r). Turf's distinction between his office and authority acknowledges that the office itself does not necessarily give authority, but it also emphasises Turf's own authority in his community. It seems, however, that Tub's revelations are not sufficient to dispel Turf's concerns:

> The Huy, and Cry, was merely counterfeit:
> The rather may you judge it to be such,
> Because the Bride-groome, was describ'd to be
> One of the theeves, first i'the velonie.
> Which, how farre 'tis from him, your selves may guesse.
> (*Tub*, sigs. M2v-M3r)

Tub uses the High Constable's knowledge of members of the local community to convince him to drop the hue and cry and prevent the wedding. This, of course, is in his own interests, not for Turf, and once again plays on the constable's loyalty to, and knowledge of, the community for personal gain.

Finally, Turf's conflicts of loyalty in this situation are resolved as Audrey marries Pol-Marten, Lady Tub's usher. Marcus reads this as evidence that 'the irrepressible energies of festival operate outside even its own mechanisms for containment – but no harm is done' (1986, p.133). However, the happy ending is, as Sanders argues, only a veneer (1997, p.443). The tension between the strict enforcement of law and the community activities is only dispelled because all responsibility is taken from Turf. Audrey's marriage takes place without the knowledge of any of the local officials, and none of the demands on him as High Constable are legitimate: the robbery was indeed a ruse, cancelling any need to prosecute Clay, or lose his own money in restitution. The fragility of this veneer is easily seen:

> Medlay: What of Iohn Clay, Ball Puppy?
>
> Puppy: He hath lost –
>
> Medlay: His life for velonie?
>
> Puppy: No, his wife by villanie.
>   (*Tub*, sig. M2v)

The urgency of Medlay's questioning and potential severity of the reply is dissolved in the comic juxtaposition of the punishment for crime and the trickery of his rivals. But that these outcomes are interchangeable, emphasised by the close similarity of 'life'/'wife' and 'velonie'/'villanie', presents the serious implications of the misuse of law.

Unusually, the play provides regular summaries of the action. Metaphor, Turf and Audrey (*Tub*, sigs. L4v-M1r, M1r and M4v respectively) all give summaries of the plot so far, which explain the changes of the groom for Audrey, and thus emphasise the contrast between the good of the community and the attempted personal gain of the Justice and Squire. The most detailed of these, however, is Medlay's masque commissioned by Squire Tub which concludes the play. The masque shifts the focus from an examination of the local to the central. Lady Tub's welcome to her 'neighbours', 'Now doth Totten-Hall / Shew like a Court' (*Tub*, sig. Q1r), aligns the Tubs firmly with the royal court rather than the local men. Their position as owners of a saltpeter mine confirms this association, and is a further example of the ways in which the centre is seen to exploit the provinces.[25] The representation of the planning and performance of the masque might go some way to explain why the play was not liked at court as Medlay is a sharply satiric caricature of Inigo Jones (Butler, 1992b, p.179). However, what the masque repeats from the play is the self-interest of those representative of central government (the Tubs and Preamble) and their abuse of legal mechanisms and authority by which Charles sought to reform law enforcement in provinces, that is, presentments to justices and active local gentry.

The implications of corruption amongst the local justices and the presentation of the imposition of central law in the provinces as unpopular and disruptive would be enough to create some discomfort at the court which sought to tighten control over localities. The problems caused by the interference of central authority in the provinces cannot be masked (masqued?) by celebratory performances (particularly, Jonson might suggest, if they lack his invention over Jones's designs), nor are they, as Butler suggests they are, 'marginalized, diffused or transcended' (1990, p.24) in the play. The manipulation of law and legal authority for personal ends in *A Tale of a Tub* critiques the Caroline court's self-interested interventions in the provinces (such as ship money and saltpeter). Importantly, it is these abuses of law and authority by those in positions higher and more central than his own that cause the divided loyalties of the High Constable, and make his task of keeping order in the provinces impossible. Whilst the play does what its prologue denies, in pretending 'State affairs', these do indeed 'shew what different things / The Cotes of Clownes, are from the Courts of Kings' (*Tub*, sig. I2v), and emphasises that these entities are not, and should not be the same.

---

[25] Saltpeter (used in gunpowder) was a contentious issue in the 1630s, as searches which were often destructive were conducted to collect hidden stores from the provinces. Central government gained at the expense of the localities (Sanders, 1997, pp.461–2).

Fragmented Authority: *A Joviall Crew*

A Tale of a Tub examines the position of the local constable and the pressures that attempts to centralise local government, particularly through central abuse of law, places upon him in the maintenance of order. The problems presented, however, are specific to the High Constable; there is little exploration of the wider picture, that is, the effect on the people and the country. Richard Brome's *A Joviall Crew* continues to advocate the mediation of the strict imposition of central law in the provinces but in doing this, I will argue, illustrates a fragmentation of authority in the polarisation of the royal court and the landowning gentry and, further, what causes, and is at stake through, this division.

The countryside authority in this play is embodied in the figure of Oldrents, who at the beginning of the play is the epitome of the benevolent gentleman landlord. His companion, Hearty, observes:

> Do you not live
> Free, out of Law, or grieving any man?
> Are you not th'onely rich man lives un-envied?
> Have you not all the praises of the *Rich*,
> And prayers of the *Poor*? Did ever any
> Servant, or Hireling, Neighbour, Kindred curse you,
> Or with one minute shorten'd of your life?
> Have you one grudging Tenant? will they not all
> Fight for you? Do they not teach their Children
> And make'em too, pray for you morn and evening,
> And in their Graces too, as duly as
> For King and Realme? The innocent things would think
> They ought not eat else.
> (*Joviall Crew*, sig. B2r-B2v)

That Oldrents can be seen as a provincial governor is suggested in the comparison made here between Oldrents and the king. As his name suggests, Oldrents represents the traditional landowning gentry, helping his tenants and exercising gentlemanly hospitality.[26] His hospitality extends to friends and strangers as well as the crew of beggars he accommodates in his barn, and in contrast with those men raised to a higher status through the purchase of titles or kingly favour, his wealth and status too are traditional, as Randall later explains that Oldrents's ancestors have held that house for more than 300 years (*Joviall Crew*, sig. I4r). Throughout the play, Oldrents's servants also give testimony to their happiness and his generosity. The butler claims that 'my Master, for his Hospitality to Gentlemen, his Charity to the Poor, and his bounty to his Servants, has not his Peer in the Kingdom' and Randall, the bailiff, comments that 'we, his Servants, live as merrily under him; and all do thrive' (*Joviall Crew*, sig. K2r, K1r).

---

[26] Sanders notes that charging old rents would indeed be kind to his tenants, as rental costs for farmlands increased threefold between 1600 and 1688 (2002a, p.4 n.12).

Oldrents's generosity and hospitality is not enjoyed by all those it affects, however; his daughters feel they suffer rather than enjoy it, claiming that the beggars are: 'Happier than we I'm sure, that are pent up and tied by the nose to the continual steam of hot Hospitality, here in our Father's house, when [the beggars] have their Aire at pleasure in all variety' (*Joviall Crew*, sig. D2r). This leads to a discussion of liberty between the ladies and their beaux:

> Hilliard: Why Ladies, you have liberty enough; or may take what you please.

> Meriel: Yes, in our Father's Rule and Government, or by his allowance. What's that to absolute freedom such as the very Beggars have; to feast and revel here today, and yonder to morrow ... ther's Liberty! (*Joviall Crew*, sig. D2r)

This idealisation of the beggars' community leads these young people to run away and join them for a short time. The reference to 'Rule and Government' reinforces Oldrents's position as a local governor, and invites comparison with the King, particularly as the vocabulary of 'absolutism' is introduced. However, it is clear throughout the play that Oldrents's government is not absolute – he allows Springlove to make his own choice whether he goes begging: 'My love shall give thy will preheminence; / And leave th'effect to Time and Providence' (*Joviall Crew*, sig. C1r) – and that his government is offered, as Sanders argues, in contrast with Charles's personal rule (Sanders, 2002a, p.5).

This implied contrast is confirmed by the other figure of authority in the play, Justice Clack, who embodies absolute authority. Unlike Oldrents's daughters' relative freedom to choose their husbands, Clack has arranged a marriage for his ward Amie, from which she is running when she meets the crew of beggars. In this Amie chose, Clack complains, 'rather to disobey me, than to displease her self. Wherein (altho' she did not altogether transgresse the Law) she did both offend and prejudice me, an Instrument; nay I may say, a Pillar thereof' (*Joviall Crew*, sig. M3r). This identification of himself with the law suggests an analogy with Charles's prerogative rule, emphasised when Clack asserts that he is 'a Justice of the *Kings*' rather than the usual Justice of the *Peace* (in fact, this comes immediately after Clack tells Martin to 'Hold [his] *own* peace') (*Joviall Crew*, sig. M3v, my emphases). In respect of royal prerogative, it is also significant that Amie is Clack's Ward, not his daughter, as wardship provided a significant amount of extra-parliamentary (prerogative) funding for the king.[27] Thus royal absolutism once again finds its way into the provinces. That Clack's son Oliver has travelled

---

[27]   At the end of James's reign, wardship was worth approximately £40,000 a year to the crown, by 1637 this was worth £62,000 and by 1640, £76,000. It was also a significant source of tension between the King and the landowners, whose wealth suffered because of it (Lockyer, 1999, pp.236, 38). Amie's complaint that in their 'inforc'd Matches' wards are often 'sold into Captivitie' (*Joviall Crew*, sig. I3r) is then not merely a comment on forced marriage, but also on the value of wardships.

from London to Amie's wedding (*Joviall Crew*, sig. H1v) cements his links with central authority.

Clack and Oldrents are also compared in terms of their hospitality. Whilst Oldrents's hospitality, as I have already illustrated, is emphasised throughout the play, Clack is shown to be particularly lacking in this respect, as Randall comments:

> Sir, my Master sends you word, and plainly, that without your Company, your Entertainment stinks. He has commanded me saddle his Nags, and away to night. If you come not at once, twice, thrice, he's gone presently, before Supper; He'll finde an Host at an Inne worth a hundred o' you. (*Joviall Crew*, sigs. N1r-N1v)

Oldrents's complaining cannot merely be explained by his desire for an excess of joviality, entered upon when his daughters ran away to join the beggars; Clack himself admits that his guests are 'scarce welcome', and drinks all of his good wine himself to avoid sharing it with his visitors (*Joviall Crew*, sigs. N1r, N3v). Far from endeavouring to maintain peace and order in the countryside through gentlemanly hospitality and neighbourly mediation – as is the case with Oldrents and Hearty to whom Oliver takes Amie's affianced in complaint when she runs away – there is, then an emphatic selfishness to absolute, prerogative rule.

Clack's dealings with Martin, the clerk who helped Amie flee her wedding, emphasise the arbitrariness of his absolutism: 'Have I not born with thee, to speak all thou pleasest in thy defence? Have I not broke mine own Rule, which is to punish before I examine; and so have the Law the surer o'my side?' (*Joviall Crew*, sig. M3v). The notion of acting without law in order to stay on the right side of it should now be familiar from Brome's *The Queen and Concubine*; it is a recurring idea in Caroline drama. Constable Busie's advice to the watch in *Wit in a Constable* also centres on this:

> You shall be sure to keep the peace; that is,
> If any quarrell, be ith' streets, sit still, and keepe
> Your rusty Bills from blood-shed; and as't began
> So let it end …
> …
> Next, if a thiefe chance to passe through your watch,
> Let him depart in peace; for should you stay him,
> To purchase his redemption he'le impart
> Some of his stolne goods, and you're apt to take them,
> Which makes you accessory to his theft,
> And so fit food for Tiburne.
> (*Wit in a Constable*, sigs. G4v-H1r)

Whereas in *The Queen and Concubine*, this idea was used to highlight the dangers of kingly disregard for law, and here in *Wit in a Constable* to suggest local law officers' susceptibility to corruption (and perhaps Busie's desire to avoid extra work as the Watch would have to present their prisoners to him), what is presented in *A Joviall Crew*'s use of this idea is a deliberate neglect of law and procedure in order to satisfy Clack's desire to punish. Access to fair and reasonable local justice has been denied through the imposition of central law, represented by the Justice, over and above the negotiation of law through the hospitality of local gentry. Clack, then, comes to embody the summation of the fears of arbitrary rule, the misapplication of law and abuse of authority.

Clack's self-seeking, arbitrary 'justice' is confirmed in his refusal to let Sentwell tell him of the beggars' arrest:

> I can inform my self, Sir, by your looks. I have taken a hundred Examinations i'
> my daies of Fellons, and other Offendors, out of their very Countenances; and
> wrote 'em down *verbatim*, to what they would have said. I am sure it has serv'd
> to hang some of 'em, and whip the rest. (*Joviall Crew*, sigs. M3v-M4r)

This inclination to judge before examination, and punish without reason is far from the ideal local justice described in Dalton's *The Countrey Justice*. Clack is guilty of 'Presumption' ('when without Law (or other sufficient rule or warrant) they (presuming of their owne wits) proceed according to their owne wills and affections') and 'Precipitation, or too much rashnesse; when they proceed hastily without due examination and consideration of the fact', both of which are listed as ways justice can be perverted by local officers (Dalton, 1635, p.7). This indiscriminate hanging and whipping also harks back to the strict imposition of central law in the provinces through the Book of Orders, regardless of the circumstances of the locality or the offender. Indeed, it is over the possible punishment of beggars that Clack and Oldrents most obviously disagree. Hearty's comment 'Pray let 'em play their Play: the Justice will not hinder 'em, you see; he's asleep' (*Joviall Crew*, sig. O1v) is a further acknowledgment of the different forms of order (provincial and central) whereby the activities of the village community can, under the eyes of Oldrents, continue whilst central law 'sleeps'. It should be noted that under the law, travelling players were classed as vagrants, and theoretically should be punished as such; they would be, as we are told twice in the play, 'well whipt and set to work, if [they] were duly and truly serv'd' for their vagrancy (*Joviall Crew*, sig. G4r), and Justice Clack is itching to 'put 'em in Stocks, and set 'em up to the Whipping-post' (*Joviall Crew*, sig. M4v). Clack agrees, however, to allow them to put on their play to entertain his visitors, on the understanding that: 'They are upon Purgation. If they can present any thing to please you [Oldrents], they may escape the Law; that is (*a hay*) If not, to morrow, Gentlemen, shall be acted, *Abuses stript and whipt*, among 'em' (*Joviall Crew*, sig. N3v). To prevent this, Oldrents is determined 'rather than they shall suffer, I will be pleas'd, let 'em Play their worst' (*Joviall Crew*, sig. N4v). That Hearty must remind his friend of this on several occasions during the performance suggests a deliberate (if well-meaning) stubbornness on Oldrents's part to thwart Clack's plans. Where central authority may be too rigid, provincial authorities compensate through leniency.

As it is the beggar crew that highlights the differences between Clack and Oldrents, it is important to understand what they represent. The children from both houses come to the beggars for their apparent liberty from absolutism (benevolent or cruelly arbitrary). Oldrents's daughters are encouraged in this by Springlove in order to fulfil benignly a prophecy given to their father by a beggar fortune-teller that his children would be beggars. They quickly come to realise that the beggars' 'freedom' is not as idyllic as they had supposed, as they have to find food and shelter, and are always potentially subject to punishment or assault by those of higher status: Vincent and Hilliard are whipped, and Rachel and Meriel are in danger of rape by Clack's son, Oliver (a further instance of the abuse of authority and exploitation of the provinces by the centre noted in *A Tale of a Tub*). Whether these liberties are what the children expected, however, is irrelevant to the idea that Clack and Oldrents disagree on the treatment of liberties of the subject. Aside from the realistic representation of a beggar's life, which does indeed cause conflict between Oldrents and Clack as representatives of different kinds of order, the '*Beggars* Commonwealth' (*Joviall Crew*, sig. E3r) presents an alternative society free from absolute rule.[28] Thus, whilst presenting the cause of contention, the beggars also present a possible solution. They are:

> The onely Freemen of a Common-wealth
> Free above *Scot-Free*; that observe no Law,
> Obey no Governour, use no Religion,
> But what they draw from their own ancient custom,
> Or constitute themselves, yet are no Rebels.
> (*Joviall Crew*, sig. E1r)

Although the beggars acknowledge Springlove as their King, they are free of the impositions of an absolute monarch as the commonwealth of beggars is ruled by customary law (common law?) or those they 'constitute themselves' (parliamentary statute?). Insisting that the beggars are not rebels despite living in this way, the play suggests a position between the extremes of deliberately obstructive country gentry and the absolutist monarch, whereby liberty can be maintained under a monarch with the rule of common law through parliament. The date of the play, after the failed short Parliament of 1640 and the calling of the long Parliament later that year, emphasises the need for such a conciliatory position.

As interlopers into the beggars' kingdom, Vincent, Hilliard, Meriel and Rachel are well placed to compare the beggars' liberties with political subjection, and their concerns are particular to Charles's reign:

> Vincent: With them there is no Grievance or Perplexity;
> No fear of war, or State Disturbances.
> No Alteration in a Common-wealth,
> Or Innovation shakes a Thought of theirs.
> ...

---

[28]   For a discussion of *A Joviall Crew* as one of several plays of this time presenting an alternative society, see Sanders (2002a, *passim*).

> Hilliard: We have no fear of lessening our Estates;
>   Nor any grudge with us (without Taxation)
>   To lend or give upon command, the whole
>   Strength of our Wealth for the publick Benefit:
>   While some, that are held rich in their Abundance,
>   (Which is their great Misery, indeed) will see
>   Rather a generall ruine upon all,
>   Then give a Scruple to prevent the Fall.
>   (*Joviall Crew*, sigs. L3r-L3v)

Vincent's observations describe a settled, peaceful state, without fear of war or rebellion or religious upheaval ('innovation'). The recent Scottish wars, personal rule and dissolved Parliaments suggest these are all fears relevant to a Caroline gentleman, and Hilliard's description of the beggars' financial freedoms also picks up this theme. The reference to lending or giving on command evokes the collection of the forced loan and ship money, and Hilliard's parenthetical 'without taxation' highlights the potential illegitimacy of such Crown demands. Nevertheless, he says, the beggars are unconcerned about them, whereas the wealthy are unprepared to contribute, regardless of the political consequences. Once again the position of the King and his wealthier subjects are set in opposition. In a political debate which essentially involves the legal rights of subjects over their own property versus the rights of the king, the beggars are free from the fears caused by these commands because they have no estate to lose. Nevertheless, whilst acknowledging the fears of those affected by Charles's laws, Hilliard's comment also notes the necessity of compliance to prevent 'general ruine', and suggests a stubbornness rather than inability in those unwilling to do so who allow a 'scruple' to prevent them. Thus, the debate is brought to centre upon the good of the commonwealth, not the rights of the individual subject or king. Polarising the prerogative position of the king ('without taxation') and the objections of the landowners ('scruple') will bring about this ruin. Only by creating compromise will the situation be rectified.

Although Hilliard leaves his listeners to speculate what the threatened 'general ruine' is, the masque written by the beggar-poet, Scribble, for the wedding of the two old beggars almost immediately ends this speculation:

> Poet: I would have the *Country*, the *City*, and the *Court*, be at great variance for *Superiority*. Then would I have *Divinity* and *Law* stretch their wide throats to appease and reconcile them: Then would I have the *Souldier* cudgel them all together, and overtop them all. (*Joviall Crew*, sig. M1v)

This is a very bleak outlook for the future; the fragmentation of the country in the division of court, city and country will become irreparable without immediate compromise. The future is not so bleak for the beggars in this masque, however, who will 'at last, overcome the *Souldier*; and bring them all to *Beggars-Hall*' (*Joviall Crew*, sig. M1v). At this point the beggars resume their position as an idealised, free, apolitical entity. Only those who have not been involved in the political wrangling for 'superiority' will emerge from it undamaged.

In disagreeing over their approach to the legal status and potential punishment of 'Statute *Beggars*' (*Joviall Crew*, sig. E1r), Clack and Oldrents represent a fragmentation of authority, caused by a split between the centre and the provinces in the dissolution of the 1640 Parliament. This fragmentation can only begin to be repaired by attention to the type of political society the same beggars represent. This compromise (monarchy ruling with parliament and in accordance with common law suggested in Springlove's beggar society) facilitates a happy ending to the play, bringing the Justice and landlord to a greater accommodation between their previously polarised positions. Oldrents's moral/legal superiority is undermined through the Patrico's disclosure that he has an illegitimate son (Springlove) by a beggar woman, and the revelation of Oldrents's ancestor's own illegitimate legal manoeuvrings to establish his position in society goes some way to levelling him with Clack's manoeuvrings. Clack, too, is brought to relax his hold over county governance, providing entertainment for his guests and 'sleeping' whilst the beggars put on their play: 'Law and Justice shall sleep, and Mirth and good Fellowship ride a *Circuit* here to night' (*Joviall Crew*, sig. N3r). Neither position in itself is particularly satisfactory: the landowner is no longer ideal, and Clack only permits this license because he is drunk. The end of the play is not unreserved in its hope for the future. However, through the marriage of Springlove and Amie (Oldrents's and Clack's children) who meet at the beggars' commonwealth which is physically and metaphorically in the space between Oldrents's and Clack's estates, a reconciliation of these polarised positions is initiated.

* * *

On the Caroline stage, the Justice of the Peace, as a figure appointed by the Crown, is often used to illustrate the spread of central authority in the imposition of impersonal and prerogative law in the provinces, and its implications for local governance. The conflicts of interest between a usually self-seeking Justice and other figures of authority suggest that Charles I's attempts to centralise the government of the localities were not always in their best interests and created an almost impossible predicament for those who attempted to maintain order – if not strictly law – in their area. *The Weeding of Covent Garden*'s Cockbrayne is able to restore order in Covent Garden through the assertion of his authority (when this is for the general good, and recognised by those he governs) because, as the only figure of judicial authority, he faces no conflicting interest and little real challenge. However, *A Tale of a Tub* highlights the difficulties faced by local officials in negotiating community and law, but provides no solution to the problem. As the period progresses, this divide between the demands of central law (increasingly identified with royal prerogative) and provincial life, and between the kingly authorities and local officials, widens on the Caroline stage. Attempts to maintain communication between the centre and the provinces through local landlords is, *A Joviall Crew* suggests, a somewhat doubtful enterprise, and unless a compromise is reached between the centre and the provinces there will be 'generall ruine' (*Joviall Crew*, sig. L3v). In the same way that Charles's attempts to impose a more absolutist regime upon the country was seen to bring about a competing authority in the common law, his attempts to centralise the government of the counties, rather than merely highlighting an existing but unthreatening discrepancy in the attitudes to law of central and local officials, created a fracture in the chain of government from the centre to the localities. This fracture, the Caroline stage suggests, potentially leads to a complete break between the centre and the provinces, and the fragmentation not only of law and government, but society as a whole.

Chapter 5
Theatre of the Courtroom

The trial and subsequent execution of Thomas Wentworth, earl of Strafford, constitutes one of the great set-piece dramas of English history: an intensely theatrical confrontation of one of Charles I's ministers with some of his most determined critics, as well as a curtain-raiser for the confrontations of the Civil War. (Kilburn and Milton, 1996, p.230)

There is an inevitable connection between the theatre and the courtroom; trials are inherently dramatic. The Earl of Strafford's trial was conducted, Terence Kilburn and Anthony Milton argue, in a public arena through printed reports of the prosecution and response (1996, *passim*), as well as in the court of Parliament. However, their opening statement focuses not on the trial itself, or indeed upon the publications surrounding it; rather, they highlight the political context of the trial and the theatricality of the occasion, describing it in explicitly theatrical terms ('set-piece drama', 'theatrical confrontation' and 'curtain raiser'). The interconnection of politics, courtroom and theatre, exemplified in Wentworth's trial, is the focus of this chapter. Trials, real and fictional, are the place of the practical imposition of the directives of the legitimate legal authorities discussed in the previous chapters. Here, I will discuss the different kinds of court, perceptions of them in drama and the courts' relationship with the King, before examining the use of trial scenes in Massinger's *The Roman Actor* (1625), Ford's *The Ladies Triall* (1638), Brome's *The Antipodes* (1638) and Shirley's *The Traytor* (1631), suggesting that these scenes not only provide an opportunity for the staged presentation of the workings of the law and legal authority – or their *perceived* workings – but also that these scenes, and the theatre, provide a forum for the trial of issues of social, cultural and political importance, including the legitimacy of legal authority itself.

Jurisdictions

Although the king held ultimate judicial power, in practice his role as judge was shared amongst his appointed judges who carried the commands of the monarch to the localities, and executed the king's justice on his behalf as discussed in the previous chapter. There were several different law courts during the early Stuart period, from the ecclesiastical courts to the courts of common law (including the Courts of Common Pleas, King's Bench and Assizes), courts of equity (Chancery) and the Conciliar or prerogative courts (Star Chamber, High Court of Admiralty, the Council in the North Parts and the Council in the Principality and the Marches of Wales), and finally the High Court of Parliament.[1]

The Court of Common Pleas had jurisdiction solely over cases concerning commoners, that is, cases of property and land disputes, and therefore not concerning the Crown. Felonies were reserved for the King's Bench and the local Courts of Assize. Although initially an itinerant court following the monarch, the Court of King's Bench finally settled in the early fifteenth century at Westminster Hall.[2] Technically, it only held jurisdiction over Middlesex, but appellants elsewhere could, with permission from the Court of Chancery, move their case to King's Bench if they felt their case would benefit from a less local hearing. The Court of King's Bench held session in the South-East corner of Westminster Hall, with no inner walls separating it from the Court of Chancery in the South-West corner, or from the general activities of 'shopkeepers, cutpurses and sightseers' (Baker, 2002, p.37) in the main body of the Hall. Their positions in Westminster Hall made trials at these courts very public events; although public attendance at trials was not always so large, the authorities expected such a large audience for the trial of the second Earl of Castlehaven in 1631 that a gallery was built in Westminster Hall to raise the official proceeding above the general public, and scaffolds for observers were also constructed (Herrup, 1999, p.50).[3] The theatrical nature of the Castlehaven trial is confirmed in Charles I's order for a full dress rehearsal of the ceremony of the trial, although this was cancelled when there was found to be no precedent for such a rehearsal (Herrup, 1999, p.51). This blending of the social and the legal, of courtroom, theatre and everyday life, is, I will argue, repeated and developed in drama of the period.

All courts were open to the public, and the Courts of Assize made sure that the forms and processes of the common law courtroom were known all over the country. Assizes took place regularly in the localities, conducted by judges from the Bench Courts of Common Pleas and King's Bench. This allowed for gaol delivery and the resolution of cases outside the capabilities of the local Justices of the Peace, as well as providing the opportunity for the dissemination of the policies of central government in the localities. It was this, Cockburn argues, that made the judiciary indistinguishable from the government whose policies they sought to

---

[1]   Unless otherwise indicated, the descriptions of the courts which follow are based upon Baker (2002, chapters 2, 3, 6 and 7), and information on the Assize Courts is based upon Cockburn (1972, pp.1–10, 219–36). I will not be discussing the activities of the ecclesiastical courts, the Court of Admiralty, or the Councils of the North and Marches here. For a discussion of ecclesiastical courts' jurisdiction and practices, see Baker (2002, pp.126–34); for Admiralty and the Councils, see Baker (2002, pp.121–4), and Sharpe (1992, pp.448–56).

[2]   For a detailed description of the development of King's Bench up to the fifteenth century, see also Sayles (1959, *passim*).

[3]   Herrup notes that '[a]dded construction was standard practice in important trials; so many observers had crowded into the Hall in 1616 during the trial of the Earl of Somerset that a scaffold had collapsed' (1999, p.50).

uphold (1972, p.236). That the judges were appointed by the king also contributed to this perception. More recently, however, Kevin Sharpe has argued that '[a]s a bench […] the judges were far less the willing agents in royal programmes than they are often presented' (1992, p.663), and indeed, a number of dismissals for failure to comply with or enforce royal policy under James VI and I and Charles I supports this argument.

Other courts lay outside the ordinary remit of the common law courts. The Court of Chancery, for example, was a court of equity. It was more concerned with individual cases and fair results than with general rules and the rigid implementation of law, and as it was not a court of record, Chancery judges (usually the Chancellor himself) need not be concerned about setting precedent with their judgements.[4] As it was concerned primarily with issues irresolvable at common law, there was initially no conflict between this court and King's Bench and the other common law courts. However, there were times when Chancery clashed with the common law courts; Lord Chancellor Ellesmere (1596–1617), for example, heard suits in Chancery which had already been concluded at common law, thus interfering with the jurisdiction of the common law courts and causing conflict between Egerton and the Judges in 1613–16. The events which followed led to the downfall of Edward Coke as Chief Justice of the King's Bench, and a royal decree which allowed the Chancellor to hear cases in Chancery after judgement had been passed at common law.[5] Indeed, the practice of moving cases from court to court was not unusual and finds its way into Caroline drama, as the lawyer in *The Antipodes* tells his client: 'Your case is cleare; I understand it fully, / And need no more instructions, this shall serve, / To firke your Adversary from Court to Court' (*Antipodes*, sig. F1r). Mihil in Brome's *The Weeding of Covent Garden* also threatens to move the Shoemaker and Taylor through several courts if they try to force him to pay them, making specific reference to Chancery court:

> Mihil: You clap a Sergeant o' my back. *I* put in bail, remove it, and carry it up into the upper Court, with *habeas Corpus;* bring it down again into the lower Court with *procedendo*; then take it from thence, and bring it into the Chancery with a *Certiorari*; *I*, and if you look not to't, bring it out of the Chancery again, and thus will *I* keep you from your money till your suite and your boots be worne out before you recover penny of me. (*Weeding of Covent Garden*, sig. C4r)

---

[4] For a more detailed discussion of courts of equity, see Baker (2002, pp.105–11), and a shorter definition with a brief history of the Court of Chancery see *ODL*, 'equity *n.*'. Courts of record are courts whose acts and judicial proceeding are permanently maintained and recorded. See *ODL*, 'court of record'.

[5] Baker summarises the chain of events which succeeded, during which Coke, as Chief Justice of the Kings Bench, entered a legal battle with Ellesmere leading finally to Coke's dismissal (Baker, 2002, pp.108–9).

The deferral of judgement brought about by the unclear limitations of each court's authority here is indicative of the wider problem of destabilised legal authority when the jurisdictional limits of law and prerogative are under question.

The Court of Star Chamber is the clearest example of the problematic combination of court and politico-legal authority. Like Chancery, the conciliar Court of Star Chamber was also initially a court of equity, but developed its criminal jurisdiction more clearly than Chancery. Jonson's *The New Inn* makes positive reference to the court for finding truth and bringing about justice:

> There is a royall Court o'the *Star-chamber*
> Will scatter all these mists, disperse these vapours,
> And cleare the truth. Let beggers match with beggers.
> That shall decide it, I will try it there.
> (*New Inn*, sig. G5r)

There is no reason to suppose that Beaufort's professed faith in the justice of this court is ironic or untrue. However, Star Chamber later became the most controversial of the extraordinary courts when it was closely associated with the enforcement of Charles I's policies. This may have been due to its shared personnel with the Privy Council (Jones, 1971, p.18), or with the rise in the number of cases at Star Chamber regarding matters of prerogative.[6] Hindle notes that by the 1630s, 'Star Chamber was being used increasingly frequently and almost exclusively for attorney-general prosecutions *pro Rege* to raise revenue by fines for malfeasance or breach of proclamation, and by persuading like offenders to compound in order to escape prosecution' (2000, p.74). The Star Chamber also developed a reputation for secrecy which was not entirely undeserved, despite the fact that, as with the common law courts, it was open to the public.[7] Although it had no authority to sentence to death (this had to be done under common law as the defendant had to be found guilty by a jury of his peers), the gruesome punishments Star Chamber was able to authorise, such as ear cropping and nose slitting, also helped establish a reputation as an instrument of autocratic government. Despite this, T. G. Barnes argues that Star Chamber did not uphold the king's prerogative any more than the established common law courts, and that defendants were more likely to have their say there than in other courts (1961, pp.4, 9). Nevertheless, as the Caroline period progressed, Star Chamber did gain a reputation as an instrument of royal policy, acting in the King's interest rather than the people's. Such a perception contributed to its abolition by Parliament in 1641 because 'the proceedings, censures, and Decrees of that Court, have by experience been found to be an intolerable burthen

---

[6]   Baker notes that the main difference between Star Chamber and the Privy Council meeting was that the Chief Justices of the two benches sat at the Star Chamber meetings, but they did not attend the Privy Council (2002, p.118n.4).

[7]   Witnesses were examined in secret and their testimonies were not made available to cross-examining counsel until all parties had completed their examination (Barnes, 1962, pp.228–9).

to the subject, and the meanes to introduce an Arbitrary power and Government' (England and Wales, 'Two acts of Parliament' 1640, sig. B2v).[8]

It is not possible to distinguish which of the courts outlined above is represented in the trial scenes discussed below, and attempting to identify particular courts, judges and trials represented in these plays is not the aim of this chapter; as Subha Mukherji has argued, 'instances in which the relation between dramatic fiction and real events is direct and intended are rare' (2006c, p.14). It is, instead, concerned with the ways in which courts and judges were *perceived* to function. What is at stake in trial scenes on the Caroline stage is not the guilt or innocence of the defendant; rather, they present a critique of social, cultural and legal issues of the period including: moral criticism of the theatre in *The Roman Actor*; social assumptions over gender and transgression in *The Ladies Triall*, and perceived practices of judges and prosecutors in *The Antipodes* and *The Traytor*. I will argue that ultimately what is at stake in the trials of these issues on the Caroline stage is the status of legitimate judicial and legal authority themselves.

Absolute Judicial Power: *The Roman Actor*

In the early action of Massinger's *The Roman Actor*, Paris, the leading actor, is summoned to appear before the Senate on charges of treason. As he is taken to trial, he encourages his colleagues not to fear the outcome:

> Nay droope not fellowes, innocence should be bould
> We that have personated in the Sceane
> The ancient Heroes, and the falles of Princes
> With loud applause, being to act our selves,
> Must doe it with undaunted confidence.
> What ere our sentence be think 'tis in sport.
> And though condemn'd lets heare it without sorrow
> As if we were to live againe to morrow.
> (*Roman Actor*, sigs. B1v-B2r)

The exhortation makes an explicit connection between the stage and his trial, exemplifying the theatre of the courtroom with which this chapter began. That Paris sees the actors' appearance at court as acting 'our selves', suggests he views the trial, and the world, as a theatrical production in which all people act a part. This is a recurrent theme in *The Roman Actor*, in which there are several plays within the play, and where the Emperor Domitian himself is often the stage manager.[9] The confidence Paris appeals for in his colleagues is evident in

---

[8]   This was not the only complaint against the Star Chamber. The anonymous *The Star Chamber epitomized* also suggests that the clerks and lawyers associated with this court were perceived to impose unreasonably high prices for their services (1641, *passim*).

[9]   For discussions of the theatricality of *The Roman Actor* and the importance of Domitian as stage-manager, see Goldberg (1989, pp.203–9) and Hartley (2001, *passim*).

his own actions at trial, as Aretinus asks 'Are you on the Stage / You talke so boldly?' (*Roman Actor*, sig. C1v), confirming the court/stage analogy. However, it is clear that his confidence lies in the theatrical possibility made available by this analogy that a protagonist condemned to death will live again in the next day's performance. Here the analogy falls short: should the actors be sentenced to death, whatever role they play, they will not live again tomorrow. Indeed, Paris's security even in theatrical resurrection also proves to be misplaced, as he is really killed in Domitian's later production of 'The False Servant' in an enactment of the Emperor's arbitrary justice.

The trial itself collapses not only the court and the stage, but also the social, political and theatrical worlds of the play:

> Aret[inus]: In thee, as being chiefe of thy profession,
>   I doe accuse the qualitie of treason,
>   As libellers against the state and Caesar.
>
> Par[is]: Meere accusations are not proofes my Lord,
>   In what are we delinquents?
>
> Aret.: You are they
>   That search into the secrets of the time,
>   And vnder fain'd names on the Stage present
>   Actions not to be toucht at; and traduce
>   Persons of rancke, and qualitie of both Sexes,
>   And with Satiricall, and bitter jests
>   Make even the Senators ridiculous
>   To the Plebeans.
>   (*Roman Actor*, sigs. C1r-C1v)

In *The Roman Actor*'s world of informers, Emperor's spies (of whom Aretinus is one (sig. B1v)) and imperial summary judgements, Paris's statement that 'accusations are not proofes' is an important distinction. However, it also feeds into Paris's defence against the libel charges, in which accusations *do* become proof, not of the guilt of the actors, but of the guilt of the accuser of the acts presented on stage:

>   And for traducing such
> That are above us, publishing to the world
> Their secret crimes we are as innocent
> As such as are borne dumbe. When we present
> An heyre, that does conspire against the life
> Of his deare parent, numbring every houre
> He lives as tedious to him, if there be
> Among the auditors one whose conscience tells him,

Hartley also discusses in this article the importance of performing obedience to Domitian's power in the play. Joanne Rochester's *Staging Spectatorship in the Plays of Philip Massinger* offers an extremely helpful overview of scholarship on this play (2010, pp.16–17).

He is of the same mould we cannot helpe it.
Or bringing on the stage a loose adultresse
…
… if a Matron
However great in fortune, birth or titles,
Guilty of such a foule unnaturall sinne,
Crie out tis writ by me, we cannot help it.
…
If any in this reverend assemblie,
Nay e'ne your selfe my Lord, that are the image
Of absent *Caesar* feele something in your bosome
That puts you in remembrance of things past,
Or things intended tis not in us to helpe it.
(*Roman Actor*, sigs. C2r-C2v)

This defence is part of a broad ranging debate over the 'application' of characters and stories on stage to contemporary people and events. Although here Paris is accused only of personal satire, Andrew Gurr argues that a 'substantial change that had taken place by 1620 was the use of plays for a larger scale of political comment than is evident earlier' and that this 'made the post of Master of the Revels as censor of plays a much hotter seat than it had been' (1996, p.133–4). Massinger himself was no stranger to censorship over political issues.[10] Paris's

---

[10] Amongst other censored plays and passages, Massinger's *Believe as You List* was censored and rewritten with the characters' names changed so as not to reflect so closely recent political occurrences in the Palatinate. Herbert noted on 11th January 1630/1: 'I did refuse to allow of a play of Messinger's because itt did contain dangerous matter, as the deposing of Sebastian king of Portugal, by Philip the [Second,] and ther being a peace sworen twixte the kings of England and Spayne' (*JCS*, IV, p.762). S. R. Gardiner gives a detailed analysis of the ways in which *Believe as You List* reflects Frederick's loss of the Palatinate in James VI and I's reign and can be seen to resemble closely Caroline negotiations with Spain regarding the Palatinate (1876, pp.499–503). Allen Gross, however, questions whether Massinger would have sufficient knowledge of contemporary court manoeuvring to give so close an analogy of Anglo-Spanish negotiations as Gardiner suggests, but admits that he cannot disagree with Gardiner's general parallel between Antiochus and Frederick (1966, *passim*, especially pp.283, 288). Massinger's *The King and Subject* (1638) was heavily censored at the King's command for an explicit comment on prerogative taxation, spoken by a Spanish king to his subjects:

> Monys? Wee'le rayse supplies what ways we please,
> And force you to subscribe to blanks, in which
> We'le mulct you as wee shall thinke fitt. The Caesars
> In Rome were wise, acknowledginge no lawes
> But what their swords did ratifye, the wives
> And daughters of the senators bowinge to
> Their wills, as deities.

According to Herbert, who noted the passage as 'for ever to bee remembered by my son and those that cast their eyes on it, in honour of Kinge Charles, my master', who himself read

defence claims that if a person or play does catch the conscience of someone in the audience, this does not prove the actors intended it, but it does suggest a guilty conscience in the accuser, or a malicious intent in the applier.

Paris's argument is, then, a wider defence of all players from such allegations. That Paris is representative of all actors – Roman and Caroline – is also evident in the other argument of his defence. He is not only concerned with political and personal application, but with a moral defence of playing:

> But 'tis urg'd
> That we corrupt youth, and traduce superiours:
> When doe we bring a vice upon the Stage,
> That does goe off unpunish'd? doe we teach
> By the successe of wicked undertakings,
> Others to tread, in their forbidden steps?
> We show no arts of *Lidian* Pandarisme,
> *Corinthian* poisons, *Persian* flatteries
> But mulcted so in the conclusion that
> Even those spectators that were so inclin'd,
> Go home chang'd men.
> (*Roman Actor*, sig. C2r)

In answering more than he was charged with (the charge against him makes no reference to corrupting youth), Paris emphasises that his trial is a trial of the theatre, not of the actor himself, and thus the platform of the stage(d) trial allows Massinger the opportunity to respond to contemporary anti-theatrical tracts, such as Alexander Leighton's 'A Short treatise Against Stage-Playes' published in 1625.[11] This treatise was dedicated to 'the High and Honourable House of Parliament Assembled May xxiii 1625' and David Reinheimer suggests that the anti-theatrical element of Parliament must have taken its arguments to heart as their first act prevented the performance of plays on Sundays (1998, p.318). It cannot be coincidence under these contemporary theatrical circumstances (and considering Charles I's extensive patronage of the arts) that it is the Senate, in the absence of the Emperor (who is Paris's patron), which brings Paris to trial. Reinheimer suggests that the scene invites this allegorical reading:

> In Rome, Paris should be judged by Domitian, not the Senate, just as the Caroline stage should be under the aegis of Charles's Master of the Revels. But Aretinus drags the actor before the Senate while Domitian is still out on campaign, trying

---

the play and marked this passage as 'too insolent, and to bee changed' (Dutton, 1991, p.91). Ironically, this is the only passage of the play that now remains. This passage and Charles's comments, read in the light of Paris's argument that the playwright and actors cannot help it if a person sees themselves in a play's character, could produce interesting speculation about Charles's own understanding of his prerogative taxation practices.

[11]   For a detailed discussion of the relationship between *The Roman Actor* and this anti-theatrical tract see Reinheimer (1998, *passim*).

a political end run. Massinger sees Parliament's legislation as the same kind of political machination, a ploy that tries to take advantage of a newly crowned king. (1998, p.330)

Aretinus's decision to 'reserve to [Domitian] / The Censure of this cause' (*Roman Actor*, sig. C3r) highlights the falsity of Paris's assertion that Aretinus is 'the image / of absent *Caesar*' (sig. C2v) and shakes the certainty of Reinheimer's analogy a little, but perhaps also suggests that in such matters Parliament should defer to the King's judgement.

Although Jonathan Goldberg claims that at the end of the scene, the Emperor exonerates Paris and the actors (1989, p.204), this is not entirely true: the Senate abandons the matter at the return of the victorious Emperor and the case is not mentioned again. We can assume that the players are acquitted because Paris returns to acting, but this is not seen on stage, and the implicit acquittal allows the theatre audience themselves to condemn or acquit the actors. The interpretive power of the audience is confirmed by the closing of Paris's defence: 'I have said, my Lord, and now as you find cause / Or censure us, or free us with applause' (*Roman Actor*, sig. C2v). This is, if one were necessary, a further iteration of the courtroom/theatre analogy in echoing the epilogue of several early Stuart plays (particularly *The Tempest*) but, more significantly, it places the responsibility for theatrical guilt on the (on and off stage) audiences' interpretation. Significantly for the broader concerns of this chapter, Rochester judiciously notes that Paris's argument 'emphasizes the fact that theatre is an open-ended process of *judgment*, intrinsically structured around representational ambiguity and freedom of interpretation' (2010, p.19, my emphasis); moreover, that in Paris's defence, 'Massinger demands that his audience be aware of their own presence, before the inset performances begin' (2010, p.23). Whatever their decision, however, for Paris, the actors and the senators, it is the Emperor/King's decision which is the most important. The deferral of the Senate to Domitian demonstrates that in this play, the absolute power of the Emperor both supersedes (in their deferral to him) and precludes the judgement of the Senate.

After Paris's Senate appearance there are no trials, but instead summary imperial judgements upon Philargus, Lamia, Sura, Rusticus and, finally, Paris. Domitian's judgement of Paris for his acquiescence in Domitia's desire for him confirms the personal and absolute nature of the Emperor's judicial authority:

Caes[ar]:   O that thy fault had bin
    But such as I might pardon; if thou hadst
    In wantonnesse (like *Nero*) fir'd proud *Rome*
    Betraide an armie, butcherd the whole Senate,
    Committed Sacriledge, or any crime
    The justice of our *Roman* lawes cals death,
    I had prevented any intercession
    And freely sign'd thy pardon.

Par[is]: But for this
 Alas you cannot, nay you must not Sir
 Nor let it to posteritie be recorded
 That *Caesar* unreveng'd sufferd a wrong,
 Which if a private man should sit downe with it
 Cowards would baffell him.
 (*Roman Actor*, sig. H4r)

That Domitian would rather pardon offences against Rome than against himself is further evidence of his arbitrary judgement and suggests that his acts toward Paris will be of personal revenge unauthorised by Roman law. This idea recurs in Shirley's *The Cardinal* (licensed 1641). In this play, the King is also more concerned with the affront to himself of Columbo's murder of Alvarez than with the murder:

 And if I should forgive
 His timeless death, I cannot the offence,
 That with such boldness struck at me. Has my
 Indulgence to your merits which are great
 Made me so cheap, your rage could meet no time
 Nor place for your revenge, but where my eys
 Must be affrighted, and affronted with
 The bloody execution? This contempt
 Of Majesty transcends my power to pardon,
 And you shall feel my anger Sir.
 (*The Cardinal*, sig. D2r)

The repeated calls for justice in this play, along with this preference of Majesty over law, demonstrate a corruption of legal authority leading away from a focus on justice to a manipulation by favourites to further personal interest. In *The Roman Actor*, the trial by the Senate must be bypassed rather than voluntarily passed over because Paris's crime is not capital according to law. His willingness to accept Domitian's sentence without offering a defence to prevent his death ('To hope for life, or pleade in the defence / Of my ingratitude were againe to wrong you' (H4r)) after his previous lengthy defence before the Senate emphasises the personal power and authority of the Emperor. Domitian's subjects should not question his authority, and those who do act against him, as demonstrated in Chapter 2, will be punished by his successor. Paris does offer something in mitigation of his crime, so that Caesar may pardon him when he is dead, giving his 'frailtie, / Her will, and the temptation of that beautie / Which you could not resist' (*Roman Actor*, sig. H4r) as his defence. The Emperor's poor example explains, although does excuse, a similar action in one of his subjects.

Domesticating Judicial Authority: *The Ladies Triall*

John Ford's *The Ladies Triall* places the personal judicial power of the Emperor of *The Roman Actor* into a domestic setting. The plot of the play centres on the relationship between Auria and his wife Spinella. Auria goes to war, returns successful and as a reward the Duke appoints him governor of Corsica. At his return, his friend Aurelio finds Spinella alone with Adurni and accuses them of adultery. Auria acts as judge at her trial. It is through his position of dual authority that the play questions the judicial power and legal position of the monarch: Auria is representative of political authority in his position as governor of Corsica, and by the husband/king analogy of patriarchalist theory and theatrical convention. Auria himself refers to his domestic kingdom in his initially happy marriage to Spinella:

> I had a kingdome once, but am depos'd
> From all that royaltie of blest content,
> by a confederacie twixt love and frailtie.
> (*Ladies Triall*, sig. F3v)

Whilst it might, in a play which conducts a trial of Spinella's virtue, be assumed that the 'frailtie' referred to here is hers, as the play progresses the social assumptions and judgements of sexual behaviour that suggest this interpretation are brought into question, and the 'frailtie' of male faith becomes a possibility. The play explores several meanings of the 'trial' in its title: the audience will see a trial (test) of Spinella's virtue, her trial (hearing) for her supposed offence, and a trial (questioning) of the contemporary social assumptions regarding gender which led to Spinella's alleged guilt. This is not merely the 'Lady's trial', but also potentially, the 'Ladies' Trial'. It is through these different kinds of trial, I will argue, that the play also presents, less obviously, a trial of legitimate legal authority.

Throughout the play, the use of legal terms maintains a close association between the domestic and politico-legal world. From the moment Aurelio finds Adurni and Spinella together, their argument over her guilt or innocence of adultery is not made in moral, but legal, terms. Adurni comments, 'Rich conquest, / To triumph on a Ladies injur'd fame, / Without a proofe or warrant' (*Ladies Triall*, sig. E3r), and Spinella herself picks up on this legal register, saying:

>   *I* must beg
> Your charities; sweet sister, yours to leave me,
> I need no fellowes now: let me appeare,
> Or mine owne lawyer, or in open court
> (Like some forsaken client) in my suit
> Be cast for want of honest plea – – oh misery.
> (*Ladies Triall*, sig. E3v)

Spinella invites a courtroom trial of her honour during which she will represent herself either as a lawyer for her defence, or appear in court without a lawyer to defend herself under presumption of her guilt ('for want of honest plea'). This refers to the legal practice that if a defendant refuses to enter a plea, the court proceeds '*pro confesso*' (as if the accused had pleaded guilty).[12] The idea of

---

[12]   At the trial of Bastwick, Burton and Prynne in Star Chamber in 1637, the gentlemen were 'injoyned to put in their answers to the Information by Munday next came sennight,

Spinella going on trial to defend her virtue is continued in her sister Castanna's concern that Spinella should not be followed:

> Ad[urni]: Her resolution's violent, quickly follow,

> Cast[anna] By no means (sir) y'ave followed her already,
>   *I* feare with too much ill successe in triall,
>   Of unbecoming courtesies.
>   (*Ladies Triall*, sig. E3v)

The word order here allows the possibility that Spinella's trial for her supposed infidelity will meet with 'ill successe' for her, before it becomes clear that Castanna is referring to the trial of Spinella's chastity in Adurni's attempt to seduce her.

It is not clear that Spinella and Adurni's 'trial' takes place in a courtroom. Indeed, in *The Ladies Triall*, the trial scenes are little more than a discussion between Spinella, Adurni, Aurelio and Auria, as accused pair, accuser and judge respectively:

> *A*dur[ni]: Stand *Aurelio*,
>   *A*nd justifie thine accusation boldly,
>   Spare me the needlesse use of my confession,
>   *A*nd having told no more, then what thy jealousie
>   Possest thee with againe before my face,
>   Urge to thy friend the breach of hospitalitie
>   *Adurni* trespast in, and thou conceavst
>   *A*gainst *Spinella*; why proofes grow faint,
>   If barely not suppos'd, Ile answere guilty.

> Aure[lio]: You come not here to brave us.

> Adur.: No *Aurelio*
>   But to reply upon that brittle evidence,
>   To which thy cunning never shall rejoyne.

---

by the advice of their counsell, and under their hands, or else the matters of the Information should be taken against them *pro confesso*' (Prynne, 1641, pp.20–21). Despite attempting to enter pleas they wrote and signed themselves, Bastwick and Prynne were tried *pro confesso* because these were not entered on their behalf and signed by their lawyers (Prynne, 1641, pp.21–33). Spinella's reference to a 'forsaken client' may make reference to this trial, as Bastwick and Prynne both claimed they were unable to give answer through their lawyers because they refused to act for them (Prynne, 1641, pp.27, 29–30). Charles I's refusal to plead at his trial created much discussion amongst the judges as to whether they should proceed, as they would in a less unusual trial, *pro confesso*, and instructions to this effect were incorporated into the ordinance passed by the Commons on 1st January 1649. This was, according to Sean Kelsey, to limit the King's options when he came to trial. Nevertheless, the King was given between nine and twelve more opportunities to enter a plea after the usual time to do so was past (Kelsey, 2004, p.4, paragraph 9; p.8, paragraph 21). This suggests a reluctance to assume the King's guilt, as this meant execution became almost inevitable.

> I make my Judge my Jurie, be accountant
> Whither withall the eagernesse of spleene
> Of a suspitious rage can plead, thou hast
> Enforc'd the likelihood of scandall.
> (*Ladies Triall*, sig. I1r)

Although the play gives no stage directions for scenery to indicate a court, their language ('confession', 'proofes', 'guilty', 'evidence') invites comparison with legal proceedings and presents Auria, whose new position as governor of Corsica makes him the obvious choice, as Judge. In his answer to Aurelio's accusation, Adurni acknowledges his fault in an intention to seduce Spinella, but denies that Aurelio has sufficient evidence other than suspicion to make a formal charge of adultery. His response becomes an accusation before his own judge and jury (Auria) that it is Aurelio, not Adurni, who has brought potential scandal to Auria's house. The collapse of judge and jury in one man suggests absolute authority, as Mukherji notes that these roles were kept scrupulously apart in common law (2006a, p.228). Auria himself says little during Adurni's trial, only intervening to ask Adurni to say more when he hears of Spinella's virtue ('On sir and doe not stop.' (*Ladies Triall*, sig. I2r)). The emphasis on 'proofes' and 'evidence' highlights the fact that Aurelio's accusation is based upon nothing more than circumstance, and brings into question the social and cultural assumption (the inevitable infidelity of unmonitored young wives) upon which his judgement is based.[13]

Spinella's language when she appears continues the movement between the trial and the domestic sphere:

> Spi[nella]: Tho prove what judge you will, till I can purge
> Objections which require beliefe and conscience,
> I have no kindred sister, husband, friend,
> Or pittie for my plea.
> (*Ladies Triall*, sig. K1r)

Whereas Adurni admits the intention to commit his crime but denies carrying out the action, Spinella, guilty in neither act nor intention, asks her family who are now the impersonal non-familial court and judge, to assume her guilt (have 'no pittie for my plea'). This draws attention to the fact that Aurelio has already done exactly that in his accusation, and highlights that the same assumption has been made of Levidolche by both Malfato and Martino during the play.[14] Spinella's next

---

[13] For an exploration of ideas of proof, rhetoric and evidence in relation to common law and Aristotelian notions of artificial and inartificial proof in this play, see Mukherji (2006a, *passim*).

[14] Dorothy Farr argues that Spinella's trial highlights the wrong conclusions Aurelio comes to about her (based upon his views on marriage for love and young brides) and Malfato's misjudgements of Levidolche's attentions to him as a response to Adurni's abandonment of her. Thus the trial makes both men question the social codes by which they came to these conclusions (Farr, 1979, pp.134–49, especially p.143). Lisa Hopkins argues that Spinella's success at her trial re-writes plays such as *Othello*, in which innocence is not an effective defence and law cannot protect the female characters (1999a, pp.59–63).

statement continues this determination to stand alone, but implicitly transfers the guilt to those who have distrusted and accused her on such slim evidence:

> *I* disclaime all benefit
> Of mercie from a charitable thought,
> If one or all the subtilties of malice,
> If any engine of faithlesse discord,
> If supposition for pretence in folly,
> Can poynt out, without injurie to goodnesse,
> A likelihood of guilt in my behaviour,
> Which may declare neglect in every dutie,
> Requir'd fit, or exacted.
> (*Ladies Triall*, sig. K1r)

The three conditional clauses here convey Spinella's confidence in her innocence, allowing three possibilities to find evidence against her. These possibilities, however, all involve underhand machinations of 'malice', 'faithlesse discord' and 'pretence in folly', setting her honesty against the dishonesty of those who might accuse her. Indeed, it is this confidence that Auria notices in Spinella's defence, saying, 'High and peremptory, / The confidence is masculine' (*Ladies Triall*, sig. K1r). For him, her innocence is confirmed in her movement away from womanly behaviour. Although Spinella later acknowledges that in this she has 'assum'd a courage / Above [her] force', she does, as Auria requires of her, 'Keepe faire, and stand the triall' (*Ladies Triall*, sigs. K2v, K1r).

Assumptions about gender roles also play an important part in Spinella's defence against Auria's assertion that infidelity is unpardonable in their marriage which was for love, not money or status. She replies:

> My thoughts in that respect are as resolute as yours,
> The same, yet herein evidence of frailtie
> Deserv'd not more a separation,
> Then doth charge of disloyaltie objected
> Without or ground or witnesse, womans faults
> Subject to punishments, and mens applauded,
> Prescribe no lawes in force.
> (*Ladies Triall*, sig. K2r)

Her alleged 'frailtie', she claims, was no worse than Auria's willingness to believe it without proper evidence. This suggests a kind of frailty in him, which could also be understood in Auria's own reference to a 'confederacie twixt love and frailtie' (*Ladies Triall*, sig. F3v) noted earlier. Spinella's argument, again blending the domestic and legal worlds, claims that men should set a good example: patriarchally-devised behavioural norms in relationships ('lawes') cannot be enforced if men are not also subject to them, or, indeed, are applauded for breaking them. This perhaps provides the clearest link between the main plot and the sub-plot of the fallen Levidolche who attempts to regain respectability having been used and abandoned by Adurni and rejected by Malfato. Spinella's comment on obeying one's own laws, following closely upon Adurni's reference to the 'power' and 'soveraignty' of Spinella's virtue to set 'bounds to rebell bloods' (*Ladies Triall*, sig. I1v) and Malfato's criticism of Auria's 'waste kinde of antique soveraigntie' (*Ladies Triall*, sig. I4v) when he pretends not to recognise his wife as she kneels to him, can also be seen as a domestically disguised reference to the necessity for the sovereign himself to set a good example in adhering to established laws.

Throughout the process of accusation and trial, Spinella's 'masculine' confidence and reasonable argument are contrasted with Aurelio's earlier unreasonable reaction when finding her with Adurni:

> Spi[nella]: What rests behind for me, out with it.
>
> Aure[lio]: Horror,
>> Becomming such a forfeit of obedience,
>> Hope not that any falsity in friendship
>> Can palliate a broken faith, it dares not
>> Leave in thy prayers (fair vow-breaking wanton)
>> To dresse thy soule new, whose purer whitenesse
>> Is sullyd by thy change, from truth to folly.
>> A feareful storme is hovering, it will fall,
>> No shelter can avoyd it, let the guilty
>> Sink under their owne ruine.
>
> Spin: How unmanly
>> His anger threatens mischiefe!
>> (*Ladies Triall*, sigs. E3r-E3v)

In describing his unsubstantiated, angry accusation as 'unmanly', the play makes explicit a connection between this unmanliness and tyranny, as Castanna challenges Aurelio to 'Use your tyranny' (*Ladies Triall*, sig. E3r) immediately before this exchange. Thus the play participates in the theatrical convention, explored in the previous chapters, which presents absolutism, tyranny and submission to will as less than manly. Spinella's questioning of patriarchal authority in calling Aurelio's outburst unmanly, and of Auria's position in undermining his charges by reminding him of his duty to her not to accept unsubstantiated accusations against her, presents the kind of questioning of legal authority by a subject which was not countenanced in Paris's willing submission to Domitian's tyranny in *The Roman Actor* ten years earlier.

Although tyranny is associated with Aurelio rather than the governor of Corsica himself, Auria's actions too are questioned and questionable. His part in Spinella's trial makes him at once 'judge of both law and fact, and converts the judge's role from that of impartial referee to that of active inquisitor' (Mukherji, 2006a, pp.228–9). Again he is in the legally problematic position of being both judge and jury, and his purpose in trying Spinella is not entirely clear. At times he seems convinced of her innocence, even before her defence:

> Revenge! for what? (uncharitable friend)
> On whom? Lets speak a little pray with reason,
> You found *Spinella* in *Adurnies* house,
> Tis like a' gave her welcome very likely,
> Her sister and another with her, so
> Invited, nobly done; but he with her
> Privatly chamberd, he deserves no wife
> Of worthy qualitie, who dares not trust
> Her virtue in the proofes of any danger.
> (*Ladies Triall*, sig. F3v)

His appeals to reason dissociate him, through legal and political discourses of the period discussed in Chapter 3, from Aurelio's tyranny. But his belief in her virtue suggests that the trial he forces her to undergo is a cruelly unnecessary testing of her loyalty to him which savours of arbitrary absolutism. For Auria, it is not enough that his wife is chaste; she must prove it through semi-public argument at law.[15]

Having declared at the end of the trial that he finds Spinella's 'vertues as [he] left them, perfect / Pure, and unflaw'd' (*Ladies Triall*, sig. K2v), Auria then, with his accepted patriarchal authority, offers her sister Castanna to Adurni in marriage. Significantly, it is made clear that Auria does not impose his authority on Castanna; rather she has chosen him as guardian of her 'faith'. Nevertheless, there is an uncomfortable convenience to this marriage. It seems it has been planned by Auria, and 'is not sudden, / But welcom'd & forethought' to Adurni (whose attempted seduction of Spinella, not Castanna, initiated the trial) but it has not been indicated to Castanna or the audience before this point. Ford draws attention to the contrivance, as Spinella comments 'The courtship's somewhat quick', but Spinella and Castanna then explain this suddenness respectively as 'the use of fate' and the 'will of heaven' (*Ladies Triall*, sig. K2v). It becomes clear though, that this is not the will of heaven so much as the will of Auria when he claims that this was his intention throughout:

> Make no scruple
> (*Castanna*) of the choice, tis firme and reall,
> Why else have I so long with tamenesse nourisht
> Reports of wrongs, but that I fixt on issue
> Of my desires, Italians use not dalliance
> But execution; herein I degenerated
> From custome of our nation.
> (*Ladies Triall*, sig. K3r)

---

[15]   Mukherji links his desire for such proof to rhetorical hierarchies understood in the period in the 'value-laden distinction in rhetoric between the superiority of artificial proof or "invention" constructed by the art of the orator, and the inferiority of external, material signs which the orator merely uses'. She argues that in testing Spinella in this way Auria 'sets himself up as a superior user of method in the project of discovery than both Aurelio, who convicts on external, circumstantial proof, and the common lookers-on, who might "construe" and "presume" guilt erroneously (I.i.)' (2006a, pp.229–30).

Auria's wording here is significant in the terms of politico-legal theatrical debate identified in this book. He has tested Spinella only to bring about the satisfaction of his will (desire), and in doing so has 'degenerated' from the custom of his nation, suggesting his absolutist leanings. 'Degenerated' is a particularly loaded word here: whilst it can mean 'to become altered in nature or character (without implying debasement)', more commonly degeneration implies deficiency or 'a fall away from ancestral virtue or excellence'.[16] In acting to satisfy his own desires, the ruler who does not follow established customary law is in some way declining from a previously superior form of legal authority. This reading is complicated by the understanding that in not following the custom of his country, Auria has brought about a peaceful resolution rather than challenging Aurelio to a duel for slandering his wife. However, the emotional cost to Spinella of the unnecessary trial, evident in Castanna's observation 'She faints' (*Ladies Triall*, sig. K2v), suggests that the governor's attempts to confirm his authority by testing subjects' loyalty and his focus on the 'issue of [*his*] desires' rather than the welfare of his subjects is an inappropriate and potentially 'degenerate' form of government.

Judicial Practices: *The Antipodes*

Whilst *The Roman Actor* and *The Ladies Triall* use trials to subject the judicial and legal authority of the monarch-as-judge to scrutiny in terms of the ultimate monarchical authority *to* judge, testing subjects' loyalty and adhering to one's own laws, the authoritative position and practices of judges themselves are not examined. The trial scene in Brome's *The Antipodes* moves the focus away from the king's judicial power and position, presenting instead a comic but critical comment on not only the perceived practices but also the position of lower ranking and local justices. Unlike the trials already discussed in this chapter, the trial in *The Antipodes* is not real: it is one of the many plays-within-the-play in which events contrary to conventional activities take place, designed by Doctor Hughball with the help of Letoy to bring Peregrine back to his senses.[17]

Having declared himself King of the Antipodes, Peregrine is witness to, and comments on, a trial conducted by Byplay as 'City Governor' (*Antipodes*, sig. G2v). The opening of the trial brings court practices and arbitrary judgement into question:

---

[16]   *OED*, 'degenerate' *v.*, 3, 1.

[17]   Although Mukherji refers to Spinella's trial as a 'false trial' (2006a, *passim*), and it is not necessarily carried out in a real court, it is a real trial in that there are real consequences for the accused, whatever the outcome. The trials in *The Antipodes* and *The Traytor* (which I will discuss shortly) are knowingly pretended trials, acted out within the play for a purpose other than judging the accused.

Byp[lay]: Call the defendant, and the Plaintiffe in.

Sword[-bearer]: Their counsell and their witnesses.

Byp: How now!
　　How long ha you beene free oth Poyntmakers,
　　Good master hilt and scaberd carrier;
　　(Which is in my hands now) do you give order
　　For counsell and for witnesses in a cause
　　Fit for my hearing, or for me to judge, haw?
　　I must be rul'd and circumscrib'd by Lawyers must I,
　　And witnesses, haw? no you shall know
　　I can give judgement, be it right or wrong,
　　Without their needlesse proving and defending:
　　So bid the Lawyers goe and shake their eares,
　　If they have any, and the witnesses,
　　Preserve their breath to prophesie of dry summers.
　　(*Antipodes*, sig. G2v)

Byplay's immediate reaction to the Swordcarrier's calling of counsel and witnesses is an attempt to maintain control: the hilt and scabbard (symbols of justice) are in *his* hands once the trial has begun, and this hearing is for *him* alone to judge. This determination to proceed with the trial in his own way is continued in his objection to being 'rul'd and circumscrib'd by Lawyers' which, echoing Domitian (*Roman Actor*, sig. D3r), hints towards a kind of absolutism in the governor of Anti-London which disregards the law when judicial expedience requires it. That this desire to be without the rule of lawyers is a practice of Anti-London, which is 'contrary in Manners' (*Antipodes*, sig. E1v) to London, suggests that it should not be the practice of the Caroline legal proceedings, thus making a critical comment on the legal manoeuvrings of Charles I and his Judges which common lawyers did attempt to circumscribe. Byplay's assertion of his ability to give a judgement 'right or wrong' without proving or defending is reminiscent of the arbitrary justice of *A Jovial Crew*'s Justice Clack who can inform himself of guilt or innocence by the defendants' countenances alone (*Joviall Crew*, sigs. M3v-M4r). Butler suggests that Byplay's 'self-opinionated judge' comes from a long tradition of such figures descending from Jonson's Justice Clement and including Clack, but that his comment on 'needlesse proving and defending' may also make reference to 'the drawn-out arguments and delayed judgement of the Ship Money case' (1987, p.216), a particularly controversial issue of prerogative rule. The brief comment about lawyers' missing ears could snipe at William Prynne, grounding this Antipodean court in contemporary London courts, specifically the Star Chamber, which had begun to gain a reputation for arbitrary royal judgement.[18] Although these practices (acting without lawyers or witnesses) are those of Antipodean Anti-London, in many cases in Caroline London, particularly those heard in Star

---

[18]　Steggle's suggestion of a date of 1636 for this play (2004, pp.105–9) would not disallow this allusion, as Prynne's ears were cropped twice, once in 1633 and once in 1637.

Chamber, witnesses did not appear in court, their testimony having been given in writing before the defendant appeared in front of the Judge (Barnes, 1962, p.229), and trials for felony in the common law courts proceeded, as Byplay will have it here, without the benefit of a lawyer for the defence. In presenting these as Anti-London, contrary practices, Brome passes comment on the (im)propriety of their inclusion in London's legal proceedings.

The association of the Antipodean court with Star Chamber is continued in Peregrine's comment on the 'equity' of Byplay's procedure:

> Byp: Bring me the plaintiffe, and defendant only.
>   But the defendant first, I will not heare
>   Any complaint before I understand
>   What the defendant can say for himselfe.
>
> Per[egrine]: I have not known such down right equity,
>   If he proceeds as he begins, ile grace him. –
>   (*Antipodes*, sigs. G2v-G3r)

Peregrine's reference to 'equity' does at least suggest a fairness in allowing the defendant to explain himself before passing judgement – something the arbitrary Justice Clack, for example, would not do – but there is, of course, something absurd about his hearing the defence before the complaint, and Peregrine's praise of this as the correct way to proceed in trial is also symptomatic of the madness, associated with arbitrary absolutism and intemperate desire, that the doctor is trying to cure in him.[19] Perhaps Star Chamber's judgements, this suggests, are not as equitable as the court's designation as a court of equity might imply.

Byplay hears the case: a merchant has brought a gentleman to court for refusing to sleep with his (the merchant's) wife in payment for the cloth he has provided. Although the gentleman offers to pay him twice its monetary value, the merchant will not accept this because it will not satisfy his wife. Byplay's judgement that he himself will take the cloth *and* satisfy the tradesman's wife is an appropriate Antipodean solution to the triviality of the case, but before examining the implications of the sentence it is worth considering the Judge's stated reasoning:

> Peace, I should
> Now give my sentence, and for your contempt,
> (which is a great one, such as if let pass
> Unpunished, may spread forth a dangerous
> Example to the breach of City custome,
> By gentlemens neglect of Tradesmens wives)
> *I* should say for this contempt commit you
> Prisoner from the sight of any other woman
> Untill you give this mans wife satisfaction,
> And she release you; justice so would have it.
> (*Antipodes*, sig. G4r)

---

[19] See Chapter 3.

The comic suggestion that it would be disastrous to the city customs in Anti-London if Byplay were to set an example allowing gentlemen *not* to sleep with tradesmen's wives suggests a wish to prevent this becoming common in London. More significantly, however, the comedy of this comment and the triviality of its cause disguise a more serious point: early modern common law legal practice (indicated again by 'custome') placed a great deal of importance on precedent, so when pronouncing difficult or controversial judgements in the common law courts of record, the judges not only had to weigh the evidence but also take into consideration the implications of the precedent it would set.

The hierarchy established in having both Peregrine (the 'King') and Byplay (the 'City Governor') of the Antipodes on stage simultaneously, encourages the audience to see Byplay as a lower ranking judge than Peregrine, Domitian, the Roman Senators or Auria, and it is the position of the local justice with which the sentence of the Antipodean trial scene is concerned. Although Byplay has stated that he knows how justice 'would have it', he chooses to adopt an alternative solution:

> But as I am a Citizen by nature,
> (For education made it so) ile use
> Urbanity in your behalfe towards you;
> And as I am a gentleman by calling,
> (For so my place must have it) ile performe
> For you the office of a gentleman
> Towards his wife, *I* therefore order thus:
> That you bring me the wares here into Court,
> (I have a chest shall hold 'hem, as mine owne)
> And you send me your wife, ile satisfie her
> My selfe. Ile do't, and set all streight and right.
> (*Antipodes*, sigs. G4r-v)

His comments upon a gentleman's position and a citizen's education is an obvious satire upon the behaviour of city traders and gentlemen, but more seriously it suggests the difficult position justices held in trying to negotiate between their position as gentlemen and local authority figures and the citizens for whom they administered justice, and upon whom they were to press, for example, Charles's potentially illegal extra-parliamentary taxation. Unable to be entirely a citizen because of his position as Judge, and constrained not to be a gentleman by his education, Byplay's solution at first appears to answer both sides of the dispute: the gentleman does not receive the goods for which he has not 'paid', and the citizen's wife is satisfied. However, it is clear that the only person really satisfied here is the Judge himself, who gains free cloth and unquestioned access to the citizen's wife, and Byplay's knowing comment immediately following the sentence, 'Justice is blinde, but Judges have their sight' (*Antipodes*, sigs. G4r-v), implies judicial corruption. Yet the fact that this comment is placed immediately after Byplay's explanation that, given his liminal position, this is the only sentence he can pass, raises the question as to whether this judgement is a result of the judge's innate corruption or of his taking advantage of the impossible situation in which he finds himself. Peregrine, the self-proclaimed King of the Antipodes who at this point is still mad, expresses satisfaction with the verdict exclaiming, 'Most admirable Justice' (*Antipodes*, sig. G4v), suggesting that only arbitrary monarchy would approve of either the self-serving action or the situation in which this Justice is placed. Peregrine's subsequent recovery and reformation of the laws of the Antipodes confirms that Antipodean practice is, or should be, an inversion of the organisation of the English courts.

The Process of Prosecution: *The Traytor*

The comedy of Brome's courtroom and the easy slippage between inverting and displaying English judicial practices highlights some of the failings of the Caroline judicial system. The lack of legal counsel hinted at in Byplay's comments, and the dramatic, adversarial aspects of trial procedure are explored in more detail in Depazzi's trial in James Shirley's *The Traytor*. Like that in *The Antipodes*, this is an imagined trial. In a similar vein to the interview between Prince Harry and King Henry in Act II of Shakespeare's *Henry IV, Part 1*, acted out by Harry and Falstaff (who each take a turn at being prince and the king) so that Harry can prepare what he will say to explain his dissolute actions to his father, Depazzi, a conspirator to treason, asks his servant Rogero to act as prosecutor in a preparatory 'trial' so that he can practise his defence.[20]

Despite Depazzi's threat of 'I will beate you, if you wonot imagine at my bidding', Rogero is reluctant to participate, claiming 'Good my Lord it will not become me, being your humble servant' (*Traytor*, sig. E2v). This concern for propriety is notably absent in the similar inversion of servant-master/mistress relations in Pru's position as Queen for the days sports in Jonson's *The New Inn*, and suggests the extent of the verbal assault which Rogero associates with treason trials, and which Depazzi expects if he is caught. In response to Rogero's concern for his humble status, Depazzi states, 'Humble Coxcombe, is't not for my good? I say, accuse me, bring it home, jerke me soundly to the quicke *Rogero*, tickle me as thou lovst thy Lord; I doe defie thee, spare me not, and the divell take thee if thou bee'st not malicious' (*The Traytor*, sigs. E2v-E3r). The series of violent and uncomfortable metaphors for this interrogation suggest the virulence of questioning Depazzi expects and perhaps the versatility his response will require, and in insisting that Rogero be 'malicious', Depazzi anticipates the worst that will confront him if his plotted treason with Lorenzo is discovered. This staged trial, with permission for the prosecutor to 'spare ... not' the defendant, allows the presentation on stage not only of an exaggerated version of Depazzi's possible trial, but also of an example of how real treason trials could be perceived by the Caroline theatrical and law-court audiences. Indeed, Depazzi's trial is not

---

[20] The interview acted by Harry and Falstaff is only a prefiguring of this sort of pretended trial, as neither of them actually offers a defence of Hal's actions; rather, as 'king' they take the opportunity either to compliment (Falstaff) or criticise (Harry) Falstaff as a companion for the Prince.

necessary for the plot of the play, suggesting that the *representation* of this trial is more important than Depazzi's part in Lorenzo's treasonous plot.

Rogero soon warms to his role, and accuses his master, without evidence, of several attempts upon the Duke's life:

> Do not interrupt mee varlet I will proove it, his hunting saddle, and woe shall be unto thy breech therefore, and finding this serpentive treason broken in the shell, doe but lend your reverend eares to his next designes I will cut em off presently. This irreligious nay Atheistical Traitor, did with his owne hands poison the Dukes prayer booke, oh impiety!
>
> ...
>
> hee hath for this fortnight or three weekes before his apprehension, walk'd up and downe the Court with a case of pistols charg'd, wherewith, as he partly confessed, hee intended to send the Duke to heaven with a powder. (*Traytor*, sig. E3v)

'[C]ut em off' has particular resonance in relation to perceived Caroline law court activities; although in the sense of the sentence, this is said in relation to expounding Depazzi's further crimes, coming so close to the reference to 'eares' it refers to the sentence of ear cropping, reminding the theatre audience of the physical punishments meted out by contemporary prerogative courts. Methods of prosecution are questioned here, too, in the mention of Depazzi's possible atheism. As Cynthia Herrup argues in her discussion of the trial of the second Earl of Castlehaven in 1631:

> adversarial law is as much about style as it is about fact .... Trials are confrontations, rhetorical swordplay within set rules. Like the swordplay of the theater, trials are constructed to persuade their audiences ... Regardless of fact and even law, the best performance is the most convincing one. And the most convincing one is usually the one most strategically attuned to the fears and ideals of the judge and jury. (1999, p.55)

Thus in stating that Depazzi is not only a traitor, but an 'atheistical' traitor, the '*ex tempore*' (*Traytor*, sig. E2v) prosecutor brings his moral character into question, playing upon contemporary fears regarding non-belief, irrespective of his crime and adding a charge of atheism to the alleged treason.[21]

In response to the accusations laid against him, Depazzi asks for evidence of his guilt:

---

[21] Such embellishments to accusations were not unusual (Hindle, 2000, p.82). Being a Catholic and possibly an atheist were accusations incorporated into the trial of the Earl of Castlehaven for rape and sodomy in 1631, shortly before the play was written (Herrup, 1999, p.3). Castlehaven's trial was such a public event that it is possible it had some influence in Shirley's play. For a discussion of the Castlehaven trial in relation to John Ford's *Perkin Warbeck*, see Hopkins (1999b, *passim*).

Dep: Will you justifie this? Did I any of these things you tadpole?

Ro: Hold your selfe contented my Lord, he that is brought t[o] the barre in case of treason, must looke to have more objected then hee can answere, or any man is able to justifie. (*Traytor*, sig. E3v)

Depazzi and Rogero here seem to step out of character from the acted trial and converse again as master and servant. However, Rogero's reply is more than a defence to his master of his insolence, also providing a comment upon the perception of State treason trials: once arrested for treason, a man becomes subject to a barrage of accusations which cannot be justified or defended, and in a trial for felony, defendants had no right to warning of the evidence against them (Herrup, 1999, p.55).

It is not merely the subject of the accusations, however, which become impossible for Depazzi to answer, but the nature of the questioning, as his defence is turned against him:

Ro: That that my Lord hath overthrowne him, he saieth hee never sought the princes life, *ergo* he sought his death, besides he hath heard of treason, now he that heareth and discovereth not is equally guilty in fact: for in offences of this nature there are not accessories, *ergo* hee is a principall, and beeing a principal Traitor, hee deserveth condemnation. (*Traytor*, sigs. E3v-E4r)

In knowing about the plot, Depazzi is automatically implicated.[22] His inadvertent admission of guilt demonstrates the dangers for the accused of *ore tenus* (oral questioning) carried out by the Attorney General in the Star Chamber rather than the more usual submission of all complaints and answers in writing:

There was much objection to the *ore tenus* procedure even then, and various safeguards were thrown around it. It is not hard to see that it was likely to lead to abuses ... A man suddenly arrested and privately and skilfully examined, overwrought, and perhaps entrapped into an unintentional and injudicious confession, then retained in the custody of a pursuivant until he was brought, without counsel, into the presence of the most dignified persons of the kingdom, was but ill provided with even such poor protection as the practice of the common-law courts then gave to a culprit'. (Cheyney, 1913, pp.740–41)

The kind of word play Rogero indulges in returns to the idea of swordplay that Herrup associates with both the theatre and the courtroom (1999, p.55), once again connecting these two forums for debate. Moreover, Depazzi's confession that he knew of treason not only confirms that he is guilty, but gives the prosecutor the opportunity to prevent him giving any further defence:

---

[22] In the same way that the earlier accusation of atheism was reminiscent of the Castlehaven trial, so here is the impossibility of being an accessory to particular crimes: all parties were tried as principals in cases of rape and sodomy (Herrup, 1999, p.26).

Dep: Shall I not speake?

Ro: No, traitors must not be sufferd to speake, for when they have leave, they have liberty, and hee that is a Traitor deserveth to bee close Prisoner.

…

Ro: I defie al the world that wil heare a Traitor speak, for himselfe, tis against the Law which provids that no man shal defend treason, and he that speakes for him being a Traitor, doth defend his treason, thou art a Capitall obstreperous malefactor. (*Traytor*, sig. E4r)

Although traitors were usually allowed to speak for themselves at trial – C. G. L. Du Cann suggests that Wentworth's 'stubborn fight and his final great speech in his own defence' might have saved him by a vote of his peers (1964, p.141) – Rogero's comment reflects upon a common contemporary argument: those accused of treason (and other felonies) were thought to have no defence, and so were not allowed to consult lawyers for their defence in point of fact, although lawyers were usually allowed for difficult points in law (Herrup, 1999, p.55).

The adversarial nature of Depazzi's acted trial is highlighted when compared with the treason trial in Shirley's *The Doubtful Heir* (1640). This is not an imagined trial; Ferdinand is on trial for his life having invaded the kingdom claiming to be the rightful King. Ferdinand is allowed to defend himself at trial, although it is made clear that this is a favour bestowed by the Queen not a right:

> Although the Queen in her own Royal power,
> And without violating Sacred Justice, where
> Treason comes to invade her, and her Crown
> With open war, need not insist upon
> The Forms, and Circumstance of Law, but use
> Her sword in present execution;
> Yet such is the sweet temper of her blood,
> And calmness of her Nature, though provok'd
> Ino [*sic*] a storm, unto the great'st offender
> She shuts up no defence, willing to give
> A satisfaction to the world how much
> She doth delight in mercy.
> (*The Doubtful Heir*, sig. C3r)

Whilst Ferdinand's crime is mentioned here, the emphasis is placed upon the Queen's goodness ('sweet temper', 'calmness', 'mercy') and her acceptance of the forms and processes of law despite having no compulsion to do so. It is in fact a demonstration of her mercy that she allows Ferdinand to speak. Later, as if to confirm this image of her justice, Olivia prevents her counsellors from interrupting his defence:

> Ferd[inand]:   I am *Ferdinand*,
>   And you the fair *Olivia*, brothers children.

Leon[ario]: What insolence is this?

Qu[een]: Oh my Lord, let him
        Be free to plead; for if it be no dream,
        His cause wil want an Orator: By my blood,
        He does talk bravely.
        (*Doubtful Heir*, sig. C3v)

In this, and the earlier emphasis placed upon her goodness, Shirley presents an idealised image of a just ruler who is prepared to hear arguments on both sides, despite the attack Ferdinand makes on her throne. Her decision to pardon him after hearing him speak, despite her courtiers' 'officious' attempts to have him executed (*Doubtful Heir*, sig. C5r), could be seen as Providential preservation of the rightful monarch, as Ferdinand is in fact the true King, not a pretender to the throne. Shirley can, therefore, allow the 'traitor' of *The Doubtful Heir* to be pardoned; he has committed no offence.

Depazzi, however, who has really conspired to commit treason, escapes execution at this point only because he pleads to an imagined judge, against a performing prosecutor and thus can easily bring his trial to an end:

Ro: Hold, hold good my Lord, I am sensible, I ha done, imagine, I ha done, I but obeyd your Lordship, whose batoone I finde stronger then my imagination, my Lord you will answer this to stricke i'th Court thus?

Dep: I Am as wearie ---- harke *Rogero*   *Knockes*
one knocks, see, see thers to make thee amends see good *Rogero*, and say nothing pray heaven it be no pursevant. (*Traytor*, sig. E4r)

Rogero's effortless list of possible criminal activities, and the comedy of his almost plaintiff admission that the 'batoone' is stronger than his imagination, draws the audience's attention away from the potentially serious prosecution Depazzi could face. The beating Depazzi administers to end the trial echoes that which he threatened if Rogero did not 'imagine at [his] bidding' (*Traytor*, sig. E2v), and this, with the emphasis on imagination in Rogero's asking him to stop, highlights that this is only a pretend trial. Rogero's question, 'will you answer this to stricke i'th' Court thus', reminds the audience that such an end to the trial – beating the prosecutor – would be impossible were he really indicted for treason against the Duke, just as Depazzi's fear of the imminent appearance of a pursuivant and his need to bribe Rogero to silence illustrates the seriousness of his crime and the trial and execution which would await him. The possibility that this fake trial will be interrupted by the appearance of a pursuivant is made more likely in the theatrical heritage of the scene: Harry and Falstaff's interview in Act II of *Henry IV, Part 1* is interrupted by a sheriff who wants to arrest Falstaff for stealing gold. For Falstaff this threat of the law is avoided because Hal first lies for him to send the Sheriff away, and then returns the gold to its rightful owner; Depazzi recants his treachery in fear for his life and pays Lorenzo half the price again of the office he had bought, hoping by doing so to 'induce your Lordship to dismisse mee' and 'have my Lordships good will' (*Traytor*, sig. H1v).

Unusually for trial scenes, there is no character on stage for Depazzi's trial playing a judge. Without interjections from a 'judge' the theatre audience are, perhaps, given more freedom to give their own comment on the activities and procedures of the trial, but the absence of a justice figure may suggest that this trial scene, unlike the trials of Paris, Spinella and the gentleman/merchant, does not comment on the judicial authority. However, Depazzi does make sure that judges are at least represented in his staged trial: 'conceive I prithee, that these chaires were Judges most grave and venerable beards and faces at my arraignment' (*Traytor*, sig. E2v). The vague description of 'venerable beards and faces' suggests that not only are the judges potentially indistinguishable one from another, but that there is little substance behind their venerable appearance, something confirmed by the fact that the accused and prosecutor in this trial make their addresses to empty chairs. Rogero's deference to 'the most understanding seates of Justice: most wise, most honourable, and most incorrupt Judges' (*Traytor*, sig. E3r) is not only comic – they are quite literally 'seates' and no more – but also potentially critical: the only wise, honourable and incorrupt seats of justice in a play so full of plotting, deception and corruption are the empty ones.

Absent Judges and Legal Authority

The empty seats of justice in *The Traytor*'s trial scene is the most obvious representation of the destabilisation of legal authority explored in all of the trial scenes examined in this chapter. Although the absolute authority of Domitian as Emperor is maintained despite the Senate's attempt to convict his favourite in his absence, from this point, figures of legitimate judicial authority come to be divided, undermined, questioned and, ultimately, absent in the trial scenes of Caroline drama. Auria's authority is brought into question by his unnecessary exercise of it, and the absolutism of patriarchal law is undermined by Aurelio's rash assumptions about Spinella's virtue; Byplay's judgement is questioned as potentially corrupt but also illustrates the divided loyalties and impossible position of those who are at once an independent legal authority and subject to the king; Olivia's trial of Frederick undermines legitimate authority as it is he, not she, who is the real monarch, and Depazzi's incorrupt, venerable judges are completely absent in the corrupt royal court in which the Duke or Prince's word is enforceable law. In place of these absent figures of legal authority, the theatre audience is invited to be judge not only of the plays and the social and cultural topics debated in them, but also, in the exploration of the use and abuse of authority each play presents, to consider the foundation and legitimate exercise of legal authority itself.

Epilogue

On 3rd February 1634, *The Triumph of Peace* was presented at court. As a masque, it may seem out of place in a book concerned with the commercial theatre; however, it would be a significant omission from any serious discussion of Caroline theatrical representations of legal authority were it to be excluded. Written by James Shirley, writer for the Queen's acting company at the commercial Cockpit, *The Triumph of Peace* was unusual in being presented not by the King to the Queen or the Queen to the King, but by the gentlemen of all four Inns of Court to their monarch.[1] Whilst it had not been unusual in previous reigns for the Inns, individually or in pairs, to present a masque constituting part of their Christmas revels to courtiers or royalty, *The Triumph of Peace* was the first (and only one) of its kind in being written to be presented by all four Inns of Court to the King and Queen at Whitehall. Equally unusual was the public element of the performance: court masques were usually private affairs, presented once on a specific occasion, to a select and invited audience; this masque, however, began with a procession of the masquers, in costume, through the streets of London to the Banqueting Hall at Whitehall, and so its very publicity sets it apart from others.[2] Moreover, *The Triumph of Peace* was presented a second time, by royal request, ten days later at Merchant Taylors' Hall. This time the masque was hosted by the city of London, enabling the city, too, to present a tribute to the King.[3] It is, in part, the public

---

[1]   There is some debate over the reasons for the presentation of the masque. The records of the Middle Temple in October 1633 suggest that the original pretext for the masque was the birth of the Duke of York; those of the Inner Temple claim it is because there has been 'no representation of any mask or show before the King's Majesty by the four Inns of Court or any of them sithens his Highness' access unto the Crown' (*JCS*, V, p.1155). However, the most commonly understood reason for producing the masque is the need for a declaration of loyalty by the Inns of Court after the publication of William Prynne's *Histriomastix*, dedicated to all four Inns, which condemned all plays and revels as inherently sinful (*passim*) and described women actors as 'notorious whores' in its Index, and to which the royal court took great offence.

[2]   No other masque presented to Charles at Whitehall included such public display. The *Memorable Masque* presented by the Middle Temple and Lincolns Inn to the Jacobean Court in 1613 as part of the celebrations for the marriage of Princess Elizabeth to the Elector Palatine began with a procession through the streets of London but this did not compare in scale to *The Triumph of Peace*. See Orgel and Strong for a contemporary description of the *Memorable Masque*'s procession (1973, p.255) and an extended description of *The Triumph of Peace*'s procession through London, giving details of the masquers and musicians, and thus an impression of the scale of the company in '[t]he manner and progression of the masque' (1973, p.538).

[3]   See Brent Whitted (2009) for a discussion of all the circumstances surrounding the production and re-production in the City of the masque.

nature of the procession that makes this masque comparable with the plays of the commercial theatre discussed in the preceding chapters. As Lauren Shohet has recently argued, 'People who witnessed the most public portion of such festivities may have had a particular interest in reading the text of other parts' (2010, p.85), and *The Triumph of Peace* was printed in quarto format, suggesting 'affordable books, and the multiple editions suggest that it sold briskly' (Shohet, 2010, p.77). Whilst the masque itself was a private performance, its printed text and public procession made it a public event, since 'publicly airing *The Triumph of Peace* (even in digested form) draws spectators into its policy commentaries' (Shohet, 2010, p.72). Like the plays of the commercial theatre discussed in the preceding chapters, then, *The Triumph of Peace* invited the public to consider the issues of law and legitimate authority with which it was concerned, as well as addressing the King on the topic of law and prerogative.

The lawyers staged their public procession through London from Holborne to Whitehall, enacting the triumph of the masque's title. The use of triumphal iconography is not unusual for the period; indeed, it borrows the imperial, triumphal iconography of Charles's court. Charles himself had previously danced as a conquering king in Aurelian Townshend's *Albion's Triumph* (1632) in which a Roman Triumph was recreated at Whitehall.[4] This association between Charles and Imperial iconography, and his peaceful reign, allows the understanding that the 'Peace' of the title refers to Charles's personal rule.[5] Because of this, Paul Raffield argues that the 'enormous procession that preceded the performance of *The Triumph of Peace* symbolised the unprecedented subservience of the Inns of Court, not only to the majesty of kingship but also (and in particular) to the putative *imperium* of Charles I' (2004, p.215). However, as is clear from Shirley's description of the masque procession, it was not Charles who rode in triumph through London, nor was it the masquer representing Irene (Peace), but rather the lawyers of the Inns of Court, and, since the public only saw the procession, not the masque's final presentation of harmony between the monarch and the Inns' representatives, it is possible to read a real triumph of the law through the Inns' successful appropriation of royal iconography. Law, not the King, holds imperial sway here. Already, then, tension is presented between the King, prerogative law and the lawyers as representatives of established law. Indeed, Raffield's reading of this masque as merely a 'vacuous entertainment, intended primarily to ingratiate the Inns with their sovereign master' (2004, p.7) seems to miss the more subtle negotiation of the relationship between monarchy and law that *The Triumph of*

---

[4]   See John Peacock (2006) for a discussion of the depiction in art and masques of Charles as a Roman emperor, and a detailed discussion of its significance in *Albion's Triumph*.

[5]   Orgel and Strong argue that as the personal rule had been underway for several years, the peace may be recognised as the King's peace. The architecture of the backdrop to the first scene of the masque too, they suggest, is, to its designer Inigo Jones, representative of the King's peace (1973, pp.65, 39).

Peace undertakes. Moreover, whilst court masques *can* be seen to offer a lavish tribute of praise and support to the King and his policies by presenting the monarch as the embodiment of perfect rule and justice, their conventions allow the presenters simultaneously to give counsel by showing in these embodiments what the King could and should be.[6]

The design of the Proscenium arch for *The Triumph of Peace* contains symbols of law, prerogative and divine right rule. Despite, or perhaps because of, Shirley's explanation that the items depicted in the arch are 'Hierogliphicks of Peace, Justice and Law' (*Triumph*, sig. A4r), they have been much neglected by critics of the masque. Mercury's caduceus is acknowledged to be the 'the sign of eloquence and peace' (Manning, 2002, p.128), the latter made clear by its combination with an olive branch in the arch's design. The caduceus is also an emblem of power and right, and the 'Festons of fruites' (*Triumph*, sig. A4r) engraved on the arch signify the plenty which accompanies good, powerful and peaceful rule.[7] The 'sharpe sighted eye' can be interpreted as a symbol of Charles's keen watchfulness and care, and the accompanying 'yoke' (*Triumph*, sig. A4r) as representative of servitude. That the yoke is golden may signify a servitude which is prosperous for the servant as well as the served under Charles, and one of ease rather than misery. However, if viewed differently, these two symbols also may have negative connotations: a sharp sighted eye may be intrusively watchful, and a golden yoke particularly heavy to bear, or suggestive of a harsh servitude gilded to give the appearance of ease. The potentially double-edged nature of Charles's attitude to law and justice is, therefore, suggested even in the smallest detail of the scenery. As with the law itself, angles of interpretation are key to understanding the extent and effect of the King's authority in the law.

Images of authority continue in the figures of Minos and Numa presented 'much bigger then the life' (*Triumph*, sig. A3v) in the niches on either side of the arch. Minos was the son of Zeus and claimed demonstrable divine support in his claim to the Cretan throne.[8] He was also 'renowned for his wisdom and justice as a lawgiver' (March, 1998, p.258), suggesting a divinely appointed royal power to make law. The description given of the statue of Minos in the masque's arch, too, contributes to an understanding of the ancient and majestic nature of the lawgiver: Minos 'held in one hand a Scepter, and in the other a Scrowle, and a picked antique crowne on his head … and his face was of a grave and joviall aspect' (*Triumph*,

---

[6]   Through watching the masque, Kevin Sharpe argues, the audience becomes what they are shown, and thus are educated in how they should behave (1987, p.196).

[7]   Alciato's *Emblema* features an emblem which shows Mercury's Caduceus entwined by two serpents and between two cornucopia. This represents the idea, the *subscriptio* explains, that the correct judgement of powerful, experienced men may be blessed with plenty and many things (1975, pp.71, 336).

[8]   To prove his claim to divine support, Minos 'prayed to Poseidon to send him a bull from the sea, promising to sacrifice it when it appeared. The god answered his prayer' (March, 1998, p.257). Minos did not fulfil his promise, and was punished.

sig. A3v). So, it is clear that Minos holds the power to rule (the sceptre) and has the law in his hand (the scroll), but this power is, although serious (grave), also benign (jovial).[9] Whilst this is an image of kingly power, it also offers an idealised representation of a king who gives equal weight to power and to law.

On the other side of the arch, the figure of Numa is depicted. Numa, too, is a figure of divine right rule, having sought the consent of the gods for his reign.[10] The belief that Numa took legal and religious advice from his lover (or wife in some versions of the story), a water-goddess called Egeria, also served to give Numa's religious and positive laws a divine status, increasing his authority. His reign was one of peace (March, 1998, p.273), making him a particularly appropriate figure to present in *The Triumph of Peace* to reflect Charles's rule. Numa also brings into focus a further aspect of Charles's reign in his influence over the religious practices of the Romans, as issues of religious faction troubled the Caroline period as the Laudian Protestants, Puritans and Catholics locked horns. As Numa is credited with bringing religion to the Romans, his depiction suggests an appeal to Charles to take a definite stand in religious matters. However, in regard to Numa's relationship with Egeria, his representation here may also suggest some concern over the influence that the Catholic Henrietta Maria held over Charles's policies.[11] There is, however, a possibility that the depiction of Egeria might also undermine Charles's claims to absolute authority, not only in that he could be unduly influenced by his French Queen, but in the arguments put forward by Livy (1600, sig. C1v) and Machiavelli in *The Discourses* (1998, p.140) that Numa merely *pretended* to visit the water goddess in order to give his edicts a stronger, divine authority. Although other versions of the story do not share this doubt, such a reading potentially undermines claims to divine right by implying false claims to divinity to give a politic man more power.

Such potential for re-reading the images of the proscenium arch is continued into the antimasques, which are hosted and performed by Fancy, Opinion, Confidence, Novelty, Admiration, Jollity and Laughter. The names of these presenters seem appropriate to the nature of antimasque, but the availability of their names to positive and negative interpretation destabilises any definite readings of the antimasques following their introduction. For example, it is clear that Fancy is the primary presenter of the antimasques and, like Brome's Letoy, he is associated positively with imagination and invention – his 'braine's nimble' (*Triumph*, sig. B2r). Yet 'Fancy' can also have negative connotations of caprice and of arbitrary notions

---

[9]   *OED*, 'jovial', 1, 5, 6.

[10]   Livy's *Roman History* explains that although Numa was chosen by his people to become the ruler after Romulus, he did not take up the position until the consent and will of the gods had been sought through the auguries. The correct flight of birds was seen and after that he was pronounced king (Livy, 1600, sigs. C1r-v).

[11]   Alternatively, Rebecca Bailey suggests that Shirley and Davenant in their dramatic texts encouraged the Queen to exert more influence over the King in matters of religion (2009, *passim*). Egeria may then be seen as an idealised image of the Queen herself.

without solid grounding (*OED*, 'fancy', 6, 7a, 8a), and, as many of the antimasques Fancy presents can be related to policies of Charles's Personal Rule, such negative connotations potentially serve to undermine prerogative interventions in law. Confidence and Opinion, too, hold diverse meanings and may present not only the court's appreciation of antimasques in Opinion's belief that Fancy will provide them, but also comment critically on hearsay and faction at court:

> *Confidence*, waite you upon *Opinion*,
> Here *Admiration*, there *Novelty*,
> This is the place for *Jollity* and *Laughter*,
> *Phansie* will dance himself too.
> (*Triumph*, sig. B2v)

These are, of course, Fancy's stage directions for his first antimasque '*expressing the natures of the Presenters*' (*Triumph*, sig. B2v), but whilst the antimasque, and indeed the court entertainment, is the place for jollity and laughter, whether confidence (in people or policy) should wait upon something as changeable as opinion is brought into question.

Opinion's wish, after the dance of the presenters, to see 'something … of other nature / To satisfie the present expectation' (*Triumph*, sig. B3r) leads Fancy to present a series of antimasques which would both satisfy any demand for variety in antimasques at court, and which are, he claims, fitting for the time and topic of the masque:

> Phansie: I imagine, nay, I'me not ignorant of proprieties
> And persons: tis a time of peace, ile fit you,
> And instantly make you a representation
> Of the effects.
>
> Opinion: Of peace? I like that well.
> (*Triumph*, sig. B3r)

A series of antimasques follow to represent the effects of peace, but like the antimasque presenters themselves, these are not unambiguous and often invite reinterpretation. The antimasques concerning tavern activities, which may be connected to Charles attempts to tighten the regulation of alehouses (Butler, 1987, p.129), begin as a representation of the effects of Peace in 'good fellowship' (*Triumph*, sig. B3r) as the master of the tavern and his wife and servants present their dance, followed by a maquerelle, two wenches and two wanton gamesters (*Triumph*, sig. B3v), who all go into the tavern. After several other antimasques have been performed, these figures return to the stage where the audience sees the gallants cheated by the wenches and 'left to dance in with a drunken repentance' (*Triumph*, sig. C1r). Whether this is an admonition to courtly gallants to regulate their own behaviour more carefully, or an endorsement of Charles's attempts to regulate drinking establishments, it is clear that 'good fellowship' can easily be corrupted to something more sinister.

Such revision and reinterpretation is also invited by the antimasque of a gentleman and beggars, in which 'The Gentleman first danceth alone: to him the Beggars, he bestows his charity, the Cripples upon his going off, throw away their legges, and dance' (*Triumph*, sig. B3v). Whilst it can be understood that the gentleman's charity allows the beggars to (metaphorically) throw away their crutches (Wigfall Green, 1931, p.129), Opinion's declaration that these are the effects of 'Corruption' (*Triumph*, sig. B3v) rather than peace suggests that the beggars should not be given the gentleman's charity; their ability to throw away their crutches suggests that they need not beg. Thus, in Butler's reading, 'the beggars are members of the idle poor, who fake disabilities to earn charity, then throw away their crutches and dance at their success' (1987, p.129). Both readings may be understood in connection with the Poor Laws as administered by local authorities which sought to distinguish between the deserving and idle poor, or could be a comment upon Charles's proclamation of 1632, 'Commaunding the gentry to keep their Residence at the Mansions in the Country, and forbidding them to make their Habitations in *London* and places adjoining', by which Charles sought to maintain better order in the provinces. Lawrence Venuti has argued, in relation to this antimasque and the tavern cheats, that there is an irony, in light of the proclamation, in the gentleman being swindled by the wenches and false beggars, in that the gentlemen themselves may be responsible for the swindlers' acts (1986, p.192) in failing to maintain hospitality and charity upon their own country estates.

In pinpointing particular laws, reforms and governmental practices, the Inns of Court are able, through Shirley's masque, to present a wider admonition regarding the importance of maintaining order and abiding by the law. In this context, the antimasque of Projectors is particularly interesting. Although monopolies had been made illegal by statute in 1624, Charles and his Attorney General had found ways around the legislation in order to raise more money for the King's coffers, 'in clear violation of the spirit of the law' (Orgel and Strong, 1973, p.64).[12] However, particular monopolies had been clearly excluded from condemnation in the Statute of 1624; monopolies held by corporations and, for limited periods, inventions were legal (Butler, 1987, p.130).[13] As several of the projectors of the

---

[12]   The controversial nature of monopolies under Charles is emphasised by their frequent and often ridiculous representation in drama of the period. Richard Brome's *The Court Begger* (licensed 1632) presents several projectors and focuses specifically upon one man trying to make his fortune in projects. In Act IV, scene I of Shirley's *The Bird in a Cage*, the idea of monopolies is made to look ridiculous when Grutti comments that it is a shame Morello cannot have a patent for his new clothes (he is punished for his attempts to visit the Princess in the tower by being made to wear his disguise of a petticoat for a month at court).

[13]   The reference to monopolies in this masque becomes increasingly significant in the light of C. E. McGee's discussion of the second performance of *The Triumph of Peace*, arguing that in part the City of London's involvement in hosting the masque was related to issues over a monopoly in soap making which affected many soap makers and laundresses of the city (1991, *passim*; especially pp.310–11, 320). See also Whitted (2009, pp.3–4, 9–10).

antimasques *are* inventors, their prospective monopoly would not necessarily be illegal. Nevertheless, the ridiculousness of many of the projects presented in *The Triumph of Peace* suggests criticism of the royal policy on monopolies, and this, indeed, was the way in which Bulstrode Whitelocke (one of the organising committee) understood the antimasque:

> Several other *Projectors* were in like manner personated in this Antimasque; and it pleased the Spectators the more, because by it an Information was covertly given to the King, of the unfitness and ridiculousness of these Projects against the Law: and the Attorney *Noy*, who had most knowledge of them, had a great hand in this Antimasque of the Projectors. (From Whitelocke's *Memorials of the English Affairs*, quoted in Orgel and Strong, 1973, pp.32–3)

This comment, importantly, provides a brief insight into the way this antimasque was understood by the public who watched the procession, and also of public opinion of monopolies. Noy's involvement contributes to the puzzling nature of Projectors' antimasques because it was Noy who had assisted Charles in the reintroduction of monopolies. He would not, therefore, have been unambiguously presenting an antimasque which showed all projectors and monopolies to be ridiculous or illegal. Venuti argues that Charles's acceptance of the masque suggests the King found nothing to offend him in this antimasque, and therefore he must have understood only compliment on his choice of appropriate projects to support (1986, p.199); Orgel and Strong, too, suggest that 'the only covert information it could have conveyed to its royal spectator had to do with the need for caution in the awarding of monopolies' (1973, p.65). Given the opportunity for counsel which masques afforded, it is possible that this was exactly what Noy intended the antimasque to do: to advise Charles to revise his approach to monopolies so as to avoid abuse of the legal negotiation he himself had accomplished for the King.[14] However, we need not necessarily assume that because the masque did not overtly displease the King that he was unaware of any criticism.

The potential for criticism of, or guidance to, the King and courtiers in matters of prerogative and law is continued into the main masque. After the antimasques presenting the 'effects / Of peace' (*Triumph of Peace*, sig. B3r), and its corruption, Irene (Peace) descends, beginning the main masque and, significantly, frightening away the disorderly, 'profane' (*Triumph*, sig. C2v) figures of Fancy and his arbitrary and subjective companions. What is to be shown now, we can understand, is to be less open to caprice and opinion to interpret. Irene wonders at the delay of her sisters' arrival, and appeals for Eunomia (Law) to arrive because, she says, 'I'm lost with them / That know not how to order me'.[15] If the preceding antimasques

---

[14] By this stage, patents and monopolies had already been granted to ridiculous schemes for the revenue they would bring (Butler, 1987, p.130).

[15] Contrary to Venuti's argument (1986, pp.202–3), there is no reason to see Eunomia as symbolic of parliamentary rule in this masque. It is clear, in both the antimasques and the main masque, that *The Triumph of Peace* is concerned with issues of law and prerogative

had been read as positive representations of Charles's prerogative interventions in law and order, such a statement suggests that whilst the King may have Peace, he cannot keep it well without recourse to a separate, embodied Law. Eunomia descends, claiming she could not have been absent for this night, but compliments Irene for her gentleness in inviting her sister, Law, to join her (*Triumph*, sig. C3r), presenting an ideal relationship between the King's peace and the law in which, despite the fact the law is necessary for a triumph of peace and *should* accompany prerogative, the courtesy of the invitation would highlight the King's graciousness. This ideal is emphasised as Eunomia and Irene proceed to compliment one another, each trying to give the other precedence:

> Ir[ene]: *Thou dost beautifie increase,*
> *And chaine security with peace.*
>
> Eu[nomia]: Irene *faire, and first devine,*
> *All my blessings spring from thine.*
>
> Ir[ene]: *I am but wilde without thee.*
> (*Triumph*, sig. C3v)

Eunomia's reference to Irene being 'first divine' may be a compliment to Charles highlighting divine kingship; however, in making her sister 'first' divine, Eunomia creates a space to highlight her own divine status, placing the claims of law alongside those of monarchy. It is clear, too, that peace can only be secure with the help of a separate figure of law, repeating again that peace has no order (is 'wilde') without it. Eunomia and Irene end this discussion with an announcement of their perfect harmony: 'The world shall give prerogative to neyther / Wee cannot flourish but together' (*Triumph*, sig. C3v).[16] The use of the language of prerogative to allow equal importance to Peace and Law does not necessarily deny Charles independent, prerogative authority; it does, however, emphasise that this prerogative cannot be held as higher than the law if peace is to produce, as it should, a 'golden harvest' (*Triumph*, sig. C3v). In this way, the main masque revises the impact of the images in the proscenium arch by making a separate but united law a necessary part of the power and plenty invoked by the caduceus and festoons of fruit.

---

rather than parliamentary government (cf. Whitted, 2009, pp.16–17). Eunomia does appear as parliamentary rule in the Anonymous *Tragedy of the Cruell Warre*, which is modelled closely on *The Triumph of Peace*. This pamphlet is an appeal for co-operation between the King and Parliament in order to bring an end to the Civil War. (See Fuzier, 1978). This re-telling of *The Triumph of Peace* foregrounds the emphasis placed on harmony in this masque.

[16]   Shohet notes that in the music of the masque, too, Irene and Eunomia are brought together in the 'parallel thirds of their duet which consistently resolves phrases in unison' (2010, pp.67–8).

Significantly, it is not until Irene and Eunomia have agreed upon this harmonious union that Dice, Justice, can descend. Kevin Sharpe argues that this part of the masque reveals that there can be no peace without law and justice (1987, p.219), but the order of the goddesses' appearances (and the association of Peace with Charles's personal rule) suggests, rather, that there can be no *Justice* without a balanced unification of prerogative and law. Whilst Minos and Numa may have issued laws directly from the gods, Charles must work within an already established law, presented here as divine in Eunomia, to maintain peace, order and justice.[17] In the context of the commercial theatre's representation of absolutism as connected with uncontrolled desires, it is significant that Dice addresses her sister as '*chast* Eunomia' (*Triumph*, sig. C4r): if law is to be just, she must be no one's mistress – not even the King's.

During her descent, Dice comments that her sisters have 'forsaken Heaven's bright gate, / To attend another state / Of gods below' (*Triumph*, sig. C4r), giving overt praise to Charles and Henrietta Maria, whom the sisters recognise as Jove and Themis, parents of the Hours and the figures of Divine Power and Divine Law. In these roles, the union of the royal couple represents the ideal union of prerogative and law (Butler, 1987, p.132) and once again the emphasis is upon their 'chaste' union (*Triumph*, sig. C4v). As with the opening triumphal procession, in highlighting the chaste marriage of the royal couple the Inns of Court appropriate royal imagery for their own argument. For a moment, the King and Queen become central to the masque's action, as the Genius draws their attention to the masquers from the Inns of Court, and comments that their attention animates the 'sons of Peace, Law and Justice' (*Triumph*, sig. D1r):

> No forraigne persons I make knowne
> But here present you with your owne,
> The Children of your Raign, not blood;
> …
> Oh smile on what your selves have made,
> These have no forme, no sunne, no shade,
> But what your vertue doth create,
> …
> That very looke into each eye
> Hath shot a soul, I saw it fly.
> (*Triumph*, sig. D1v)

In describing the lawyers as the children of Charles's reign, Shirley again presents an idealised relationship between the King and the law. The lawyers should not be 'forraigne' to Charles's rule; rather, he should foster and protect the law as if it were part of his own family. Significantly, the King's recognition of the lawyers

---

[17] Minos was thought to be on intimate terms with his father, Zeus, who received him every nine years on Mount Ida and gave him laws to impose upon the people of Crete (Grant and Hazel, 1999, p.223).

makes the Hours (Peace, Law and Justice) happy (*Triumph*, sigs. D1v-D2r). Moreover, in claiming that the lawyers have no being (form, sun or shade) without the King's virtue, the Genius subtly reminds Charles that a virtuous king will rule according to established law. The invitation to the monarch to look and smile upon the lawyers allows him to participate in the masque in animating their dance, and actively realises the notion that the King must acknowledge the law and lawyers to create the harmonious union of the court and Inns which follows in the revels.

This renewed harmony between the court and law is, however, disrupted by a strange sound behind the scenes as 'a cracke is heard in the workes, as if there were some danger by some piece of the Machines falling' (*Triumph*, sig. D2r); the illusory world of the masque, for a moment, seems as if it will literally come crashing down. This is, however, followed by the ungainly and comic appearance of a group of craftsmen and their wives who, having participated in creating the masque, now insist on being allowed to watch it:

> Painter: I, come, be resolute, we know the worst, and let us challenge a
>   privelledge, those stairs were of my Paynting.

> Carpenter: And that Timber I set up: some body is my witness.
> (*Triumph*, sig. D2v)

The language of their complaint is significant; it is the language of prerogative. Their contribution to the creation of the masque gives them a right ('privelledge') to be present at the performance, but their unexpected presence also challenges the privileged exclusivity of the invited audience, and their (mis)use of the language of privilege also suggests a challenge to the King's prerogative over law. The point at which this disruption occurs is also significant, reminding the audience that, although in the world of the masque the relationship between the King and lawyers is natural, familial and harmonious, the masque is only a performance, engineered through machinery and costume. In the practical world outside the masque, this ideal relationship must also be realised and practised. The craftsmen and their wives, understanding that the masque will not continue while they remain in the hall, decide to 'dance a figary' themselves so that the audience will think they are another antimasque, and they can avoid punishment for their intrusion ('we may else kisse the Porter's lodge for 't') (*Triumph*, sig. D3r). Order then is restored and the masquers of the Inns are encouraged to take the ladies of the court to dance. The contrast in grace and order between the craftsmen's 'figary' and the courtly dancing highlights the difference between a country ordered by law and one in which the language of 'privilege' is misused.

In accordance with the order promulgated by the masque, the revels come to an end with the arrival of the morning in the figure of Amphiluche. Sharpe suggests that this indicates that the invasion of her 'unwelcome light' (*Triumph*, sig. D3v) brings about the realisation that 'reality, the outside world, must dawn' (1987, p.220), continuing the negotiation between real and ideal instigated by the craftsmen's intrusion. However, her appearance also presents the lawyers' hope that the real and ideal may now begin to coincide; Amphiluche is 'that glimpse of the light which is seen when the night is past, and the day is not yet appearing' (*Triumph*, sig. D3v). As much as *The Triumph of Peace* comments upon the problems with Charles's personal rule in relation to law by presenting an idealised relationship between Peace and Law, the monarch and the masquers, it also anticipates a more constructive relationship between the lawyers and the King in the future.

* * *

The harmony presented between the monarch and the lawyers, the prerogative and the law in *The Triumph of Peace* is increasingly absent from drama of the commercial theatre. Charles I's attempts to gain greater and tighter control over the laws of the kingdom, asserting himself as the authoritative legitimate legal power, led to an increased emphasis on the legitimacy of the common law and local custom as meaningful alternatives to the King's will as law in maintaining order. Such assertions, Caroline dramatists suggest, bring about conflict between the King, the law and local governors which culminates in the destabilisation, fragmentation and, potentially, the disintegration of any legitimate legal authority. Whilst arguments over good governance and political and legal authority can take place in the public, political realm of parliament, law court, legal tract and political action, these activities and utterances have real-life consequences for Charles and his subjects, perhaps the most dramatic of which was the execution of the King in 1649. The Caroline commercial theatre, however, offered a space where political theory could be played out without real consequence: the actor playing Massinger's Paris will rise to play him again, even though within the play the actor (Paris) will not rise to play the False Servant again. Moreover, public theatre offers a clear and lively presentation of the politics of law throughout the Caroline period, making arguments over the foundation and legitimacy of legal authority accessible to a wider public, and continuing such debate, even, or perhaps particularly, when the more conventional venue for political debate – Parliament – had been dissolved.

Bibliography

Primary Texts

Alciato [1549] (1975). *Emblemas*. Madrid: Editora Nacional.
Anonymous. (1601). [*The A B C with the catechism that is to saie the instruction ... to be learned of everie childe*]. London. STC (2nd ed.) 20.7.
———— (1637). *The Complete justice a compendium of the particulars incident to justices of the peace, either in sessions or out of sessions; gathered out of the statutes, reports, late resolutions of the judges, and other approved authorities. Abstracted and cited alphabetically for their ready helpe, and the ease of inferiour Officers, and for the general good of the Kingdome.* STC (2nd ed.) 14887.5.
———— (1641). *The Star-chamber epitomized or. A dialogue between Inquisition, a news-Smeller, and Christopher Cob-web, a Keeper of the Records, for the Star-Chamber, as they met at the Office in Gayes-Inne. Wherein they Discourse how the Clerkes used to exact Fees, and of the likely alteration.* London. Wing (2nd ed.) S5264A.
———— (1649). *The Divine Right and Irresistibility of Kings and Supreme Magistrates clearly evidenced, not from any private authority, but from the publique confessions of the reformed churches, and the homilies of the Church of England.* Oxford. Wing D1732.
Bacon, Sir F. [1597] (1630). *The elements of the common lawes of England branched into a double tract: the one containing a collection of some principall rules and maximes of the common law, with their latitude and extent. Explicated for the more facile introduction of such as are studiously addicted to that noble profession. The other the vse of the common law, for the preservation of our persons, goods, and good names. According to the lawes and customes of this land.* London. STC (2nd ed.) 1134.
Bodin, J. (1606). *The Six Bookes of a Common-weale. Written by J Bodin a famous lawyer, and a man of great experience in matters of state. Out of the French and Latine copies, done into English, by Richard Knolles.* London. STC (2nd ed.) 3193.
Bracton, H. (1968–77). *De Legibus et Consuetudinibus Angliae* (On the Laws and Customs of England). (S. Thorne, trans and notes). 4 Vols. Published in association with the Selden Society. Cambridge, Massachusetts and London, England: The Belknap Press of Harvard University Press.
Brome, R. (1632). *The Northern Lasse, A Comoedie. As it hath beene often Acted with good Applause, at the Globe, and Black-Fryers. By his Majesties Servants.* London. STC (2nd ed.) 3819.

———— (1640). *The Antipodes: A Comedie. Acted in the yeare 1638 by the Queenes Majesties Servants, at Salisbury Court in Fleet Street*. London. STC (2nd ed.) 3818.

———— (1652). *A Joviall Crew: or The Merry Beggars. Presented in a Comedie at the Cock-pit in Drury Lane in the yeer 1641*. London. Wing B4873.

———— (1653). *The Court Begger. A Comedie Acted at the Cock-pit, by his Majesties servants, Anno 1632*. London. Wing B4867.

———— (1657). *The Queenes Exchange, A Comedy Acted with generall applause at the Black-friers by His Majesties Servants*. London. Wing B4882.

———— [1657] (2010). *The Queens Exchange* (Marion O'Connor, Ed.) Modern Text. *Richard Brome Online* <http://www.hrionline.ac.uk/brome>.

———— [1658] (1980). *The Weeding of Covent Garden. In A Critical Edition of The Weeding of Covent Garden and The Sparagus Garden* (Donald S. McClure, Ed.). New York and London: Garland Publishing.

———— (1659). *The Love-sick Court. Or the Ambitious Politique. A Comedy in Five Nevv Playes*. London. Wing B4872.

———— (1659). *The Queen and Concubine. A Comedy in Five Nevv Playes*. London. Wing B4872.

———— (1659). *The Weeding of Covent-Garden Or the Middlesex-Justice of Peace in Five New Playes*. London. Wing (2nd ed.) B4872.

———— [1640] (1995). *The Antipodes*. In A. Parr (Ed.), *Three Renaissance Travel Plays* (pp.217–326). Manchester: Manchester University Press.

Buchanan, G. (2004). *A Dialogue on the law of Kingship among the Scots. A Critical edition and translation of George Buchanan's De Iure Regni apud Scotos Dialogus*. (R. Mason and M. S. Smith, Eds and trans). Aldershot: Ashgate.

Carew, T. [1634] (1995). *Coelum Brittanicum*. In D. Lindley (Ed.), *Court Masques. Jacobean and Caroline Entertainments 1605–1640* (pp.166–93). Oxford: Oxford University Press.

Chapman, G. [1613] (1987). *The Memorable Masque of the two honourable houses or inns of Court; The Middle Temple, and Lincoln's Inn*. In R. Dutton (Ed.), *Jacobean and Caroline Masques*. 2 Vols. Nottingham Drama Texts. Nottingham: Nottingham University Press.

Charles I. (1627). *By the King a proclamation for the better making of saltpeter within this kingdome*. London. Bonham Norton and John Bill, printers to the Kings most Excellent Majestie. STC (2nd ed.) 8848.

———— (1630). *Orders and Directions, together with a commission for the better administration of Justice, and more perfect Information of His majestie; How and by whom the Lawes and statutes tending to the reliefe of the Poore, the well ordering and training up of youth in trades, and the reformation of Disorders and disordered persons, are executed throughout the Kingdome: Which his Royall Majestie hath commanded to be Published and Inquired of, by the Body of His Privie Councell, whom He hath made principall Commissioners for this purpose*. London. STC (2nd ed.) 9252.4.

——— (1648). *Eikon Basilike, The Pourtraicture of His Sacred Majestie in his solitudes and sufferings.* Wing E268.

Coke, Sir E. (1611). *La huictme part des reports de Sr Edvv. Coke Chevalier, chief Justice del Common Banke des divers resolutions & jugements donez sur solemne arguments & avec grand deliberation & conference des tresreverend juges & sages de la ley, de cases en ley queux ne fueront unques resolus ou adjudgez par devant: et les raisons & causes des dits resolutions & judgements.* London. Printed for the Societie of Stationers. STC (2nd ed.) 5513.

——— (1629). *The first part of the Institutes of the Lawes of England. Or A Commentarie upon Littleton, not the name of a Lawyer onely, but of the Law it selfe. The second Edition, corrected: With an Alphabeticall Table thereunto added.* London. STC (2nd ed.) 15785.

——— (1635a). *Le second part des reports del Edward Coke Lattorney general le roigne de divers matters en ley, avec graunde & mature consideration resolve, & adjudge, queux ne fueront unques resolve ou adjudge par devant, & les raison & causes de yceux, Durant le raigne de tresillustre & renomes roygne Elizabeth, le fountaine de tout iustice, & la vie de la ley.* London. STC (2nd ed.) 5498.5.

——— (1635b). *Le Tierce part des reportes del Edward Coke lattorney general le roigne de diuers resolutions & judgements donnes avec graud deliberation, per les trereverend judges, & sages de la ley, de cases & matters en ley, queux ne fueront unques resolue, ou adjudges par devant, & les reasons & causes des dits resolutions & judgements, Durant les tresheureux regiment de tresillustre & renomes roigne Elizabeth, le fountaine de tout iustice, & la vie de la ley.* London. STC (2nd ed.) 5501.5.

——— (1635c). *Le quart part des reportes del Edward Coke chivalier, lattorney general le roy de divers resolutions & judgements dones sur solemnes arguments, & avec graund deliberation & conference des tresreverend judges & sages de la ley de cases difficult, en queux sont graund diversities des opinions, & queux ne fueront unques resolves, ou adjudges, & reporte par devant, et les raisons & causes des dits resolutions & judgements.* London. STC (2nd ed.) 5503.7.

——— (1636). *La size part des reports Sir Edw. Coke chivaler, chiefe justice del Common banke des divers resolutions & judgements dones sur solemne arguments, & avec grand deliberation & conference des tresreverend judges & sages de la ley, des cases en ley queux ne fueront unques resolve ou adjudges par devant: et les raisons & causes des dits resolutions & judgements.* London. STC (2nd ed.) 5494.8.

Dalton, M. (1635). *The countrey justice containing the practice of the justices of the peace out of their sessions; gathered for the better help of such justices of the peace as have not been much conversant in the studie of the lawes of this realme; now the fifth time published, revised, in many things corrected, and much inlarged.* London. STC (2nd ed.) 6210.

Davies, Sir J. (1615). *Le Primer Report des cases & Matters en Ley resolves & adjudges en les Courts del Roy en Ireland.* Dublin. Iohn Franckton, printer to the Kings most excellent Maiestie. STC (2nd ed.) 6361.

Dickinson, W. (1619). *The Kings Right, Briefly set downe in a Sermon preached before the Reverend Judges at the Assizes held in Reading for the County of Berks*, June 28. 1619. London. STC (2nd ed.) 6821.

Doddridge, Sir J. (1631). *The English Lawyer. Describing the method for the managing of the lawes of this land. And expressing the best qualities requisite in the student practizer judges and fathers of the same.* London. STC (2nd ed.) 6981.

England and Wales. (1640). *Two acts of parliament, the one for the preventing of the Inconveniences happening by the long intermission of Parliament. And the other for regulating of the Privie Councell, and for the taking away the Court, commonly called, The Star-Chamber.* London. Wing (2nd ed.) E2382C.

Filmer, R. (1680). *Patriarcha, or the Natural Power of Kings.* London. Wing F922.

———— [1680] (1991). *Patriarcha.* In Johann P. Somerville (Ed.), *Sir Robert Filmer. Patriarcha and Other Works* (pp.1–68). Cambridge: Cambridge University Press.

Finch, Sir H. (1627). *Law, or a Discourse thereof, in four Bookes. Written in French by Sir Henrie Finch Knight, his Maiesties Serjeant at Law. And done into English by the same Author.* London, Printed for the Societie of Stationers. STC (2nd ed.) 10871.

Ford, J. (1639). *The Ladies Triall. Acted by both their Majesties Servants at the private house in Drury Lane.* London. STC (2nd ed.) 11161.

Fortescue, Sir J. [1545-6] (1942). *De Laudibus Legum Angliae* (S. B. Chrimes, Ed. and trans). Cambridge: Cambridge University Press.

Fuzier, J. (1978). The Tragedy of the Cruell Warre in English Political Dialogues 1641–1651: A Suggestion for Research with a Critical Edition of 'The Tragedy of the Cruell Warre'. *Cahiers Elisabethains, 14,* 9–68.

Glapthorne, H. (1640). *Wit in a Constable: A Comedy written 1639. And now Printed as it was lately Acted at the Cock-pit in Drury lane, by their Majesties Servants, with good allowance.* London. STC (2nd ed.) 11914.

Hare, J. (1647). *St. Edwards Ghost: or, Anti-Normanisme: being a patheticall Complaint and Motion in the behalfe of our English nation against her grand (yet neglected) Grievance, Normanisme.* London. Wing (2nd ed.) H765.

Heywood, T. and Brome, R. (1634). *The Late Lancashire Witches. A well received Comedy, lately acted at the Globe on the Bank-side by the Kings Majesties Actors.* London. STC (2nd ed.) 13373.

———— [1634] (1979). *An Edition of 'The Late Lancashire Witches' by Thomas Heywood and Richard Brome* (Laird H. Barber, Ed.). New York and London: Garland Publishing.

James VI and I. (1599). *Basilikon Doron.* Edinburgh. STC (2nd ed.) 14348.

———— (1603). *The True Lawe of Free Monarchies. Or The Reciprock and Mutuall dutie betwixt a free King, and his naturall Subjects.* London. STC (2nd ed.) 14410.5.

———— (1609). *The Kings Majesties Speach to the Lords and Commons of this present Parliament at Whitehall on Wednesday the xxj of march, Anno Dom. 1609*. London. STC (2nd ed.) 14396.3.

———— (1615). *By the King a proclamation for the confirmation of all Authorized Orders, tending to the Universall publishing and teaching, or a certain Religious Treatise, compiled by Authoritie, And Intituled by the Name of GOD, And the KING*. London. STC (2nd ed.) 8531.

Jonson, B. (1631). *The New Inne. Or The Light Heart. A Comoedy. As it was never acted, but most negligently play'd, by some, the Kings Servants. And more squeamishly beheld, and censured by others, the Kings Subjects, 1629. Now, at last, set at liberty to the Readers, his Maties Servants, and Subjects, to be judg'd*. London. STC (2nd ed.) 14780.

———— (1641). *A Tale of a Tub* in *The Workes of Benjamin Jonson*. London. Printed for Richard Meighen. STC (2nd ed.) 14754.

———— (1984). *The New Inn* (Michael Hattaway, Ed.). Manchester: Manchester University Press.

Lambarde, W. (1581). *Eirenarcha: or of the office of the Justices of Peace in two bookes: gathered. 1579. and now revised, and firste published, in the 24. yeare of the peaceable reigne of our gratious Queene Elizabeth*. London. STC (2nd ed.) 15163.

Leighton, A. (1625). *A Shorte Treatise Against Stage-Playes*. Amsterdam. STC (2nd ed.) 15431.

Livy, T. (1600). *The Romane historie written by T. Livius of Padua. Also, the Breviaries of L. Florus: with a chronologie to the whole historie: and the Topographie of Rome in old tile. Translated out of Latine into English, by Philemon Holland, Doctor in Physicke*. London. STC (2nd ed.) 16613.

Machiavelli, N. [1531] (1998). *The Discourses* (B. Crick, Ed.; L.J. Walker and B. Richardson, trans). London: Penguin.

Massinger, P. (1629). *The Roman Actor. A tragedie. As it hath divers times beene with good allowance Acted, at the private Play-house in the Black-Friers by the Kings Majesties Servants*. London. STC (2nd ed.) 17642.

———— (1630). *The Picture, A tragaecomaedie, As it was often presented with good allowance, at the Globe, and Blackefriers play-houses, by the Kings Majesties servants*. London. STC (2nd ed.) 17640.

———— (1632). *The Emperour of the East A Tragae-Comoedie. The scene Constantinople. As it hath bene divers times acted, at the Black-friers, and Globe Play-houses, by the Kings Majesties Servants*. London. STC (2nd ed.) 17636.

———— (1655). *The Guardian in Three New Playes, viz. The Bashful Lover, The Guardian, The Very Woman. As they have been often Acted at the Private-House in Black-friers, by His late MAJESTIES Servants, with great applause*. London. Wing (2nd ed.) M1050.

———— (1655). *The Very Woman in Three New Playes, viz. The Bashful Lover, The Guardian, The Very Woman. As they have been often Acted at the Private-*

House in Black-friers, by His late MAJESTIES Servants, with great applause.
London. Wing (2nd ed.) M1050.

——— (1976). *Believe as You List* in P. Edwards and C. Gibson (Eds.), *The Plays and Poems of Philip Massinger* (Vol. III, pp.303–90). Oxford: Clarendon Press.

——— (1976). *The Plays and Poems of Philip Massinger* (P. Edwards and C. Gibson, Eds.). 5 Vols. Oxford: Clarendon Press.

Maxwell, J. (1644). *Sacro-sancta Regum Majestas: or; The Sacred and Royall Prerogative of Christian Kings. Wherein Soveraigntie is by Holy Scriptures, Reverend Antiquitie, and sound reason asserted, by discussing of five Questions. And, The Puritanicall, Jesuiticall, Antimonarchicall grounds are disproved, and the untruth and weaknesse of their new-devised-State-principles are discovered.* Oxford. Wing M1384.

Mocket, R. (1615). *God and the King: or a dialogue shewing that our soveraigne Lord King James, being immediate under god within his dominions, doth rightfully claim whatsoever is required by the Oath of Allegeance.* London: Imprinted by his majesties speciall priviledge and command. STC (2nd ed.) 14419.

Nabbes, T. (1638). *Covent garden a pleasant comedie: acted in the yeare, MDCXXXIII. By the Queenes Majesties Servants.* London. STC (2nd ed.) 18339.

Noy, W. (1642). *A treatise of the principal grounds and maximes of the lawes of the kingdome. Very usefull and commodious for all Students, and such others as desire the Knowledge, and Understanding of the Lawes.* London. Wing N1452.

Prynne, W. [1633] (1974). *Histriomastix.* New York and London: Garland Publishing.

——— (1641). *A new discovery of the prelates tyranny, in their late prosecutions of Mr William Pryn, an eminent Lawyer; Dr. Iohn Bastwick, a learned physitian; and Mr. Henry Burton, a reverent divine.* London. Wing (2nd ed.) P4018.

Rutherford, S. (1644). *Lex, Rex: The Law and the prince. A Dispute for the just prerogative of the King and People. Containing the reasons and causes of the most necessary Defensive Wars of the Kingdom of SCOTLAND, and of their Expedition for the ayd and help of their dear Brethren of ENGLAND. In which their Innocency is asserted, and a full ANSWER is given to a Seditious Pamphlet, Intituled, Sacro-sancta Regum Majestas, or The sacred and Royall Prerogative of Christian Kings.* London. Printed for John Field. Wing R2386.

Selden, Sir J. (1616). 'Notes upon Sir John Fortescue Knight, L. Chief Iustice of England, *De laudibus legum Angliae*' in *De Laudibus Legum Angliae*. London. Printed for the Companie of Stationers. STC (2nd ed.) 11197.

Shakespeare, W. (1988). *The Oxford Shakespeare. The Complete Works* (S. Wells and G. Taylor, Eds.). Oxford: Oxford University Press.

Shirley, J. (1633). *The Bird in a Cage. A Comedie. As it hath beene Presented at the Phoenix in Drury-Lane.* London.. STC (2nd ed.) 22436.

———— (1634). *The Triumph of Peace. A masque presented by the Foure Honourable Houses, or Innes of Court. Before the King and Queenes Majesties, in the Banquetting-house at White Hall, February the third, 1633*. London. STC (2nd ed.) 22459b.

———— [1634] (1980). *The Triumph of Peace*. In C. Leech (Ed.), *A Book of Masques In Honour of Allardyce Nicoll* (pp.277–313). Cambridge: Cambridge University Press.

———— (1635). *The Traytor. A tragedie*, written by James Shirley. Acted by her Majesties Servants. London. STC (2nd ed.) 22458.

———— (1637). *The Lady of Pleasure. A Comedie, As it was Acted by her Majesties Servants, at the private House in Drury Lane*. London.. STC (2nd ed.) 22448.

———— (1638). *The Dukes Mistris. As it was presented by her Majesties Servants, At the private house in Drury Lane*. London. STC (2nd ed.) 22441b.

———— (1652). *The Cardinal, a tragedie, as it was acted at the private house in Black Fryers. Not printed before*. London. Wing S3461.

———— (1652). *The Doubtful Heir. A tragi-comedie, as it was Acted at the private House in Blackfriers*. London. Wing S3466.

Spelman, Sir H. (1698). *'Two Discourses: I. Of the Ancient Government of England. II. Of Parliaments' in Reliquiae Spelmannianae. The posthumous works of Sir Henry Spelman, Kt., relating to the laws and antiquities of England: published from the original manuscripts: with the life of the author*. London. Wing S4930.

Suetonius. (1606). *The History of Twelve Caesars, emperours of Rome: written in Latine C. Suetonius Tranquillis, and newly translated into English by Philemon Holland, Doctor in Physicke. Together with a marginal glosse, and other brief annotations there-upon*. London. STC (2nd ed.) 23423.

Townshend, A. (1632). *Albion's Triumph. Personated in a Maske at Court. By the Kings majestie and his Lords. The Sunday after Twelfe Night. 1631*. London. STC (2nd ed.) 24155.

———— (1632). *Tempe Restord. A masque Presented by the Queene, and foureteene Ladies, to the Kings Majestie at Whitehall on Shrove-Tuesday 1631*. London. STC (2nd ed.) 24156.

———— [1632] (1973). *Albion's Triumph*. In S. Orgel and R. Strong, *Inigo Jones and the Theatre of the Stuart Court* (pp.453–8). London: Sotheby Park Bernet.

Virgil. (1991). *The Aeneid: A New Prose Translation*(D. West, trans). Middlesex: Penguin.

Secondary texts

Adler, D. (1987). *Philip Massinger*. Boston, Massachusetts: Twayne Publishers, G. K. Hall and Co.

Andrews, C. E. (1981). *Richard Brome: A Study of his Life and Works*. Michigan and London: Ann Arbor.

Atherton, I. and Sanders, J. (Eds.). (2006). *The 1630s. Interdisciplinary essays on Culture and Politics in the Caroline Era*. Manchester: Manchester University Press.

Bailey, R. (2009). *Staging the Old Faith: Queen Henrietta Maria and the Theatre of Caroline England, 1625–42*. Manchester: Manchester University Press.

Baker, J. H. (1985). Law and Legal Institutions. In John F. Andrews (Ed.), *William Shakespeare. His World. His Work. His Influence*. Volume I (pp.41–54). New York: Charles Scribner's Sons.

———— (2000). *The Common Law Tradition: Lawyers, Books and the Law*. London and Rio Grande: The Hambledon Press.

———— (2002). *An Introduction to English Legal History* (4th ed.). London: Butterworths, Lexis Nexis.

Barnes, T. G. (1961). Star Chamber Mythology. *American Journal of Legal History*, *5*, 1–11.

———— (1962). Due Process and Slow Process in the Late Elizabethan-Early Stuart Star Chamber. *American Journal of Legal History*, *6*, 221–49.

———— (2004). Introduction to Coke's 'Commentary on Littleton'. In Allen D. Boyer (Ed.), *Law, Liberty and Parliament. Selected Essays on the Writings of Sir Edward Coke* (pp.1–25). Indianapolis: published by the Liberty Fund.

Barton, A. (1981). Harking Back to Elizabeth: Ben Jonson and Caroline Nostalgia. *ELH*, *48*(4), 706–31.

Bentley, G. E. (1956). *The Jacobean and Caroline Stage*. 7 Vols. Oxford: Clarendon Press.

Boynton, L. (1964). Martial Law and the Petition of Right. *English Historical Review*, *79*, 255–84.

Britland, K. (2006). *Drama at the Courts of Queen Henrietta Maria*. Cambridge: Cambridge University Press.

Brooks, C. and Sharpe, K. (1976). History, English Law and the Renaissance. *Past and Present*, *72*, 133–42.

Burgess, G. (1992). *The Politics of the Ancient Constitution: An Introduction to English Political Thought, 1603–1642*. London: Macmillan Press Ltd.

Butler, M. (1984). *Theatre and Crisis 1632–1642*. Oxford: Oxford University Press.

———— (1985). Romans in Britain: *The Roman Actor* and the Early Stuart Classical Play. In Douglas Howard (Ed.), *Philip Massinger: A Critical Reassessment* (pp.139–70). Cambridge: Cambridge University Press.

———— (1987). Politics and the masque: *The Triumph of Peace*. *Seventeenth Century*, *2*(2), 117–41.

———— (1990). Stuart Politics in Jonson's *A Tale of a Tub*. *The Modern Language Review*, *85*(1), 12–28.

———— (1992a). Ecclesiastical Censorship of Early Stuart Drama: The Case of Jonson's *The Magnetic Lady*. *Modern Philology*, *89*(4), 469–81.

———— (1992b). Late Jonson. In G. McMullan and J. Hope (Eds.), *The Politics of Tragicomedy* (pp.166–88). London and New York: Routledge.

Cheyney, E. P. (1913). The Court of Star Chamber. *The American Historical Review*, *18*(4), 727–50.

Christianson, P. (1985). John Selden, the Five Knights' Case, and Discretionary Imprisonment in Early Stuart England. *Criminal Justice History*, *6*, 65–87.

Clark, I. (1992). *Professional Playwrights: Massinger, Ford, Shirley and Brome*. Lexington: University of Kentucky Press.

———— (1993). *The Moral Art of Philip Massinger*. Lewisburg: Bucknell University Press; London and Toronto: Associated University Presses.

Cockburn, J. S. (1972). *A History of English Assizes 1558–1714*. Cambridge: Cambridge University Press.

Cogswell, T. (1998). *Home Divisions. Aristocracy, the State and Provincial Conflict*. Manchester: Manchester University Press.

Collinson, P. (1987). The Monarchical Republic of Queen Elizabeth I. *Bulletin of the John Rylands University Library of Manchester*, *69*(2), 394–424.

Cormack, B. (2008). *A Power to Do Justice: Jurisdiction, English Literature and the Rise of the Common Law 1509–1625*. Chicago: University of Chicago Press.

Cromartie, A. (2006). *The Constitutionalist Revolution: An Essay on the History of England 1450–1642*. Cambridge: Cambridge University Press.

Cust, R. (2005). *Charles I: A Political Life*. Harlow: Pearson Education.

———— (1987). *The Forced Loan and English Politics 1626–1628*. Oxford: Clarendon Press.

Cust, R. and Lake, P. (1981). Sir Richard Grosvenor and the Rhetoric of Magistracy. *Bulletin of the Institute of Historical Research*, *54*(129), 40–53.

Daly, J. (1979). *Sir Robert Filmer and English Political Thought*. Toronto, Buffalo and London: University of Toronto Press.

Dawson, L. (2002). 'New Sects of Love': Neoplatonism and Constructions of Gender in Davenant's *The Temple of Love* and *The Platonick Lovers*. *Early Modern Literary Studies*, *8*(1) <http://extra.shu.ac.uk/emls/08_1/dawsnew.html>.

Du Cann, C. G. L. (1964). *English Treason Trials*. London: Frederick Muller Limited.

Dutton, R. (1991). *Mastering the Revels. The Regulation and Censorship of English Renaissance Drama*. Hampshire and London: Macmillan Press Ltd.

———— (2000). *Licensing, Censorship and Authorship in Early Modern England*. Hampshire: Palgrave.

Edwards, P. (1963). Massinger the Censor. In R. Hosley (Ed.), *Essays on Shakespeare and Elizabethan Drama in honour of Hardin Craig* (pp.341–50). London: Routledge and Kegan Paul Ltd.

Farr, D. M. (1979). *John Ford and the Caroline Theatre*. London and Basingstoke: Macmillan Press Ltd.

Finkelpearl, P. J. (1969). *John Marston of the Inner Temple*. Cambridge, Massachusetts: Harvard University Press.

Fletcher, A. (1986). *Reform in the Provinces: the Government of Stuart England*. New Haven and London: Yale University Press.

Ford, J. D. (1994). *Lex, rex iusto posita*: Samuel Rutherford on the origins of government. In Roger Mason (Ed.), *Scots and Britons. Scottish Political Thought and the Union of 1603* (pp.262–90). Cambridge: Cambridge University Press.

Foster, E. (1974). Petitions and the Petition of Right. *The Journal of British Studies*, *14*(1), 21–45.

Gardiner, S. R. (1876). The Political Element in Massinger. *Contemporary Review*, *28*, 495–507.

Garrett, M. (2007). Massinger, Philip (1583–1640). In *Oxford Dictionary of National Biography*. (H. C. G. Matthew and B. Harrison, Eds). Oxford: Oxford University Press. <http://www.oxforddnb.com/view/article/18306>.

Goldberg, J. (1989). *James I and the Politics of Literature. Jonson, Shakespeare, Donne and their Contemporaries*. Stanford, California: Stanford University Press.

Grant, M. and Hazel, J. (1999). *Who's Who in Classical Mythology*. London: Routledge.

Gross, A. (1966). Contemporary Politics in Massinger. *Studies in English Literature 1500–1900*, *6*, 279–90.

Gurr, A. (1996). *The Shakespearean Playing Companies*. Oxford: Clarendon Press.

Guy, J. A. (1982). The Origins of the Petition of Right Reconsidered. *The Historical Journal*, *25*(2), 289–312.

Hadfield, A. (Ed.) (2001). *Literature and Censorship in Renaissance England*. Hampshire: Palgrave.

Hartley, A. J. (2001). Philip Massinger's *The Roman Actor* and the Semiotics of Censored Theater. *ELH*, *68*(2), 359–76.

Hattaway, M. (1984). 'Introduction' to *The New Inn*. Manchester: Manchester University Press.

Herrup, C. B. (1999). *A House in Gross Disorder. Sex, Law and the 2nd Earl of Castlehaven*. Oxford: Oxford University Press.

Hill, C. (1958). *Puritanism and Revolution: studies in interpretation of the English Revolution of the Seventeenth century*. London: Secker and Warburg.

———— (1997). *Liberty Against the Law. Some Seventeenth-Century Controversies*. London: Penguin.

Hill, L. M. (1973). County Government in Caroline England 1625–1640. In C. Russell (Ed.), *The Origins of the English Civil War* (pp.66–90). London: Macmillan Press Ltd.

Hindle, S. (2000). *The State and Social Change in Early Modern England, 1550–1640*. Basingstoke: Palgrave Macmillan.

Hopkins, L. (1994). *John Ford's Political Theatre*. Manchester: Manchester University Press.

———— (1999a). Ladies' Trials: Women and the Law in Three Plays of John Ford. *Cahiers Elisabethains*, *56*, 49–64.

———— (1999b). Touching Touchets: Perkin Warbeck and the Buggery Statute. *Renaissance Quarterly*, *52*(2), 384–401.

Howard, D. (1985). Massinger's Political Tragedies. In D. Howard (Ed.), *Philip Massinger. A Critical Reassessment* (pp.117–37). Cambridge: Cambridge University Press.

Hughes, A. (1991). *The Causes of the English Civil War*. Basingstoke and London: Macmillan Press Ltd.

Hutson, L. (2007). *The Invention of Suspicion: Law and Mimesis in Shakespeare and Renaissance Drama*. Oxford: Oxford University Press.

——— (2010). Law, crime and punishment. In J. Sanders (Ed.), *Ben Jonson in Context* (pp.221–8). Cambridge: Cambridge University Press.

Jones, W. J. (1971). *Politics and the Bench. The Judges and the Origins of the English Civil War*. London: George Allen and Unwin Ltd.

Julius, A. (1999). Introduction. In Michael Freeman and Andrew D. E. Lewis (Eds.), *Law and Literature* (pp.xi-xxvi). Oxford: Oxford University Press.

Kaufmann, R. J. (1981). *Richard Brome: Caroline Playwright*. Michigan: Ann Arbor; London: University Microfilms.

Keeton, G. W. (1966). *The Norman Conquest and the Common Law*. London: Earnest Benn Ltd; New York: Barnes and Noble Inc.

Kelley, D. R. (1974). History, English Law and the Renaissance. *Past and Present*, *65*, 24–51.

——— (1976). A Rejoinder. *Past and Present*, *72*, 143–6.

Kelsey, S. (2004). Politics and Procedure in the Trial of Charles I. *Law and History Review*, *22*(1), 31 paragraphs. <http://www.historycooperative.org/journals/lhr/22.1/kelsey.html>.

Kent, J. (1986). *The English Village Constable 1580–1642*. Oxford: Clarendon Press.

Kenyon, J. P. (Ed.) (1986). *The Stuart Constitution 1603–1688. Documents and Commentary* (2nd ed.). Cambridge: Cambridge University Press.

Kewes, P. (2002). Julius Caesar in Jacobean England. *The Seventeenth Century*, *17*(2), 155–86.

Khan, V. and Hutson, L. (Eds.) (2001). *Rhetoric and Law in Early Modern Europe*. New Haven and London: Yale University Press.

Kilburn, T. and Milton, A. (1996). The public context of the trial and execution of Strafford. In J. F. Merritt, J. F. (Ed.) *The Political World of Thomas Wentworth, Earl of Strafford 1621–1641* (pp.230–50). Cambridge: Cambridge University Press.

Kleber Monod, P. (2001). *The Power of Kings: Monarchy and Religion in Europe 1589–1715*. New Haven and London: Yale University Press.

Lake, P. (1981). The Collection of Ship Money in Cheshire During the Sixteen-Thirties: A Case Study of Relations Between Central and Local Government. *Northern History, A Review of the History of the North of England*, *17*, 44–71.

Lane, M. (1981). Law and Consciousness in Early Seventeenth Century England. In F. Barker *et al* (Eds.), *1642: Literature and Power in the Seventeenth Century* (pp.274–82). Essex: University of Essex.

Leech, C. (Ed.) (1967). *A Book of Masques in Honour of Allardyce Nicoll*. Cambridge: Cambridge University Press.

Lockyer, R. (1999). *The Early Stuarts: A Political History of England 1603–1642* (2nd ed.). Essex: Longman.

Loxley, J. (2002). *The Complete Critical Guide to Ben Jonson*. London: Routledge.

Lynch, K. M. (1967). *The Social Mode of Restoration Comedy*. London: Frank Cass and Company Ltd.

Manning, J. (2002). *The Emblem*. London: Reaktion Books.

March, J. (1998). *Dictionary of Classical Mythology*. London: Cassell.

Marcus, L. (1986). *The Politics of Mirth. Jonson, Herrick, Milton, Marvell, and the Defence of Old Holiday Pastimes*. Chicago and London: University of Chicago Press.

McGee, C. E. (1991). 'Strangest consequence from remotest cause': The Second Performance of *The Triumph of Peace. Medieval and Renaissance Drama in England, 5*, 309–42.

Merritt, J. (2005). *The Social World of Early Modern Westminster*. Manchester: Manchester University Press.

Miller, P. W. (1990). The Historical Moment of Caroline Topographical Comedy. *Texas Studies in Literature and Language, 32*(3), 345–74.

Mukherji, S. (2006a). False Trials in Shakespeare, Massinger, and Ford. *Essays in Criticism, 56*(3), 219–40.

——— (2006b). Jonson's *The New Inn* and a revisiting of the amorous jurisdiction. *Law and Literature, 18*(2), 149–69.

——— (2006c). *Law and Representation in Early Modern Drama*. Cambridge: Cambridge University Press.

Neill, M. (2007). 'Ford, John (*bap.* 1586, *d.* 1639x53?)'. In *Oxford Dictionary of National Biography* (H. C. G. Matthew and B. Harrison, Eds).. Oxford: Oxford University Press. <http://www.oxforddnb.com/view/article/9861>.

Norbrook, D. (1999). *Writing the English Republic: Poetry, Rhetoric and Politics 1627–1660*. Cambridge: Cambridge University Press.

O'Callaghan, M. (2004). Tavern Societies, the Inns of Court, and the Culture of Conviviality in Early Seventeenth-Century London. In Adam Smyth (Ed.), *A Pleasing Sinne. Drink and Convivilaity in 17th Century England* (pp.37–51). Cambridge: D. S. Brewer.

Orgel, S. and Strong, R. (1973). *Inigo Jones and the Theatre of the Stuart Court*. London: Sotheby Park Bernet.

Parr, A. (Ed.) (1995). *Three Renaissance Travel Plays*. Manchester: Manchester University Press.

Parry, G. (1981). *The Golden Age Restor'd. The Culture of the Stuart Court, 1603–42*. Manchester: Manchester University Press.

Peacock, J. (2006). The Image of Charles I as a Roman Emperor. In Ian Atherton and Julie Sanders (Eds.), *The 1630s. Interdisciplinary essays on Culture and Politics in the Caroline Era* (pp.50–73). Manchester: Manchester University Press.

Peltonen, M. (1995). *Classical Humanism and Republicanism in English Political Thought 1570–1640*. Cambridge: Cambridge University Press.

Pocock, J. G. A. (1987). *The Ancient Constitution and the Feudal Law. A Study of English Historical Thought in the Seventeenth Century. A Reissue with a Retrospect*. Cambridge: Cambridge University Press.

Posner, R. (1988). *Law and Literature. A Misunderstood Relation*. Cambridge, Massachusetts and London, England: Harvard University Press.

Prest, W. (1972). *The Inns of Court under Elizabeth I and the Early Stuarts 1590–1640*. London: Longman.

Raffield, P. (2004). *Images and Cultures of Law in Early Modern England: Justice and Political Power, 1558–1660*. Cambridge: Cambridge University Press.

Reeve, L. J. (1986). The Legal Status of the Petition of Right. *The Historical Journal, 29*(2), 257–77.

Reinheimer, D. A. (1998). The Roman Actor, Censorship, and Dramatic Autonomy. *Studies in English Literature 1500–1900, 38*(2), 317–32.

Roberts Peters, B. (2004). *Marriage in Seventeenth-Century English Political Thought*. Basingstoke: Palgrave Macmillan.

Rochester, J. (2010). *Staging Spectatorship in the Plays of Philip Massinger*. Aldershot: Ashgate.

Russell, C. (1979). *Parliaments and English Politics 1626–1629*. Oxford: Clarendon Press.

Sanders, J. (1996). 'The Day's Sports Devised in the Inn': Jonson's *The New Inn* and Theatrical Politics. *Modern Language Review, 91*(3), 545–60.

———— (1997). 'The Collective Contract is a Fragile Structure': Local Government and Personal Rule in Jonson's *A Tale of a Tub. English Literary Renaissance, 27*(3), 443–67.

———— (1998). *Ben Jonson's Theatrical Republics*. Hampshire: Palgrave.

———— (1999a). *Caroline Drama. The Plays of Massinger, Ford, Shirley and Brome*. Plymouth: Northcote House Publishers Ltd.

———— (1999b). The politics of escapism: fantasies of travel and power in Richard Brome's *The Antipodes* and Ben Jonson's *The Alchemist*. In Ceri Sullivan and Barbara White (Eds.), *Writing and Fantasy* (pp.137–50). London and New York: Longman.

———— (2000). Caroline Salon Culture and Female Agency: The Countess of Carlisle, Henrietta Maria, and Public Theatre. *Theatre Journal, 52*(4), 449–64.

———— (2002a). Beggars Commonwealths and the Pre-civil war stage: Suckling's *The Goblins*, Brome's *A Jovial Crew*, and Shirley's *The Sisters. Modern Language Review, 97*(1), 1–14.

———— (2002b). 'Wardrobe Stuffe': Clothes, Costume and the Politics of Dress in Ben Jonson's *The New Inn. Renaissance Forum, 6*(1). <http://www.hull.ac.uk/renforum/v6no1/sanders.htm>.

Sayles, G. O. (1959). *The Court of King's Bench in Law and History*. Selden Society Lecture. London: Bernard Quaritch.

Schochet, G. (1975). *Patriarchalism in Political Thought*. Oxford: Basil Blackwell.

Sharpe, J. A. (1980). Enforcing the Law in the Seventeenth-Century English Village. In V. A. C. Gatrell, Bruce Lenman and Geoffrey Parker (Eds.), *Crime* and the Law. *The Social History of Crime in Western Europe Since 1500* (pp.97–119). London: Europa Publications Ltd.

Sharpe, K. (1987). *Criticism and Compliment: the politics of literature in the England of Charles I*. Cambridge: Cambridge University Press.

———— (1992). *The Personal Rule of Charles I*. New Haven and London: Yale University Press.

———— (2000). *Remapping Early Modern England. The Culture of Seventeenth-Century Politics*. Cambridge: Cambridge University Press.

Shaw, C. (1980). *Richard Brome*. Boston, Massachusetts: Twayne Publishers, G. K. Hall and Co.

Sheen, E. and Hutson, L. (Eds.) (2005). *Literature, Politics and Law in Renaissance England 1580–1660*. Hampshire: Palgrave Macmillan.

Shohet, L. (2010). *Reading Masques: The English Masque and Public Culture in the Seventeenth Century*. Oxford: Oxford University Press.

Skinner, Q. (1965). History and Ideology in the English Revolution. *The Historical Journal*, *8*(2), 151–78.

Smyth, A. (2004). 'Introduction'. In Adam Smyth (Ed.), *A Pleasing Sinne. Drink and Conviviality in 17th Century England* (pp.xiii-xxv). Cambridge: D. S. Brewer.

Sommerville, J. P. (1986). History and Theory: the Norman Conquest in Early Stuart Political Thought. *Political Studies*, *34*, 249–61.

———— (1996). The ancient constitution reassessed: the common law, the court and the languages of politics in early modern England. In R. Malcolm Smuts (Ed.), *The Stuart Court and Europe. Essays in politics and political culture* (pp.39–64). Cambridge: Cambridge University Press.

———— (1999). *Royalists and Patriots: Politics and Ideology in England 1603–1640* (2nd ed.). New York and London: Longman.

Stater, V. (1994). *Noble Government. The Stuart Lord Lieutenancy and the Transformation of English Politics*. Athens, Georgia and London, England: University of Georgia Press.

Steggle, M. (2001). Brome, Covent Garden, and 1641. *Renaissance Forum*, *5*(2). <http://www.hull.ac.uk/renforum/v5no2/steggle.htm>.

———— (2004). *Richard Brome: Place and Politics on the Caroline Stage*. Manchester: Manchester University Press.

———— (2006). Placing Caroline politics on the professional comic stage. In Ian Atherton and Julie Sanders (Eds), *The 1630s. Interdisciplinary essays on Culture and Politics in the Caroline Era* (pp.154–70). Manchester: Manchester University Press.

Strong, R. (1972). *Van Dyck – 'Charles I on Horseback'*. London: Allen Lane.

Tubbs, J. W. (1998). Custom, Time and Reason: Early Seventeenth-Century Conceptions of the Common Law. *History of Political Thought*, *19*(3), 363–406.

Usher, R. G. (1903). James I and Sir Edward Coke. *The English Historical Review*, *18*, 664–75.

Venuti, L. (1986). The Politics of Allusion: The Gentry and Shirley's *The Triumph of Peace. English Literary Renaissance*, *16*(1), 182–205.

Walsh, S. M. (1999). 'But yet the lady, th'heir, enjoys the land': Heraldry, Inheritance and Nat(ion)al Households in Jonson's *The New Inn. Medieval and Renaissance Drama in England*, *11*, 226–63.

Ward, I. (1995). *Law and Literature: Possibilities and Perspectives*. Cambridge: Cambridge University Press.

Weston, C. (1991). England: Ancient Constitution and Common Law. In J. H. Burns and Mark Goldie (Eds.), *The Cambridge History of Political Thought 1450–1700* (pp.374–411). Cambridge: Cambridge University Press.

Whitted, B. (2009). Street Politics: Charles I and the Inns of Court's *Triumph of Peace. The Seventeenth Century*, *24*(1), 1–25.

Wigfall Green, A. (1931). *The Inns of Court and Early English Drama*. London: Humphrey Milford, Oxford University Press.

Wilson, L. (2000). *Theaters of Intention: Drama and Law in Early Modern England*. Stanford, California: Stanford University Press.

Woolf, D. R. (1985). Two Elizabeths? James I and the Late Queen's Famous Memory. *The Canadian Journal of History*, *20*, 167–91.

Wrightson, K. (1980). Two concepts of order: justices, constables and jurymen in seventeenth-century England. In John Brewer and John Styles (Eds.), *An Ungovernable People. The English and their Law in the Seventeenth and Eighteenth Centuries* (pp.21–46). London: Hutchinson and Co. Ltd.

Zaret, D. (1992). Religion, Science, and Printing in the Public Spheres in Seventeenth-Century England. In Craig Calhoun (Ed.), *Habermas and the Public Sphere* (pp.212–35). London, England and Cambridge, Massachusetts: MIT Press.

Zucker, A. and Farmer, A. (Eds.) (2006). *Localizing Caroline Drama: Politics and Economics of the Early Modern English Stage, 1625–1642*. Basingstoke: Palgrave Macmillan.

Reference works

The Bible. Authorized King James Version with Apocrypha. [1611] (1997). Oxford: Oxford University Press.

Martin, E. A. and Law, J. (Eds.) (2006). *Oxford Dictionary of Law*. Oxford: Oxford University Press. <http://www.oxfordreference.com/views/SUBJECT_SEARCH.html?subject=s12>.

Oxford Dictionary of National Biography. Oxford: Oxford University Press, 2007. <http://www.oxforddnb.com/>.

Oxford English Dictionary Online. Oxford: Oxford University Press, 2007. <http://dictionary.oed.com/entrance.dtl>.

Index